NYSTCE®

Teachers of Early Childhood Exam Success

By Lewis Morris

www.insiderswords.com/NYSTCEEarly

ISBN-13: 978-1793456991

Table of Contents

What is "Insider Language"?

Recent research has confirmed what we have known for decades: The strongest students and leaders in industry have a mastered an Insider Language in their subject and field. This Insider language is made up of the technical terms and vocabulary necessary to communicate effectively in classes or the workplace. For those who master it, learning is easier, faster, and much more enjoyable.

Most students who are surveyed report that the greatest challenge to any course of study is learning the vocabulary. When we examine typical college courses, we discover that there is, on average, 250 Insider Terms a student must learn over the course of a semester. Further, most exams rely heavily on this set of words for assessment purposes. The structure of multiple choice exams lends itself perfectly to the testing of this Insider Language. Students who can differentiate between Insider Language terms can handle challenging exam questions with ease and confidence.

From recent research on learning and vocabulary we have learned:

- Your knowledge of any subject is contained in the content-specific words you know. The more of these terms that you know, the easier it is to understand and recall important information; the easier it will be to communicate your ideas to peers, professors, supervisors, and co-workers. The stronger your content-area vocabulary is, the higher your scores will be on your exams and written assignments.

- Students who develop a strong Insider Language perform better on tests, learn faster, retain more information, and express greater satisfaction in learning.

- Familiarizing yourself with subject-area vocabulary before formal study (pre-learning) is the most effective way to learn this language and reap the most benefit.

- The vocabulary on standardized exams come directly from the stated objectives of the test-makers. This means that the vocabulary found on standardized exams is predictable. Our books focus on this vocabulary.

- Most multiple-choice exams are glorified vocabulary quizzes. Think about the format of a multiple-choice question. The question stem is a definition of a term and the choices (known as distractors) are 4 or 5 similar words. Your task is to differentiate between the meanings of those terms and choose the correct word.

- It takes a person several exposures to a new word to be able to use it with confidence in conversation or in writing. You need to process these words several different ways to make them part of your long-term memory.

The goals of this book are:

- To give you an "Insider Language" for your subject.
- Pre-teach the most important words before you set out on a traditional course of review or study.
- Teach you the most important words in your subject area.
- Teach you strategies for learning subject-area words on your own.
- Boost your confidence in your ability to master this language and support you in your study.
- Reduce the stress of studying and provide you with fun activities that work.

How it works:

The secret to mastering Insider Language is through repetition and exposure. We have eleven steps for you to follow:

1. Read the word and definition in the glossary out loud. "See it, Say it"
2. Identify the part of speech the word belongs to such as noun, verb, adverb, or adjective. This will help you group the word and identify similar words.
3. Place the word in context by using it in a sentence. Write this sentence down and read it aloud.
4. Use "Chunking" to group the words. Make a diagram or word cloud using these groups.
5. Make connections to the words by creating analogies.
6. Create mnemonics that help you recognize patterns and orders of words by substituting the words for more memorable items or actions.
7. Examine the morphology of the word, that is, identify the root, prefix, and suffix that make up the word. Identify similar and related words.
8. Complete word games and puzzles such as crosswords and word searches.
9. Complete matching questions that require you to differentiate between related words.
10. Complete Multiple-choice questions containing the words.
11. Create a visual metaphor or "memory cartoon" to make a mental picture of the word and related processes.

By completing this word study process, you will be exposed to the terminology in various ways that will activate your memory and create a lasting understanding of this language.

The strategies in this book are designed to make you an independent expert at learning insider language. These strategies include:

- Verbalizing the word by reading it and its definition aloud ("See It, Say It"). This allows you to make visual, auditory, and speech connections with its meaning.

- Identifying the type of word (Noun, verb, adverb, and adjective). Making this distinction helps you understand how to visualize the word. It helps you "chunk" the words into groups, and gives you clues on how to use the word.

- Place the word in context by using it in a sentence. Write this sentence down and read it aloud. This will give you an example of how the word is used.

- "Chunking". By breaking down the word list into groups of closely related words, you will learn them better and be able to remember them faster. Once you have group the terms, you can then make word clouds using a free online service. These word clouds provide visual cues to remembering the words and their meanings.

- Analogies. By creating analogies for essential words, you will be making connections that you can see on paper. These connections can trigger your memory and activate your ability to use the word in your writing as you begin to use them. Many of these analogies also use visual cues. In a sense, you can make a mental picture from the analogy.

- Mnemonics. A device such as a pattern of letters, ideas, or associations that assists in remembering something. A mnemonic is especially useful for remembering the order of a set of words or the order of a process.

- Morphology. The study of word roots, prefixes, and suffixes. By examining the structure of the words, you will gain insight into other words that are closely related, and learn how to best use the word.

- Visual metaphors. This is the most sophisticated and entertaining strategy for learning vocabulary. Create a "memory cartoon" using one or more of the vocabulary terms. This activity triggers the visual part of your memory and makes fast, permanent, imprints of the word on your memory. By combining the terms in your visual metaphor, you can "chunk" the entire set of vocabulary terms into several visual metaphors and benefit from the brain's tendency to group these terms.

The activities in this book are designed to imprint the words and their meanings in your memory in different ways. By completing each activity, you will gain the necessary exposures to the word to make it a permanent part of your vocabulary. Each activity uses a different part of your memory. The result is that you will be comfortable using these words and be able to tell the difference between closely related words. The activities include:

A. Crossword Puzzles and Word Searches- These are proven to increase test scores and improve comprehension. Students frequently report that they are fun and engaging, while requiring them to analyze the structure and meaning of the words.

B. Matching- This activity is effective because it forces you to differentiate between many closely related terms.

C. Multiple Choice- This classic question format lends itself to vocabulary study perfectly. Most exams are in this format because they are simple to make, easy to score, and are a reliable type of assessment. (Perfect for the Vocabulary Master!) One strategy to use with multiple choice questions that enhance their effectiveness is to cover the answer choices while you read the question. After reading the question, see if you can answer it before looking at the choices. Then look at the choices to see if you match one of them.

Conducting a thorough "word study" of your insider language will take time and effort, but the rewards will be well worth it. By following this guide and completing the exercises thoughtfully, you will become a stronger, more effective, and satisfied student. Best of luck on your mastery of this Insider Language!

Insider Language Strategies

"See It, Say It!" Reading your Insider Language set aloud

"It is better to fail in originality than to succeed in imitation."
–Herman Melville

Reading aloud is the foundation for the development of an Insider Language. It is the single most important thing you can do for vocabulary acquisition. Done correctly, it engages the visual, auditory, and speech centers of the brain and hastens its storage in your long-term memory.

Reading aloud demonstrates the relationship between the printed word and its meaning.

You can read aloud on a higher level than you can initially understand, so reading aloud makes complex ideas more accessible and exposes you to vocabulary and patterns that are not part of your typical speech. Reading aloud helps you understand the complicated text better and makes more challenging text easier to grasp and understand. Reading aloud helps you to develop the "habits of mind" the strongest students use.

Reading aloud will make connections to concepts in the reading that requires you to relate the new vocabulary to things you already know. Go to the glossary at the end of this book and for each word complete the five steps outlined below:

1. Read the word and its definition aloud. Focus on the sound of the word and how it looks on the paper.
2. Read the word aloud again try to say three or four similar words; this will help you build connections to closely related words.
3. Read the word aloud a third time. Try to make a connection to something you have read or heard.
4. Visualize the concept described in the term. Paint a mental picture of the word in use.
5. Try to think of the opposite of the word. Discovering a close antonym will help you place this word in context.

Create a sentence using the word in its proper context

"OPPORTUNITIES DON'T HAPPEN. YOU CREATE THEM." -CHRIS GROSSER

Context means the circumstances that form the setting for an event, statement, or idea, and which it can be fully understood and assessed. Synonyms for context include conditions, factors, situation, background, and setting.
Place the word in context by using it in a sentence. Write this sentence down and read it aloud. By creating sentences, you are practicing using the word correctly. If you strive to make these sentences interesting and creative, they will become more memorable and effective in activating your long-term memory.

Identify the Parts of Speech

"SUCCESS IS NOT FINAL; FAILURE IS NOT FATAL: IT IS THE COURAGE TO CONTINUE THAT COUNTS." -WINSTON S. CHURCHILL

Read through each term in the glossary and make a note of what part of speech each term is. Studying and identifying parts of speech shows us how the words relate to each other. It also helps you create a visualization of each term. Below are brief descriptions of the parts of speech for you to use as a guide.

VERB: A word denoting action, occurrence, or existence. Examples: walk, hop, whisper, sweat, dribbles, feels, sleeps, drink, smile, are, is, was, has.

NOUN: A word that names a person, place, thing, idea, animal, quality, or action. Nouns are the subject of the sentence. Examples: dog, Tom, Florida, CD, pasta, hate, tiger.

ADJECTIVE: A word that modifies, qualifies, or describes nouns and pronouns. Generally, adjectives appear immediately before the words they modify. Examples: smart girl, gifted teacher, old car, red door.

ADVERB: A word that modifies verbs, adjectives and other adverbs. An "ly" ending almost always changes an adjective to an adverb. Examples: ran swiftly, worked slowly, and drifted aimlessly. Many adverbs do not end in "ly." However, all adverbs identify when, where, how, how far, how much, etc. Examples: run hot, lived hard, moved right, study smart.

Chunking

"YOUR POSITIVE ACTION COMBINED WITH POSITIVE THINKING RESULTS IN SUCCESS." SHIV KHERA

Chunking is when you take a set of words and break it down into groups based on a common relationship. Research has shown that our brains learn by chunking information. By grouping your terms, you will be able to recall large sets of these words easily. To help make your chunking go easily use an online word cloud generator to make a set of word clouds representing your chunks.

1. Study the glossary and decide how you want to chunk the set of words. You can group by part of speech, topic, letter of the alphabet, word length, etc. Try to find an easy way to group each term.
2. Once you have your different groups, visit www.wordclouds.com to create a custom word cloud for each group. Print each one of these clouds and post it in a prominent place to serve as constant visual aids for your learning.

Analogies

"CHOOSE THE POSITIVE. YOU HAVE CHOICE, YOU ARE MASTER OF YOUR ATTITUDE, CHOOSE THE POSITIVE, THE CONSTRUCTIVE. OPTIMISM IS A FAITH THAT LEADS TO SUCCESS."– BRUCE LEE

An analogy is a comparison in which an idea or a thing is compared to another thing that is quite different from it. Analogies aim at explaining an idea by comparing it to something that is familiar. Metaphors and similes are tools used to create analogies.

Analogies are useful for learning vocabulary because they require you to analyze a word (or words), and then transfer that analysis to another word. This transfer reinforces the understanding of all the words.

As you analyze the relationships between the analogies you are creating, you will begin to understand the complex relationships between the seemingly unrelated words.

_A__ is to __B_ as __C_ is to __D_

This can be written using colons in place of the terms "is to" and "as."

A:B::C:D

The two items on the left (items A & B) describe a relationship and are separated by a single colon. The two items on the right (items C & D) are shown on the right and are also separated by a colon. Together, both sides are then separated by two colons in the middle, as shown here: Tall: Short :: Skinny: Fat. The relationship used in this analogy is the antonym.

How to create an analogy

Start with the basic formula for an analogy:

____ : ____ :: ____ : ____

Next, we will examine a simple synonym analogy:

automobile : car :: box : crate

The key to figuring out a set of word analogies is determining the relationship between the paired set of words.

Here is a list of the most common types of Analogies and examples

Synonym	Scream : Yell :: Push : Shove
Antonym	Rich : Poor :: Empty : Full
Cause is to Effect	Prosperity : Happiness :: Success : Joy
A Part is to its Whole	Toe : Foot :: Piece : Set
An Object to its Function	Car : Travel :: Read : Learn
A Item is to its Category	Tabby : House Cat :: Doberman : Dog
Word is a symptom of the other	Pain : Fracture :: Wheezing : Allergy
An object and it's description	Glass : Brittle :: Lead : Dense
The word is lacking the second word	Amputee : Limb :: Deaf : Hearing
The first word Hinders the second word	Shackles : Movement :: Stagger : Walk
The first word helps the action of the second	Knife : Bread :: Screwdriver : Screw
This word is made up of the second word	Sweater : Wool :: Jeans : Denim
A word and it's definition	Cede: Break Away :: Abolish : To get rid of

Using words from the glossary, make a set of analogies using each one. As a bonus, use more than one glossary term in a single analogy.

___________________ : ________________ :: _______________________ : __________________

Name the relationship between the words in your analogy:_______________________________

___________________ : ________________ :: ____________________ : _____________________

Name the relationship between the words in your analogy:_______________________________

___________________ : ________________ :: _______________________ : __________________

Name the relationship between the words in your analogy:_______________________________

Mnemonics

"IT ISN'T THE MOUNTAINS AHEAD TO CLIMB THAT WEAR YOU OUT; IT'S THE PEBBLE IN YOUR SHOE." -MUHAMMAD ALI

A mnemonic is a learning technique that helps you retain and remember information. Mnemonics are one of the best learning methods for remembering lists or processes in order. Mnemonics make the material more meaningful by adding associations and creating patterns. Interestingly, mnemonics may work better when they utilize absurd, startling, or shocking examples and references. Mnemonics help organize the information so that you can easily retrieve it later. By giving you associations and cues, mnemonics allow you to form a mental structure ordering a list or process to help you remember it better. This mental structure allows you to create a structure of association between items that may not appear to have any relationship. Mnemonics typically use references that are easy to visualize and thus easier to remember. Through visualization of vivid images and references, the information is much easier to imprint into long-term memory. The power of making mnemonics lies in converting dull, inert and uninspiring information into something vibrant and memorable.

How to make simple and effective mnemonics

Some of the best mnemonics help us remember simple rules or lists in order.

Step 1. Take a list of terms you are trying to remember in order. For example, we will use the scientific method:

observation, question, hypothesis, methods, results, and conclusion.

Next, we will replace each word on the list with a new word that starts with the same letter. These new words will together form a vivid sentence that is easy to remember:

Objectionable Queens Haunted Macho Rednecks Creatively.

As silly as the above sentence seems, it is easy to remember, and now we can call on this sentence to remind us of the order of the scientific method.

Visit http://www.mnemonicgenerator.com/ and try typing in a list of words. It is fun to see the mnemonics that it makes and shows how easy it is to make great mnemonics to help your studying.

Using vivid words in your mnemonics allows you to see the sentence you are making. Words that are gross, scary, or name interesting animals are helpful. Profanity is also useful because the shock value can trigger memory. The following are lists of vivid words to use in your mnemonics:

Gross words
Moist, Gurgle, Phlegm, Fetus, Curd, Smear, Squirt, Chunky, Orifice, Maggots, Viscous, Queasy, Bulbous, Pustule, Putrid, Fester, Secrete, Munch, Vomit, Ooze, Dripping, Roaches, Mucus, Stink, Stank, Stunk, Slurp, Pus, Lick, Salty, Tongue, Fart, Flatulence, Hemorrhoid.

Interesting Animals
Aardvark, Baboon, Chicken, Chinchilla, Duck, Dragonfly, Emu, Electric Eel, Frog, Flamingo, Gecko, Hedgehog, Hyena, Iguana, Jackal, Jaguar, Leopard, Lynx, Minnow, Manatee, Mongoose, Neanderthal, Newt, Octopus, Oyster, Pelican, Penguin, Platypus, Quail, Racoon, Rattlesnake, Rhinoceros, Scorpion, Seahorse, Toucan, Turkey, Vulture, Weasel, Woodpecker, Yak, Zebra.

Superhero Words
Diabolical, Activate, Boom, Clutch, Dastardly, Dynamic, Dynamite, Shazam, Kaboom, Zip, Zap, Zoom, Zany, Crushing, Smashing, Exploding, Ripping, Tearing.

Scary Words
Apparition, Bat, Chill, Demon, Eerie, Fangs, Genie, Hell, Lantern, Macabre, Nightmare, Owl, Ogre, Phantasm, Repulsive, Scarecrow, Tarantula, Undead, Vampire, Wraith, Zombie.

There are several types of mnemonics that can help your memory.

1. Images
Visual mnemonics are a type of mnemonic that works by associating an image with characters or objects whose name sounds like the item that must be memorized. This is one of the easiest ways to create effective mnemonics. An example would be to use the shape of numbers to help memorize a long list of them. Numbers can be memorized by their shapes, so that: 0 -looks like an egg; 1 -a pencil, or a candle; 2 -a snake; 3 -an ear; 4 -a sailboat; 5 -a key; 6 -a comet; 7 -a knee; 8 -a snowman; 9 -a comma.

Another type of visual mnemonic is the word-length mnemonic in which the number of letters in each word corresponds to a digit. This simple mnemonic gives pi to seven decimal places:

3.141582 becomes "How I wish I could calculate pi."

Of course, you could use this type of mnemonic to create a longer sentence showing the digits of an important number. Some people have used this type of mnemonic to memorize thousands of digits.

Using the hands is also an important tool for creating visual objects. Making the hands into specific shapes can help us remember the pattern of things or the order of a list of things.

2. Rhyming

Rhyming mnemonics are quick ways to make things memorable. A classic example is a mnemonic for the number of days in each month:

"30 days hath September, April, June, and November.
All the rest have 31
Except February, my dear son.
It has 28, and that is fine
But in Leap Year it has 29."

Another example of a rhyming mnemonic is a common spelling rule:

"I before e except after c
or when sounding like a
in neighbor and weigh."

Use **rhymer.com** to get large lists of rhyming words.

3. Homonym

A homonym is one of a group of words that share the same pronunciation but have different meanings, whether spelled the same or not.

Try saying what you're attempting to remember out loud or very quickly, and see if anything leaps out. If you know other languages, using similar-sounding words from those can be effective.

You could also browse this list of homonyms at http://www.cooper.com/alan/homonym_list.html.

4. Onomatopoeia

An Onomatopeia is a word that phonetically imitates, resembles or suggests the source of the sound that it describes. Are there any noises made by the thing you're trying to memorize? Is it often associated with some other sound? Failing that, just make up a noise that seems to fit.

Achoo, ahem, baa, bam, bark, beep, beep beep, belch, bleat, boo, boo hoo, boom, burp, buzz, chirp, click clack, crash, croak, crunch, cuckoo, dash, drip, ding dong, eek, fizz, flit, flutter, gasp, grrr, ha ha, hee hee, hiccup, hiss, hissing, honk, icky, itchy, jiggly, jangle, knock knock, lush, la la la, mash, meow, moan, murmur, neigh, oink, ouch, plop, pow, quack, quick, rapping, rattle, ribbit, roar, rumble, rustle, scratch, sizzle, skittering, snap crackle pop, splash, splish splash, spurt, swish, swoosh, tap, tapping, tick tock, tinkle, tweet, ugh, vroom, wham, whinny, whip, whooping, woof.

5. Acronyms

An acronym is a word or name formed as an abbreviation from the initial components of a word, such as NATO, which stands for North Atlantic Treaty Organization. If you're trying to memorize something involving letters, this is often a good bet. A lot of famous mnemonics are acronyms, such as ROYGBIV which stands for the order of colors in the light spectrum (Red, Orange, Yellow, Green, Blue, Indigo, and Violet).

A great acronym generator to try is: www.all-acronyms.com.

A different spin on an acronym is a backronym. A **backronym** is a specially constructed phrase that is supposed to be the source of a word that is an acronym. A backronym is constructed by creating a new phrase to fit an already existing word, name, or acronym.

The word is a combination of *backward* and *acronym*, and has been defined as a "reverse acronym." For example, the United States Department of Justice assigns to their Amber Alert program the meaning "**A**merica's **M**issing: **B**roadcast **E**mergency **R**esponse." The process can go either way to make good mnemonics.

Visit: https://arthurdick.com/projects/backronym/ to try out a simple backronym generator.

6. Anagrams

An anagram is a direct word switch or word play, the result of rearranging the letters of a word or phrase to produce a new word or phrase, using all the original letters exactly once; for example, the word anagram can be rearranged into nag-a-ram.

Try re-arranging letters or components and see if anything memorable emerges. Visit http://www.nameacronym.net/ to use a simple anagram generator.

One particularly memorable form of anagram is the spoonerism, where you swap the initial syllables or letters of words to make new phrases. These are usually humorous, and this makes them easier to remember. Here are some examples:

"Is it kisstomary to cuss the bride?" (as opposed to "customary to kiss")
"The Lord is a shoving leopard." (instead of "a loving shepherd")
"A blushing crow." ("crushing blow")
"A well-boiled icicle" ("well-oiled bicycle")
"You were fighting a liar in the quadrangle." ("lighting a fire")
"Is the bean dizzy?" (as opposed to "is the dean busy?")

7. Stories

Make up quick stories or incidents involving the material you want to memorize. For larger chunks of information, the stories can get more elaborate. Structured stories are particularly good for remembering lists or other sequenced information. Have a look at https://en.wikipedia.org/wiki/Method_of_loci for a more advanced memory sequencing technique.

Visual Metaphors

"LIMITS, LIKE FEAR, IS OFTEN AN ILLUSION." –MICHAEL JORDAN

What is a Metaphor?

A metaphor is a figure of speech that refers to one thing by mentioning another thing. Metaphors provide clarity and identify hidden similarities between two seemingly unrelated ideas. A visual metaphor is an image that creates a link between different ideas.

Visual metaphors help us use our understanding of the world to learn new concepts, skills, and ideas. Visual metaphors help us relate new material to what we already know. Visual metaphors must be clear and simple enough to spark a connection and understanding. Visual metaphors should use familiar things to help you be less fearful of new, complex, or challenging topics. Metaphors trigger a sense of familiarity so that you are more accepting of the new idea. Metaphors work best when you associate a familiar, easy to understand idea with a challenging, obscure, or abstract concept.

How to make a visual metaphor

1. Brainstorm using the words of the concept. Use different fonts, colors, or shapes to represent parts of the concept.

2. Merge these images together

3. Show the process using arrows, accents, etc.

4. Think about the story line your metaphor projects.

Examples of visual metaphors:

A skeleton used to show a framework of something.

A cloud showing an outline.

A bodybuilder whose muscles represent supporting ideas and details.

A sandwich where the meat, tomato, and lettuce represent supporting ideas.

A recipe card to show a process.

Your metaphor should be accurate. It should be complex enough to convey meaning, but simple and clear enough to be easily understood.

Morphology

"SCIENCE IS THE CAPTAIN, AND PRACTICE THE SOLDIERS." LEONARDO DA VINCI

Morphology is the study of the origin, roots, suffixes, and prefixes of the words. Understanding the meaning of prefixes, suffixes, and roots make it easier to decode the meaning of new vocabulary. Having the ability to decode using morphology increases text comprehension when initially reading as well.

The capability of identifying meaningful parts of words (morphemes), including prefixes, suffixes, and roots can be helpful. Identifying morphemes improves decoding accuracy and fluency. Reading speed improves when you can decode larger chunks of text quickly. When you can recognize morphemes in words, you will be better able to make sense of new words in context. Below are charts containing the most common prefixes, suffixes, and root words. Use them to help you decode your vocabulary terms.

Prefixes

Prefix	Meaning	Example words and meanings	
a, ab, abs	away from	absent abdicate	not to be present, to give up an office or throne.
ad, a, ac, af, ag, an, ar, at, as	to, toward	Advance advantage	To move forward To have the upper hand
anti	against	Antidote antisocial antibiotic	To repair poisoning refers to someone who's not social
bi, bis	two	bicycle binary biweekly	two-wheeled cycle two number system every two weeks
circum, cir	around	circumnavigate circle	Travel around the world a figure that goes all around
com, con, co, col	with, together	Complete Complement	To finish To go along with
de	away from, down, the opposite of	depart detour	to go away from to go out of your way
dis, dif, di	apart	dislike dishonest distant	not to like not honest away
En-, em-	Cause to	Entrance	the way in.
epi	upon, on top of	epitaph epilogue epidemic	writing upon a tombstone speech at the end, on top of the rest
equ, equi	equal	equalize equitable	to make equal fair, equal
ex, e, ef	out, from	exit eject exhale	to go out to throw out to breathe out
Fore-	Before	Forewarned	To have prior warning

Prefix	Meaning	Example Words and Meanings	
in, il, ir, im, en	in, into	Infield Imbibe	The inner playing field to take part in
in, il, ig, ir, im	not	inactive ignorant irreversible irritate	not active not knowing not reversible to put into discomfort
inter	between, among	international interact	among nations to mix with
mal, male	bad, ill, wrong	malpractice malfunction	bad practice fail to function, bad function
Mid	Middle	Amidships	In the middle of a ship
mis	wrong, badly	misnomer	The wrong name
mono	one, alone, single	monocle	one lensed glasses
non	not, the reverse of	nonprofit	not making a profit
ob	in front, against, in front of, in the way of	Obsolete	No longer needed
omni	everywhere, all	omnipresent omnipotent	always present, everywhere all powerful
Over	On top	Overdose	Take too much medication
Pre	Before	Preview	Happens before a show.
per	through	Permeable pervasive	to pass through, all encompassing
poly	many	Polygamy polygon	many spouses figure with many sides
post	after	postpone postmortem	to do after after death
pre	before, earlier than	Predict Preview	To know before To view before release
pro	forward, going ahead of, supporting	proceed pro-war promote	to go forward supporting the war to raise or move forward
re	again, back	retell recall reverse	to tell again to call back to go back
se	apart	secede seclude	to withdraw, become apart to stay apart from others
Semi	Half	Semipermeable	Half-permeable

Prefix	Meaning	Example Words and Meanings	
Sub	under, less than	Submarine	under water
super	over, above, greater	superstar superimpose	a start greater than her stars to put over something else
trans	across	transcontinental transverse	across the continent to lie or go across
un, uni	one	unidirectional unanimous unilateral	having one direction sharing one view having one side
un	not	uninterested unhelpful unethical	not interested not helpful not ethical

Roots

Root	Meaning	Example words & meanings	
act, ag	to do, to act	Agent Activity	One who acts as a representative Action
Aqua	Water	Aquamarine	The color of water
Aud	To hear	Auditorium	A place to hear music
apert	open	Aperture	An opening
bas	low	Basement Basement	Something that is low, at the bottom A room that is low
Bio	Living thing	Biological	Living matter
cap, capt, cip, cept, ceive	to take, to hold, to seize	Captive Receive Capable Recipient	One who is held To take Able to take hold of things One who takes hold or receives
ced, cede, ceed, cess	to go, to give in	Precede Access Proceed	To go before Means of going to To go forward
Cogn	Know	Cognitive	Ability to think
cred, credit	to believe	Credible Incredible Credit	Believable Not believable Belief, trust
curr, curs, cours	to run	Current Precursory Recourse	Now in progress, running Running (going) before To run for aid
Cycle	Circle	Lifecycle	The circle of life
dic, dict	to say	Dictionary Indict	A book explaining words (sayings)

Root	Meaning	Examples and meanings	
duc, duct	to lead	Induce Conduct Aqueduct	To lead to action To lead or guide Pipe that leads water somewhere
equ	equal, even	Equality Equanimity	Equal in social, political rights Evenness of mind, tranquility
fac, fact, fic, fect, fy	to make, to do	Facile Fiction Factory Affect	Easy to do Something that is made up Place that makes things To make a change in
fer, ferr	to carry, bring	Defer Referral	To carry away Bring a source for help/information
Gen	Birth	Generate	To create something
graph	write	Monograph Graphite	A writing on a particular subject A form of carbon used for writing
Loc	Place	Location	A place
Mater	Mother	Maternity	Expecting birth
Mem	Recall	Memory	The recall experiences
mit, mis	to send	Admit Missile	To send in Something sent through the air
Nat	Born	Native	Born in a place
par	equal	Parity Disparate	Equality No equal, not alike
Ped	Foot	Podiatrist	Foot doctor
Photo	Light	Photograph	A picture
plic	to fold, to bend, to turn	Complicate Implicate	To fold (mix) together To fold in, to involve
pon, pos, posit, pose	to place	Component Transpose Compose Deposit	A part placed together with others A place across To put many parts into place To place for safekeeping
scrib, script	to write	Describe Transcript Subscription	To write about or tell about A written copy A written signature or document
sequ, secu	to follow	Sequence	In following order

Root	Meaning	Examples and Meanings	
Sign	Mark	Signal	to alert somebody
spec, spect, spic	to appear, to look, to see	Specimen Aspect	An example to look at One way to see something
sta, stat, sist,	to stand, or make stand	Constant	Standing with
stit, sisto	Stable, steady	Status Stable Desist	Social standing Steady (standing) To stand away from
Struct	To build	Construction	To build a thing
tact	to touch	Contact Tactile	To touch together To be able to be touched
ten, tent, tain	to hold	Tenable Retentive Maintain	Able to be held, holding Holding To keep or hold up
tend, tens, tent	to stretch	Extend Tension	To stretch or draw out Stretched
Therm	Temperature	Thermometer	Detects temperature
tract	to draw	Attract Contract	To draw together An agreement drawn up
ven, vent	to come	Convene Advent	To come together A coming
Vis	See	Invisible	Cannot be seen
ver, vert, vers	to turn	Avert Revert Reverse	To turn away To turn back To turn around

Crossword Puzzles

1. Using the Across and Down clues, write the correct words in the numbered grid below.

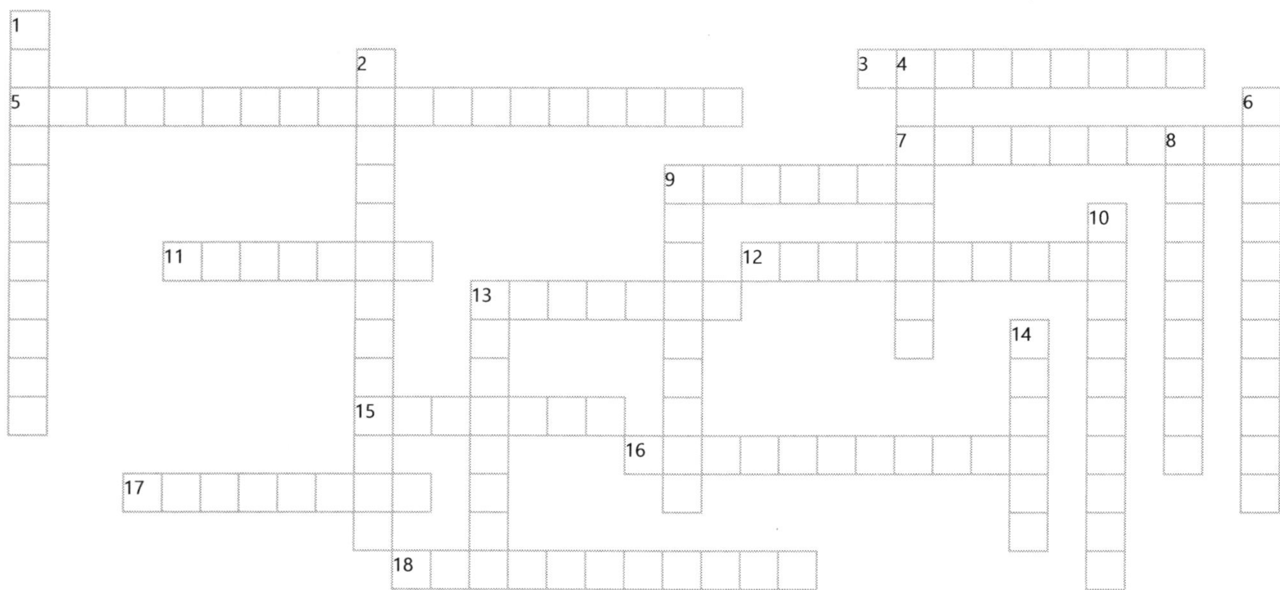

ACROSS

3. Determine (the amount or number of something) mathematically.
5. The process by which cells use oxygen to produce energy from food.
7. The ability to see, hear, or become aware of something through the senses.
9. inspect (someone or something) in detail to determine their nature or condition.
11. Estimate, measure, or note the similarity or dissimilarity between.
12. Place in a particular class or group.
13. Assigning human qualities to objects "the sun was mad and burned me".
15. A comparison of two things based on their being alike in some way.
16. Clearly show the existence or truth of (something) by giving proof or evidence.
17. The state of being strikingly different from something else.
18. Recognize or treat (someone or something) as different.

DOWN

1. Family of classroom.
2. A condition characterized by paralysis, weakness, lack of coordination.
4. A type of autism characterized by normal cognitive and language development and impaired social skills.
6. Combine one thing with another so that they become a whole.
8. Acting or done without forethought.
9. Influence of external aspects on development.
10. Interaction of two microsystems.
13. Breakdown information into parts and use those parts.
14. Emotion or desire, especially as influencing behavior or action.

A. Compare
B. Asperger
C. Examine
D. Contrast
E. Demonstrate
F. Mesosystem
G. Perception
H. Cerebral Palsy
I. Affect
J. Distinguish
K. Microsystem
L. Animism
M. Impulsive
N. Categorize
O. Exosystem
P. Analogy
Q. Calculate
R. Cellular Respiration
S. Integration
T. Analysis

2. Using the Across and Down clues, write the correct words in the numbered grid below.

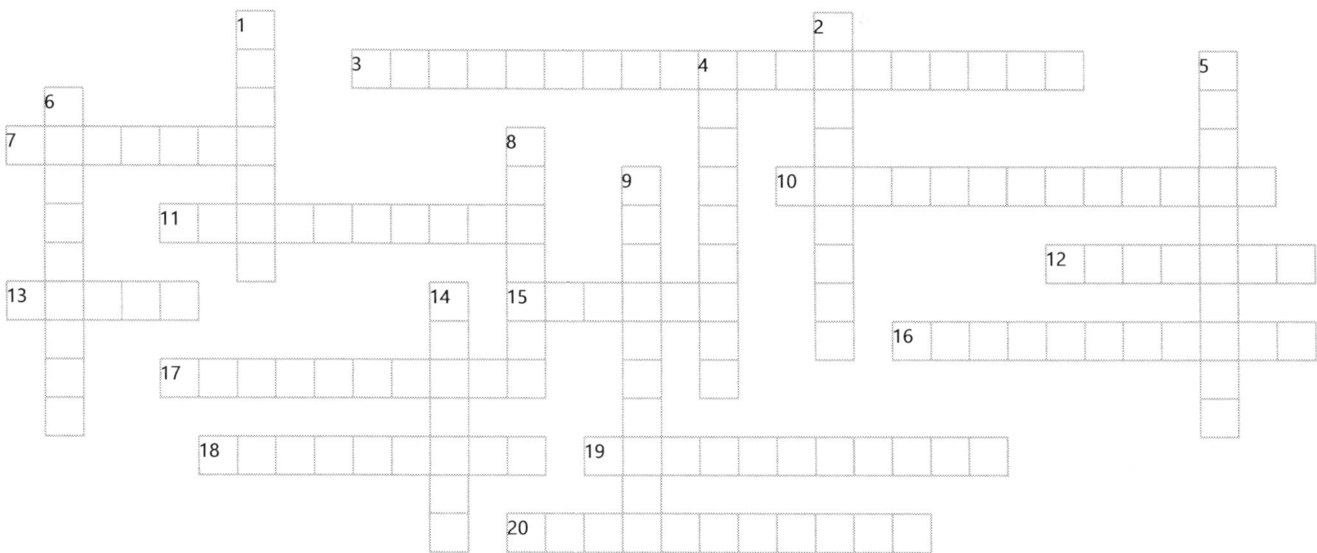

ACROSS

3. The process by which cells use oxygen to produce energy from food.
7. An uncontrolled outburst of anger and frustration, typically in a young child.
10. Leader in field of child psychology and development, outlined 4 types of nested systems.
11. Interaction of two microsystems.
12. A comparison of two things based on their being alike in some way.
13. Detailed classification of critical thinking and learning skills and objectives into tiered levels.
15. Emotion or desire, especially as influencing behavior or action.
16. Recognize or treat (someone or something) as different.
17. Explain or make (something) clear by using examples, charts, pictures, etc.
18. Indicate the faults of (someone or something) in a disapproving way.
19. Clearly show the existence or truth of (something) by giving proof or evidence.
20. Recognize or treat (someone or something) as different.

DOWN

1. Assigning human qualities to objects "the sun was mad and burned me".
2. Reports events about someone's life.
4. Influence of external aspects on development.
5. Place in a particular class or group.
6. Determine (the amount or number of something) mathematically.
8. Estimate, measure, or note the similarity or dissimilarity between.
9. A scientific procedure undertaken to make a discovery, test a hypothesis, or demonstrate a fact.
14. inspect (someone or something) in detail to determine their nature or condition.

A. Cellular Respiration	B. Bloom	C. Analogy	D. Illustrate
E. Tantrum	F. Mesosystem	G. Exosystem	H. Calculate
I. Brofenbrenner	J. Biography	K. Demonstrate	L. Affect
M. Experiment	N. Animism	O. Compare	P. Distinguish
Q. Distinguish	R. Criticize	S. Examine	T. Categorize

3. Using the Across and Down clues, write the correct words in the numbered grid below.

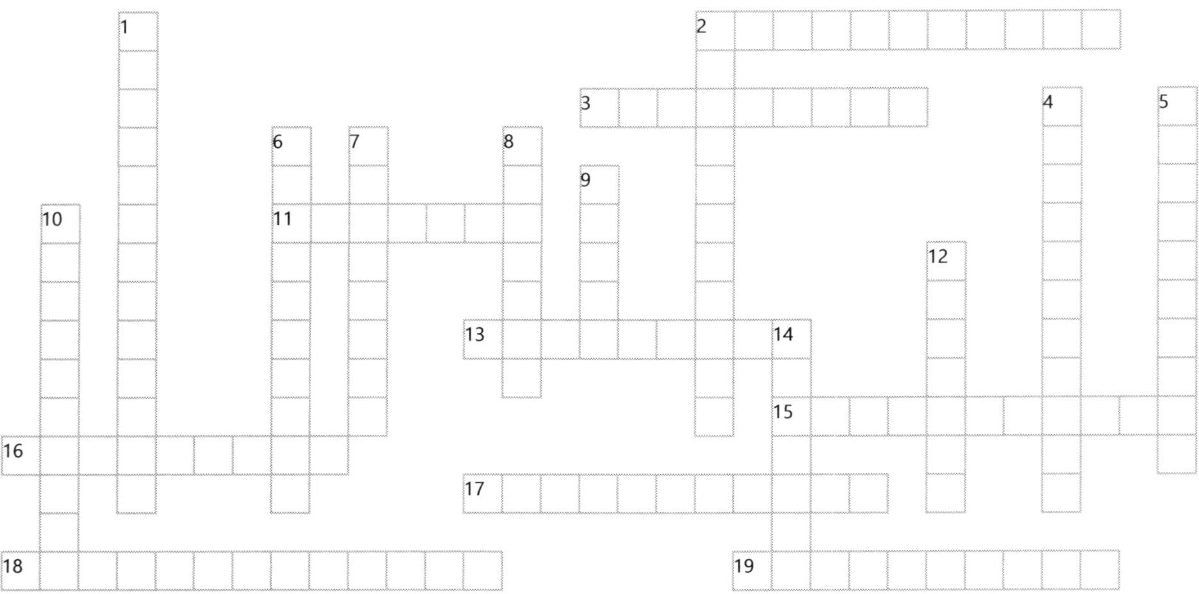

ACROSS

2. Clearly show the existence or truth of (something) by giving proof or evidence.
3. Influence of external aspects on development.
11. An uncontrolled outburst of anger and frustration, typically in a young child.
13. Adapt a novel or present a particular incident as a play or movie.
15. Bloom's 3rd level, take previous learning and use it in a new way.
16. Indicate the faults of (someone or something) in a disapproving way.
17. Recognize or treat (someone or something) as different.
18. A condition characterized by paralysis, weakness, lack of coordination.
19. The ability to see, hear, or become aware of something through the senses.

DOWN

1. The condition of being abnormally or extremely active.
2. Recognize or treat (someone or something) as different.
4. The whole socio-cultural context.
5. A scientific procedure undertaken to make a discovery, test a hypothesis, or demonstrate a fact.
6. Place in a particular class or group.
7. The state of being strikingly different from something else.
8. Estimate, measure, or note the similarity or dissimilarity between.
9. Detailed classification of critical thinking and learning skills and objectives into tiered levels.
10. Explain or make (something) clear by using examples, charts, pictures, etc.
12. Assigning human qualities to objects "the sun was mad and burned me".
14. inspect (someone or something) in detail to determine their nature or condition.

A. Dramatize	B. Hyperactivity	C. Contrast	D. Illustrate	E. Macrosystem
F. Distinguish	G. Animism	H. Criticize	I. Cerebral Palsy	J. Perception
K. Tantrum	L. Exosystem	M. Application	N. Distinguish	O. Bloom
P. Demonstrate	Q. Compare	R. Experiment	S. Categorize	T. Examine

4. Using the Across and Down clues, write the correct words in the numbered grid below.

ACROSS

2. The whole socio-cultural context.
4. Breakdown information into parts and use those parts.
5. The process by which cells use oxygen to produce energy from food.
8. inspect (someone or something) in detail to determine their nature or condition.
11. The condition of being abnormally or extremely active.
13. Explain or make (something) clear by using examples, charts, pictures, etc.
15. Interaction of two microsystems.
16. Recognize or treat (someone or something) as different.
17. A condition characterized by paralysis, weakness, lack of coordination.
18. Indicate the faults of (someone or something) in a disapproving way.
19. An uncontrolled outburst of anger and frustration, typically in a young child.

DOWN

1. Leader in field of child psychology and development, outlined 4 types of nested systems.
3. A comparison of two things based on their being alike in some way.
4. Bloom's 3rd level, take previous learning and use it in a new way.
6. Emotion or desire, especially as influencing behavior or action.
7. Family of classroom.
9. Influence of external aspects on development.
10. Place in a particular class or group.
12. Determine (the amount or number of something) mathematically.
14. Assigning human qualities to objects "the sun was mad and burned me".

A. Mesosystem	B. Examine	C. Analogy	D. Animism
E. Criticize	F. Affect	G. Tantrum	H. Distinguish
I. Categorize	J. Cerebral Palsy	K. Analysis	L. Cellular Respiration
M. Macrosystem	N. Calculate	O. Microsystem	P. Hyperactivity
Q. Illustrate	R. Exosystem	S. Brofenbrenner	T. Application

5. Using the Across and Down clues, write the correct words in the numbered grid below.

ACROSS

3. Recognize or treat (someone or something) as different.
6. Bloom's 3rd level, take previous learning and use it in a new way.
7. Assigning human qualities to objects "the sun was mad and burned me".
9. The process by which cells use oxygen to produce energy from food.
11. Indicate the faults of (someone or something) in a disapproving way.
13. A scientific procedure undertaken to make a discovery, test a hypothesis, or demonstrate a fact.
14. Estimate, measure, or note the similarity or dissimilarity between.
16. Interaction of two microsystems.
17. Clearly show the existence or truth of (something) by giving proof or evidence.
18. Place in a particular class or group.
19. Explain or make (something) clear by using examples, charts, pictures, etc.
20. Detailed classification of critical thinking and learning skills and objectives into tiered levels.

DOWN

1. Adapt a novel or present a particular incident as a play or movie.
2. Determine (the amount or number of something) mathematically.
4. An uncontrolled outburst of anger and frustration, typically in a young child.
5. Breakdown information into parts and use those parts.
8. Leader in field of child psychology and development, outlined 4 types of nested systems.
10. Influence of external aspects on development.
12. The state of being strikingly different from something else.
15. Emotion or desire, especially as influencing behavior or action.

A. Brofenbrenner	B. Cellular Respiration	C. Bloom	D. Criticize
E. Contrast	F. Application	G. Affect	H. Calculate
I. Demonstrate	J. Exosystem	K. Dramatize	L. Compare
M. Distinguish	N. Animism	O. Illustrate	P. Tantrum
Q. Experiment	R. Analysis	S. Mesosystem	T. Categorize

6. Using the Across and Down clues, write the correct words in the numbered grid below.

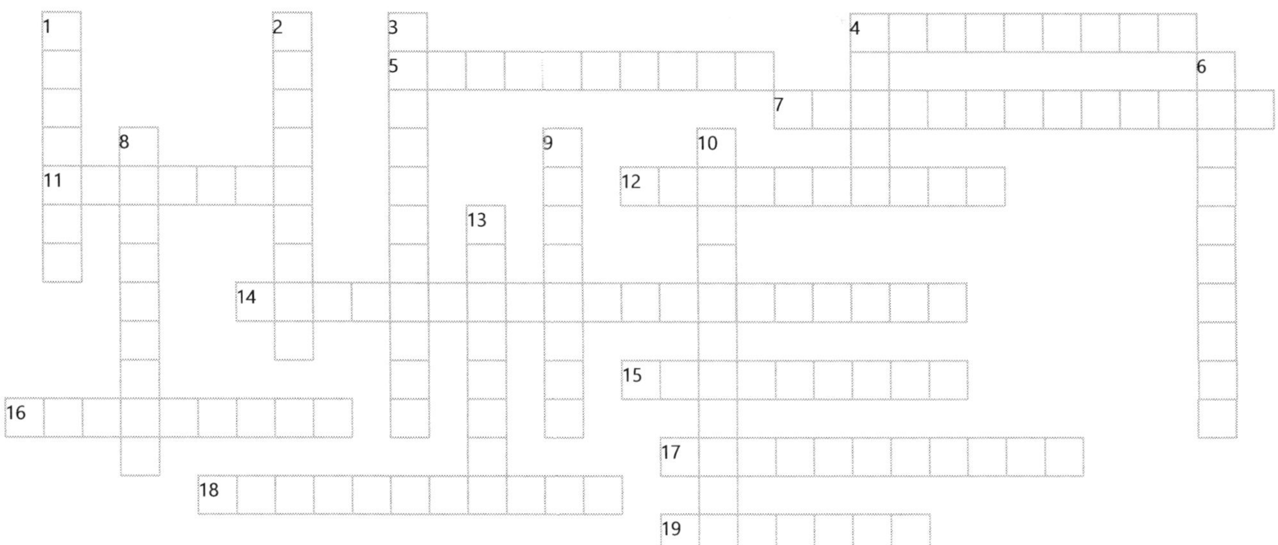

ACROSS

4. Reports events about someone's life.
5. Explain or make (something) clear by using examples, charts, pictures, etc.
7. Leader in field of child psychology and development, outlined 4 types of nested systems.
11. A comparison of two things based on their being alike in some way.
12. A scientific procedure undertaken to make a discovery, test a hypothesis, or demonstrate a fact.
14. The process by which cells use oxygen to produce energy from food.
15. Adapt a novel or present a particular incident as a play or movie.
16. Indicate the faults of (someone or something) in a disapproving way.
17. Recognize or treat (someone or something) as different.
18. Family of classroom.
19. Assigning human qualities to objects "the sun was mad and burned me".

DOWN

1. Estimate, measure, or note the similarity or dissimilarity between.
2. Influence of external aspects on development.
3. Recognize or treat (someone or something) as different.
4. Detailed classification of critical thinking and learning skills and objectives into tiered levels.
6. Interaction of two microsystems.
8. Determine (the amount or number of something) mathematically.
9. The state of being strikingly different from something else.
10. Bloom's 3rd level, take previous learning and use it in a new way.
13. Breakdown information into parts and use those parts.

A. Cellular Respiration
B. Exosystem
C. Illustrate
D. Dramatize
E. Analysis
F. Microsystem
G. Mesosystem
H. Brofenbrenner
I. Contrast
J. Distinguish
K. Calculate
L. Application
M. Experiment
N. Compare
O. Biography
P. Criticize
Q. Animism
R. Distinguish
S. Analogy
T. Bloom

7. Using the Across and Down clues, write the correct words in the numbered grid below.

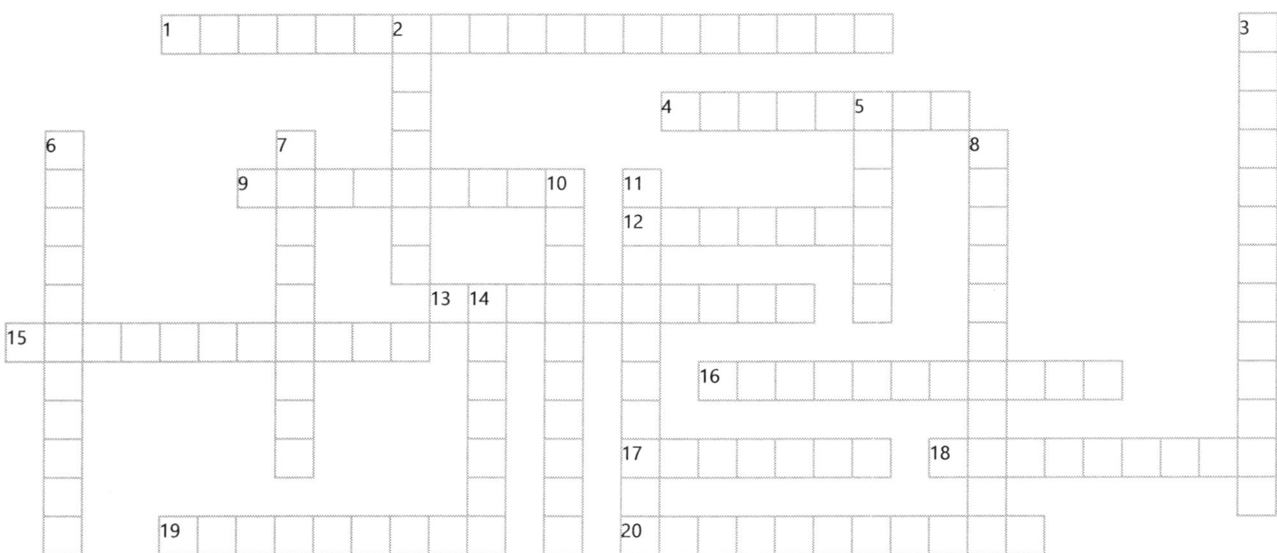

ACROSS

1. The process by which cells use oxygen to produce energy from food.
4. The state of being strikingly different from something else.
9. Indicate the faults of (someone or something) in a disapproving way.
12. inspect (someone or something) in detail to determine their nature or condition.
13. Place in a particular class or group.
15. Combine one thing with another so that they become a whole.
16. Bloom's 3rd level, take previous learning and use it in a new way.
17. An uncontrolled outburst of anger and frustration, typically in a young child.
18. Determine (the amount or number of something) mathematically.
19. Reports events about someone's life.
20. Family of classroom.

DOWN

2. Assigning human qualities to objects "the sun was mad and burned me".
3. Leader in field of child psychology and development, outlined 4 types of nested systems.
5. Emotion or desire, especially as influencing behavior or action.
6. Recognize or treat (someone or something) as different.
7. Adapt a novel or present a particular incident as a play or movie.
8. Clearly show the existence or truth of (something) by giving proof or evidence.
10. A scientific procedure undertaken to make a discovery, test a hypothesis, or demonstrate a fact.
11. Interaction of two microsystems.
14. A comparison of two things based on their being alike in some way.

A. Application	B. Biography	C. Tantrum	D. Brofenbrenner
E. Demonstrate	F. Contrast	G. Dramatize	H. Cellular Respiration
I. Categorize	J. Mesosystem	K. Distinguish	L. Criticize
M. Experiment	N. Animism	O. Calculate	P. Integration
Q. Analogy	R. Microsystem	S. Affect	T. Examine

8. Using the Across and Down clues, write the correct words in the numbered grid below.

ACROSS

4. The ability to see, hear, or become aware of something through the senses.
6. The process by which cells use oxygen to produce energy from food.
10. A scientific procedure undertaken to make a discovery, test a hypothesis, or demonstrate a fact.
11. inspect (someone or something) in detail to determine their nature or condition.
12. A type of autism characterized by normal cognitive and language development and impaired social skills.
14. Place in a particular class or group.
16. The state of being strikingly different from something else.
17. Leader in field of child psychology and development, outlined 4 types of nested systems.
18. Breakdown information into parts and use those parts.
19. Emotion or desire, especially as influencing behavior or action.
20. A condition characterized by paralysis, weakness, lack of coordination.

DOWN

1. Clearly show the existence or truth of (something) by giving proof or evidence.
2. A comparison of two things based on their being alike in some way.
3. Detailed classification of critical thinking and learning skills and objectives into tiered levels.
5. The condition of being abnormally or extremely active.
7. Recognize or treat (someone or something) as different.
8. Recognize or treat (someone or something) as different.
9. Combine one thing with another so that they become a whole.
13. Estimate, measure, or note the similarity or dissimilarity between.
15. An uncontrolled outburst of anger and frustration, typically in a young child.

A. Analysis	B. Asperger	C. Categorize	D. Perception
E. Cerebral Palsy	F. Affect	G. Compare	H. Demonstrate
I. Brofenbrenner	J. Experiment	K. Distinguish	L. Tantrum
M. Integration	N. Analogy	O. Bloom	P. Distinguish
Q. Examine	R. Contrast	S. Hyperactivity	T. Cellular Respiration

9. Using the Across and Down clues, write the correct words in the numbered grid below.

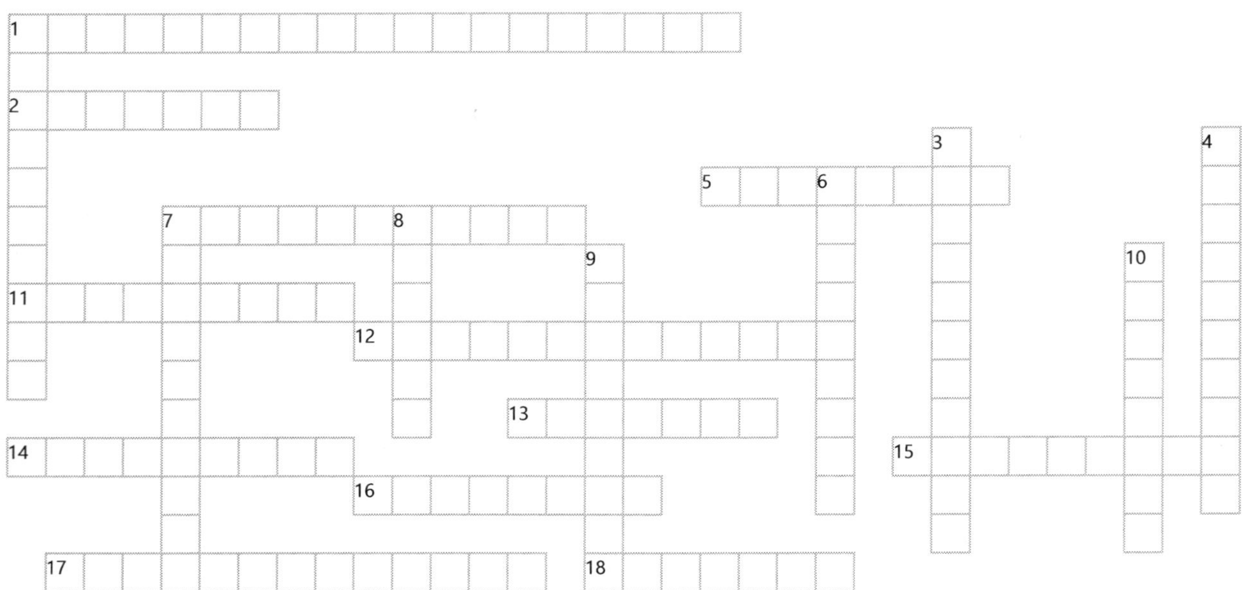

ACROSS

1. The process by which cells use oxygen to produce energy from food.
2. An uncontrolled outburst of anger and frustration, typically in a young child.
5. A type of autism characterized by normal cognitive and language development and impaired social skills.
7. Combine one thing with another so that they become a whole.
11. Acting or done without forethought.
12. A condition characterized by paralysis, weakness, lack of coordination.
13. A comparison of two things based on their being alike in some way.
14. Reports events about someone's life.
15. Determine (the amount or number of something) mathematically.
16. Breakdown information into parts and use those parts.
17. The condition of being abnormally or extremely active.
18. inspect (someone or something) in detail to determine their nature or condition.

DOWN

1. Place in a particular class or group.
3. Clearly show the existence or truth of (something) by giving proof or evidence.
4. Interaction of two microsystems.
6. Influence of external aspects on development.
7. Explain or make (something) clear by using examples, charts, pictures, etc.
8. Emotion or desire, especially as influencing behavior or action.
9. Adapt a novel or present a particular incident as a play or movie.
10. The state of being strikingly different from something else.

A. Demonstrate	B. Impulsive	C. Illustrate	D. Dramatize
E. Examine	F. Categorize	G. Tantrum	H. Calculate
I. Integration	J. Asperger	K. Affect	L. Analogy
M. Contrast	N. Biography	O. Cellular Respiration	P. Cerebral Palsy
Q. Mesosystem	R. Hyperactivity	S. Exosystem	T. Analysis

10. Using the Across and Down clues, write the correct words in the numbered grid below.

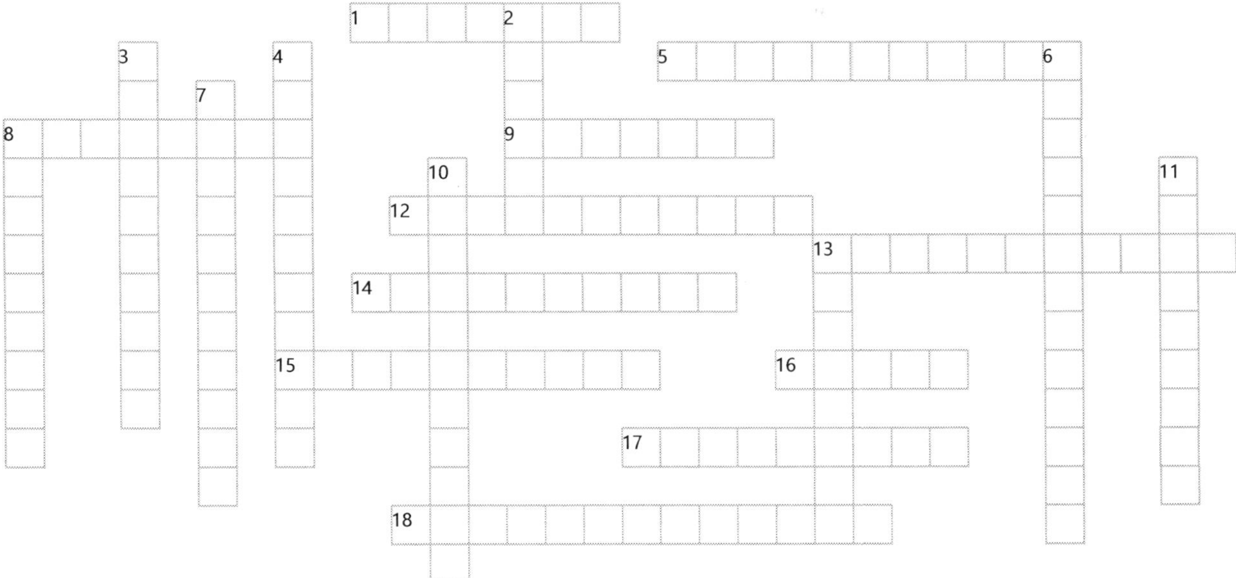

ACROSS

1. Estimate, measure, or note the similarity or dissimilarity between.
5. Recognize or treat (someone or something) as different.
8. The state of being strikingly different from something else.
9. inspect (someone or something) in detail to determine their nature or condition.
12. Recognize or treat (someone or something) as different.
13. Bloom's 3rd level, take previous learning and use it in a new way.
14. The ability to see, hear, or become aware of something through the senses.
15. Explain or make (something) clear by using examples, charts, pictures, etc.
16. Detailed classification of critical thinking and learning skills and objectives into tiered levels.
17. Acting or done without forethought.
18. A condition characterized by paralysis, weakness, lack of coordination.

DOWN

2. Emotion or desire, especially as influencing behavior or action.
3. Place in a particular class or group.
4. Combine one thing with another so that they become a whole.
6. The condition of being abnormally or extremely active.
7. The whole socio-cultural context.
8. Determine (the amount or number of something) mathematically.
10. Family of classroom.
11. Influence of external aspects on development.
13. Breakdown information into parts and use those parts.

A. Compare	B. Calculate	C. Affect	D. Application	E. Impulsive
F. Analysis	G. Examine	H. Integration	I. Hyperactivity	J. Microsystem
K. Perception	L. Macrosystem	M. Distinguish	N. Contrast	O. Categorize
P. Distinguish	Q. Cerebral Palsy	R. Bloom	S. Exosystem	T. Illustrate

11. Using the Across and Down clues, write the correct words in the numbered grid below.

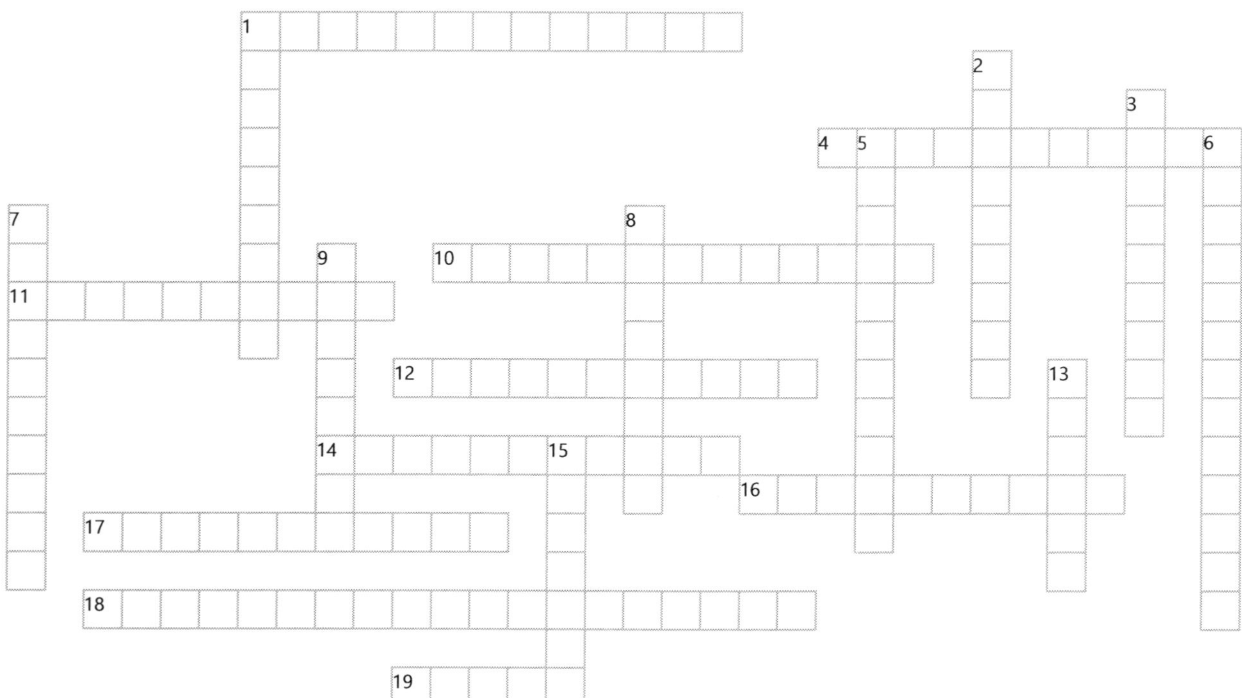

ACROSS

1. A condition characterized by paralysis, weakness, lack of coordination.
4. Recognize or treat (someone or something) as different.
10. Leader in field of child psychology and development, outlined 4 types of nested systems.
11. The ability to see, hear, or become aware of something through the senses.
12. Family of classroom.
14. Bloom's 3rd level, take previous learning and use it in a new way.
16. Interaction of two microsystems.
17. Clearly show the existence or truth of (something) by giving proof or evidence.
18. The process by which cells use oxygen to produce energy from food.
19. Detailed classification of critical thinking and learning skills and objectives into tiered levels.

DOWN

1. Determine (the amount or number of something) mathematically.
2. Indicate the faults of (someone or something) in a disapproving way.
3. Reports events about someone's life.
5. Combine one thing with another so that they become a whole.
6. The condition of being abnormally or extremely active.
7. A scientific procedure undertaken to make a discovery, test a hypothesis, or demonstrate a fact.
8. Breakdown information into parts and use those parts.
9. The state of being strikingly different from something else.
13. Emotion or desire, especially as influencing behavior or action.
15. Assigning human qualities to objects "the sun was mad and burned me".

A. Cerebral Palsy
B. Analysis
C. Distinguish
D. Experiment
E. Criticize
F. Calculate
G. Contrast
H. Biography
I. Brofenbrenner
J. Animism
K. Mesosystem
L. Application
M. Microsystem
N. Perception
O. Hyperactivity
P. Demonstrate
Q. Integration
R. Bloom
S. Affect
T. Cellular Respiration

12. Using the Across and Down clues, write the correct words in the numbered grid below.

ACROSS

1. The whole socio-cultural context.
5. Assigning human qualities to objects "the sun was mad and burned me".
6. Leader in field of child psychology and development, outlined 4 types of nested systems.
10. The process by which cells use oxygen to produce energy from food.
13. A condition characterized by paralysis, weakness, lack of coordination.
14. The ability to see, hear, or become aware of something through the senses.
15. A type of autism characterized by normal cognitive and language development and impaired social skills.
16. Reports events about someone's life.
17. A scientific procedure undertaken to make a discovery, test a hypothesis, or demonstrate a fact.
18. inspect (someone or something) in detail to determine their nature or condition.
19. Family of classroom.

DOWN

2. Estimate, measure, or note the similarity or dissimilarity between.
3. Adapt a novel or present a particular incident as a play or movie.
4. Breakdown information into parts and use those parts.
7. The condition of being abnormally or extremely active.
8. Explain or make (something) clear by using examples, charts, pictures, etc.
9. An uncontrolled outburst of anger and frustration, typically in a young child.
10. Place in a particular class or group.
11. Interaction of two microsystems.
12. The state of being strikingly different from something else.

A. Experiment
B. Dramatize
C. Cellular Respiration
D. Examine
E. Asperger
F. Mesosystem
G. Analysis
H. Hyperactivity
I. Cerebral Palsy
J. Microsystem
K. Contrast
L. Tantrum
M. Animism
N. Categorize
O. Illustrate
P. Macrosystem
Q. Brofenbrenner
R. Compare
S. Perception
T. Biography

13. Using the Across and Down clues, write the correct words in the numbered grid below.

ACROSS

1. A condition characterized by paralysis, weakness, lack of coordination.
6. The whole socio-cultural context.
8. Assigning human qualities to objects "the sun was mad and burned me".
9. Interaction of two microsystems.
11. The process by which cells use oxygen to produce energy from food.
13. Reports events about someone's life.
14. Recognize or treat (someone or something) as different.
15. Explain or make (something) clear by using examples, charts, pictures, etc.
16. Emotion or desire, especially as influencing behavior or action.
17. Family of classroom.
18. Determine (the amount or number of something) mathematically.

DOWN

2. inspect (someone or something) in detail to determine their nature or condition.
3. Detailed classification of critical thinking and learning skills and objectives into tiered levels.
4. Place in a particular class or group.
5. Leader in field of child psychology and development, outlined 4 types of nested systems.
7. Recognize or treat (someone or something) as different.
8. Breakdown information into parts and use those parts.
10. The state of being strikingly different from something else.
11. Indicate the faults of (someone or something) in a disapproving way.
12. An uncontrolled outburst of anger and frustration, typically in a young child.

A. Illustrate	B. Brofenbrenner	C. Calculate	D. Affect
E. Biography	F. Contrast	G. Cerebral Palsy	H. Microsystem
I. Examine	J. Distinguish	K. Bloom	L. Criticize
M. Cellular Respiration	N. Animism	O. Categorize	P. Mesosystem
Q. Distinguish	R. Analysis	S. Tantrum	T. Macrosystem

14. Using the Across and Down clues, write the correct words in the numbered grid below.

ACROSS

2. The ability to see, hear, or become aware of something through the senses.
7. Determine (the amount or number of something) mathematically.
11. inspect (someone or something) in detail to determine their nature or condition.
12. A condition characterized by paralysis, weakness, lack of coordination.
15. Reports events about someone's life.
16. Breakdown information into parts and use those parts.
18. The process by which cells use oxygen to produce energy from food.
19. Emotion or desire, especially as influencing behavior or action.
20. The state of being strikingly different from something else.

DOWN

1. A comparison of two things based on their being alike in some way.
3. Leader in field of child psychology and development, outlined 4 types of nested systems.
4. Clearly show the existence or truth of (something) by giving proof or evidence.
5. Combine one thing with another so that they become a whole.
6. Estimate, measure, or note the similarity or dissimilarity between.
8. Family of classroom.
9. Recognize or treat (someone or something) as different.
10. Indicate the faults of (someone or something) in a disapproving way.
13. A scientific procedure undertaken to make a discovery, test a hypothesis, or demonstrate a fact.
14. Explain or make (something) clear by using examples, charts, pictures, etc.
17. Detailed classification of critical thinking and learning skills and objectives into tiered levels.

A. Illustrate	B. Distinguish	C. Criticize	D. Biography
E. Cerebral Palsy	F. Compare	G. Integration	H. Examine
I. Brofenbrenner	J. Bloom	K. Demonstrate	L. Analogy
M. Perception	N. Analysis	O. Affect	P. Contrast
Q. Calculate	R. Cellular Respiration	S. Experiment	T. Microsystem

15. Using the Across and Down clues, write the correct words in the numbered grid below.

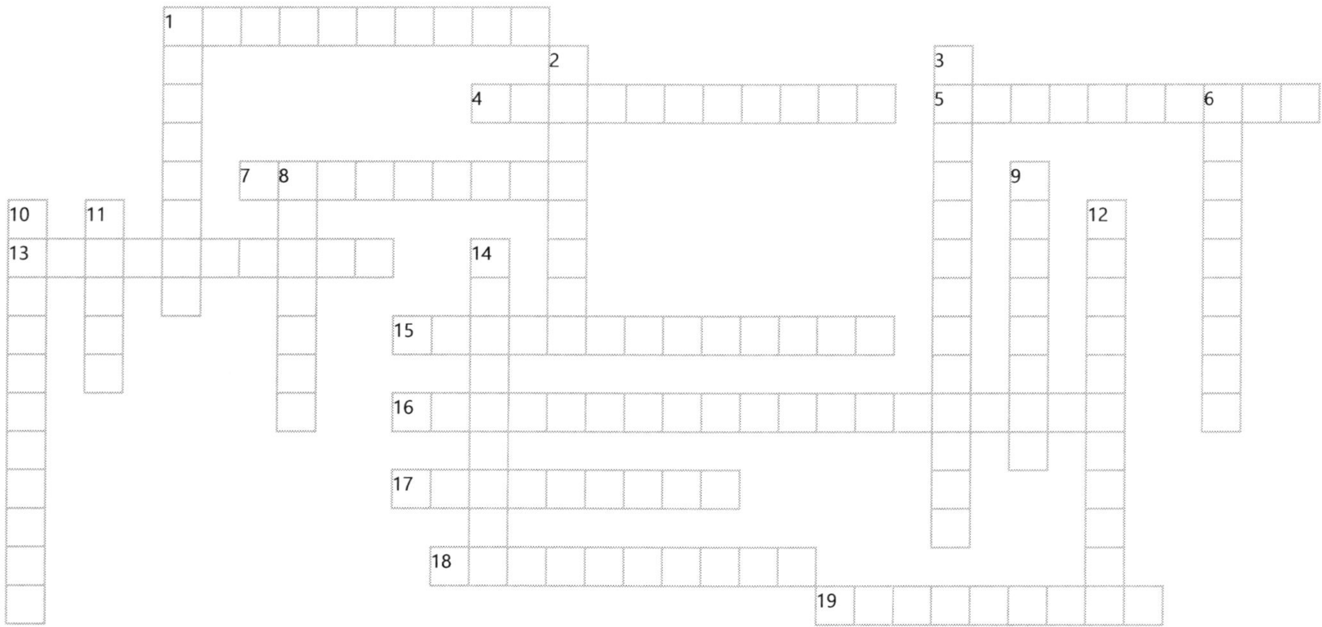

ACROSS

1. Place in a particular class or group.
4. Recognize or treat (someone or something) as different.
5. A scientific procedure undertaken to make a discovery, test a hypothesis, or demonstrate a fact.
7. Determine (the amount or number of something) mathematically.
13. Explain or make (something) clear by using examples, charts, pictures, etc.
15. The condition of being abnormally or extremely active.
16. The process by which cells use oxygen to produce energy from food.
17. Indicate the faults of (someone or something) in a disapproving way.
18. Interaction of two microsystems.
19. Reports events about someone's life.

DOWN

1. The state of being strikingly different from something else.
2. A type of autism characterized by normal cognitive and language development and impaired social skills.
3. A condition characterized by paralysis, weakness, lack of coordination.
6. Influence of external aspects on development.
8. A comparison of two things based on their being alike in some way.
9. Breakdown information into parts and use those parts.
10. Family of classroom.
11. Detailed classification of critical thinking and learning skills and objectives into tiered levels.
12. Recognize or treat (someone or something) as different.
14. Acting or done without forethought.

A. Categorize
B. Criticize
C. Cellular Respiration
D. Illustrate
E. Contrast
F. Microsystem
G. Hyperactivity
H. Experiment
I. Asperger
J. Mesosystem
K. Distinguish
L. Analysis
M. Exosystem
N. Analogy
O. Calculate
P. Bloom
Q. Impulsive
R. Distinguish
S. Cerebral Palsy
T. Biography

16. Using the Across and Down clues, write the correct words in the numbered grid below.

ACROSS

3. A condition characterized by paralysis, weakness, lack of coordination.
5. Adapt a novel or present a particular incident as a play or movie.
6. Determine (the amount or number of something) mathematically.
10. inspect (someone or something) in detail to determine their nature or condition.
12. Detailed classification of critical thinking and learning skills and objectives into tiered levels.
14. Bloom's 3rd level, take previous learning and use it in a new way.
17. Interaction of two microsystems.
18. The process by which cells use oxygen to produce energy from food.
19. Estimate, measure, or note the similarity or dissimilarity between.

DOWN

1. Leader in field of child psychology and development, outlined 4 types of nested systems.
2. Recognize or treat (someone or something) as different.
4. A scientific procedure undertaken to make a discovery, test a hypothesis, or demonstrate a fact.
7. The whole socio-cultural context.
8. Clearly show the existence or truth of (something) by giving proof or evidence.
9. Family of classroom.
11. Explain or make (something) clear by using examples, charts, pictures, etc.
13. A comparison of two things based on their being alike in some way.
14. Assigning human qualities to objects "the sun was mad and burned me".
15. Emotion or desire, especially as influencing behavior or action.
16. An uncontrolled outburst of anger and frustration, typically in a young child.

A. Calculate	B. Illustrate	C. Tantrum	D. Examine
E. Compare	F. Affect	G. Bloom	H. Application
I. Demonstrate	J. Cellular Respiration	K. Mesosystem	L. Brofenbrenner
M. Analogy	N. Cerebral Palsy	O. Dramatize	P. Macrosystem
Q. Microsystem	R. Animism	S. Experiment	T. Distinguish

17. Using the Across and Down clues, write the correct words in the numbered grid below.

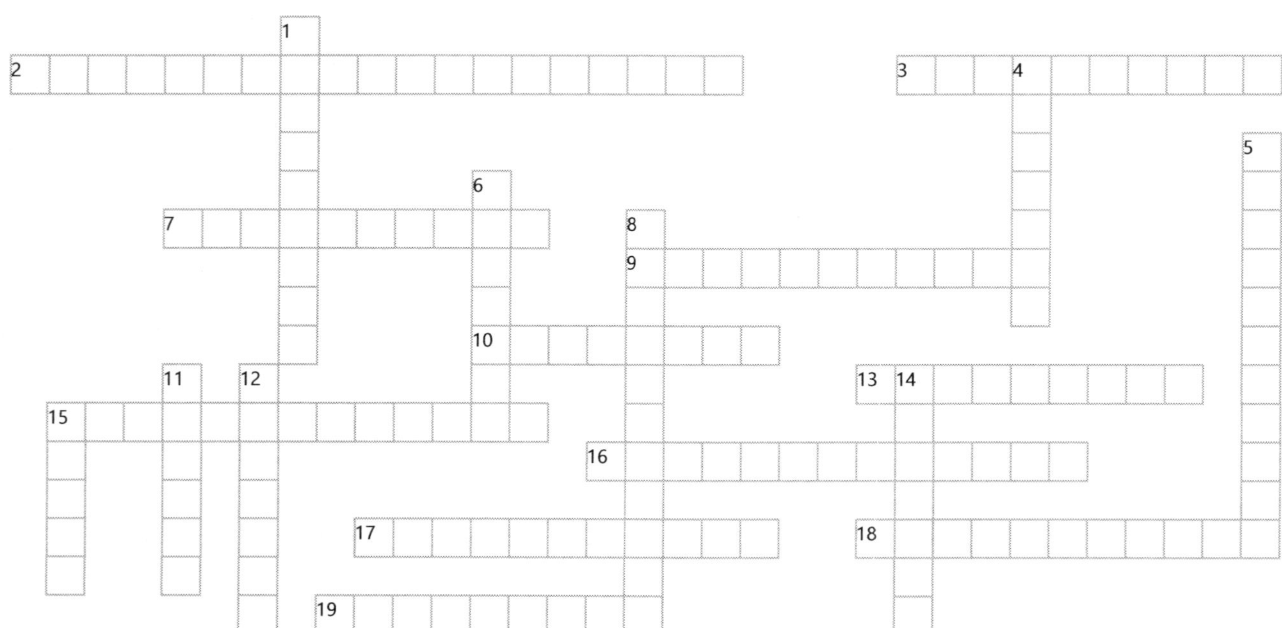

ACROSS

2. The process by which cells use oxygen to produce energy from food.
3. A scientific procedure undertaken to make a discovery, test a hypothesis, or demonstrate a fact.
7. The ability to see, hear, or become aware of something through the senses.
9. Combine one thing with another so that they become a whole.
10. A type of autism characterized by normal cognitive and language development and impaired social skills.
13. Determine (the amount or number of something) mathematically.
15. Leader in field of child psychology and development, outlined 4 types of nested systems.
16. The condition of being abnormally or extremely active.
17. Bloom's 3rd level, take previous learning and use it in a new way.
18. Recognize or treat (someone or something) as different.
19. Influence of external aspects on development.

DOWN

1. Indicate the faults of (someone or something) in a disapproving way.
4. inspect (someone or something) in detail to determine their nature or condition.
5. Recognize or treat (someone or something) as different.
6. Estimate, measure, or note the similarity or dissimilarity between.
8. Family of classroom.
11. Emotion or desire, especially as influencing behavior or action.
12. A comparison of two things based on their being alike in some way.
14. Assigning human qualities to objects "the sun was mad and burned me".
15. Detailed classification of critical thinking and learning skills and objectives into tiered levels.

A. Integration
B. Calculate
C. Animism
D. Exosystem
E. Asperger
F. Affect
G. Examine
H. Compare
I. Experiment
J. Distinguish
K. Brofenbrenner
L. Application
M. Bloom
N. Perception
O. Analogy
P. Hyperactivity
Q. Distinguish
R. Cellular Respiration
S. Criticize
T. Microsystem

18. Using the Across and Down clues, write the correct words in the numbered grid below.

ACROSS

1. Estimate, measure, or note the similarity or dissimilarity between.
4. The condition of being abnormally or extremely active.
8. Interaction of two microsystems.
10. Determine (the amount or number of something) mathematically.
12. Detailed classification of critical thinking and learning skills and objectives into tiered levels.
13. Emotion or desire, especially as influencing behavior or action.
14. A comparison of two things based on their being alike in some way.
15. A type of autism characterized by normal cognitive and language development and impaired social skills.
16. The ability to see, hear, or become aware of something through the senses.
17. Breakdown information into parts and use those parts.
18. Recognize or treat (someone or something) as different.
19. Reports events about someone's life.

DOWN

1. Indicate the faults of (someone or something) in a disapproving way.
2. An uncontrolled outburst of anger and frustration, typically in a young child.
3. The whole socio-cultural context.
5. Bloom's 3rd level, take previous learning and use it in a new way.
6. A condition characterized by paralysis, weakness, lack of coordination.
7. Explain or make (something) clear by using examples, charts, pictures, etc.
9. Recognize or treat (someone or something) as different.
11. inspect (someone or something) in detail to determine their nature or condition.

A. Bloom	B. Distinguish	C. Compare	D. Macrosystem	E. Mesosystem
F. Affect	G. Criticize	H. Hyperactivity	I. Application	J. Perception
K. Analysis	L. Distinguish	M. Analogy	N. Asperger	O. Tantrum
P. Examine	Q. Cerebral Palsy	R. Calculate	S. Biography	T. Illustrate

19. Using the Across and Down clues, write the correct words in the numbered grid below.

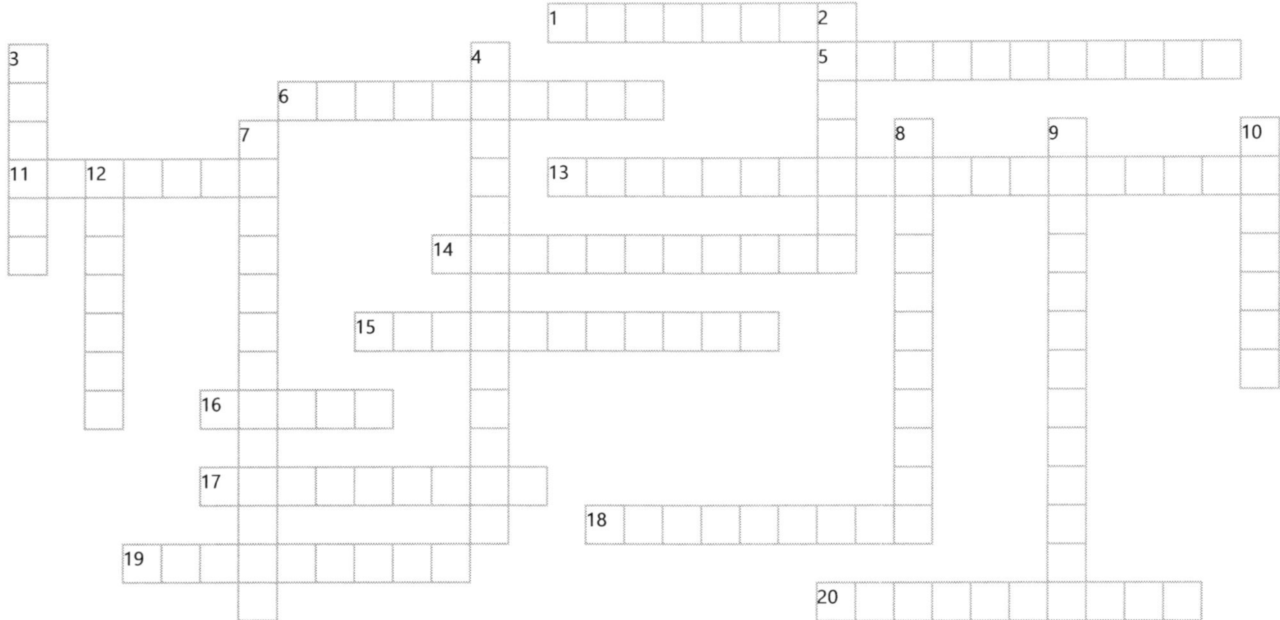

ACROSS

1. The state of being strikingly different from something else.
5. Bloom's 3rd level, take previous learning and use it in a new way.
6. Interaction of two microsystems.
11. inspect (someone or something) in detail to determine their nature or condition.
13. The process by which cells use oxygen to produce energy from food.
14. The whole socio-cultural context.
15. Recognize or treat (someone or something) as different.
16. Detailed classification of critical thinking and learning skills and objectives into tiered levels.
17. Determine (the amount or number of something) mathematically.
18. Adapt a novel or present a particular incident as a play or movie.
19. Influence of external aspects on development.
20. Place in a particular class or group.

DOWN

2. An uncontrolled outburst of anger and frustration, typically in a young child.
3. Emotion or desire, especially as influencing behavior or action.
4. The condition of being abnormally or extremely active.
7. A condition characterized by paralysis, weakness, lack of coordination.
8. Clearly show the existence or truth of (something) by giving proof or evidence.
9. Leader in field of child psychology and development, outlined 4 types of nested systems.
10. Assigning human qualities to objects "the sun was mad and burned me".
12. A comparison of two things based on their being alike in some way.

A. Bloom	B. Animism	C. Hyperactivity	D. Categorize
E. Brofenbrenner	F. Tantrum	G. Mesosystem	H. Contrast
I. Analogy	J. Examine	K. Affect	L. Cellular Respiration
M. Calculate	N. Distinguish	O. Cerebral Palsy	P. Demonstrate
Q. Exosystem	R. Dramatize	S. Macrosystem	T. Application

20. Using the Across and Down clues, write the correct words in the numbered grid below.

ACROSS

5. Assigning human qualities to objects "the sun was mad and burned me".
7. Recognize or treat (someone or something) as different.
10. An uncontrolled outburst of anger and frustration, typically in a young child.
14. The process by which cells use oxygen to produce energy from food.
15. A type of autism characterized by normal cognitive and language development and impaired social skills
16. The condition of being abnormally or extremely active.
17. Adapt a novel or present a particular incident as a play or movie.
18. Influence of external aspects on development.
19. inspect (someone or something) in detail to determine their nature or condition.

DOWN

1. A scientific procedure undertaken to make a discovery, test a hypothesis, or demonstrate a fact.
2. Recognize or treat (someone or something) as different.
3. The state of being strikingly different from something else.
4. Leader in field of child psychology and development, outlined 4 types of nested systems.
6. A condition characterized by paralysis, weakness, lack of coordination.
8. The whole socio-cultural context.
9. Clearly show the existence or truth of (something) by giving proof or evidence.
11. Detailed classification of critical thinking and learning skills and objectives into tiered levels.
12. Place in a particular class or group.
13. Reports events about someone's life.
14. Determine (the amount or number of something) mathematically.

A. Animism	B. Hyperactivity	C. Examine	D. Calculate
E. Brofenbrenner	F. Dramatize	G. Asperger	H. Bloom
I. Macrosystem	J. Distinguish	K. Distinguish	L. Biography
M. Categorize	N. Experiment	O. Cellular Respiration	P. Exosystem
Q. Contrast	R. Tantrum	S. Cerebral Palsy	T. Demonstrate

21. Using the Across and Down clues, write the correct words in the numbered grid below.

ACROSS

1. Bloom's 3rd level, take previous learning and use it in a new way.
6. Emotion or desire, especially as influencing behavior or action.
11. inspect (someone or something) in detail to determine their nature or condition.
13. The whole socio-cultural context.
16. A scientific procedure undertaken to make a discovery, test a hypothesis, or demonstrate a fact.
17. The state of being strikingly different from something else.
18. Determine (the amount or number of something) mathematically.
19. Recognize or treat (someone or something) as different.
20. Family of classroom.

DOWN

2. Acting or done without forethought.
3. Detailed classification of critical thinking and learning skills and objectives into tiered levels.
4. Adapt a novel or present a particular incident as a play or movie.
5. The condition of being abnormally or extremely active.
7. English natural scientist who formulated a theory of evolution by natural selection.
8. An uncontrolled outburst of anger and frustration, typically in a young child.
9. Leader in field of child psychology and development, outlined 4 types of nested systems.
10. A condition characterized by paralysis, weakness, lack of coordination.
12. A type of autism characterized by normal cognitive and language development and impaired social skills.
14. Breakdown information into parts and use those parts.
15. Recognize or treat (someone or something) as different.

A. Macrosystem
B. Hyperactivity
C. Impulsive
D. Asperger
E. Distinguish
F. Tantrum
G. Experiment
H. Distinguish
I. Affect
J. Examine
K. Bloom
L. Microsystem
M. Calculate
N. Analysis
O. Application
P. Dramatize
Q. Brofenbrenner
R. Cerebral Palsy
S. Contrast
T. Charles Darwin

22. Using the Across and Down clues, write the correct words in the numbered grid below.

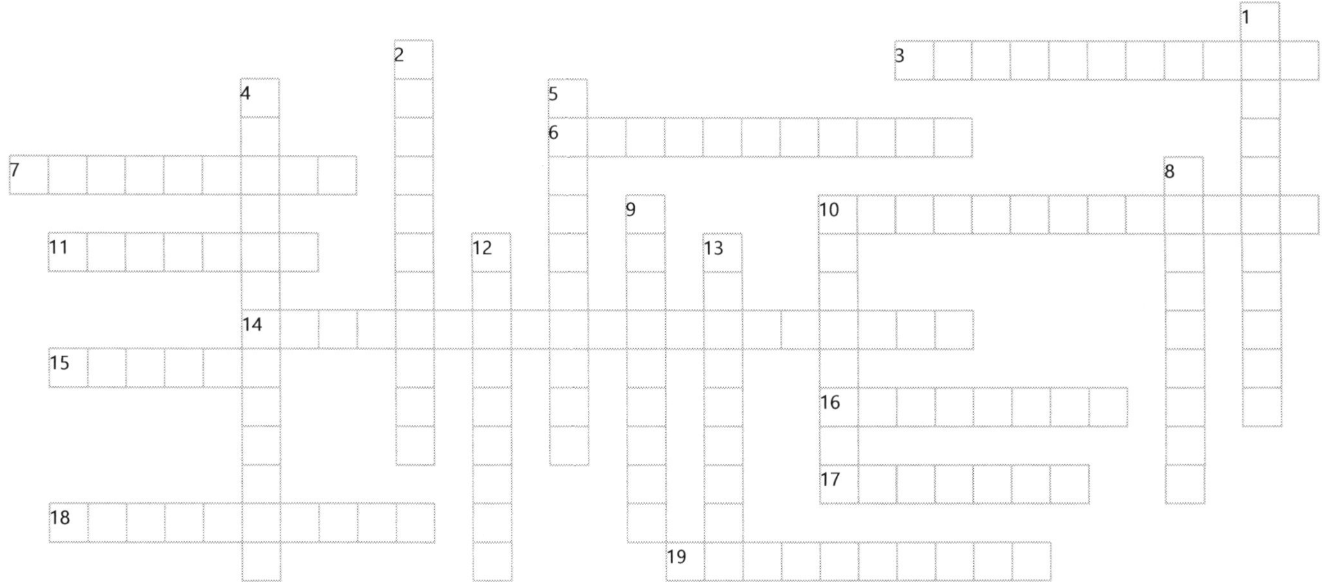

ACROSS

3. Family of classroom.
6. Bloom's 3rd level, take previous learning and use it in a new way.
7. Reports events about someone's life.
10. A condition characterized by paralysis, weakness, lack of coordination.
11. Estimate, measure, or note the similarity or dissimilarity between.
14. The process by which cells use oxygen to produce energy from food.
15. Emotion or desire, especially as influencing behavior or action.
16. A type of autism characterized by normal cognitive and language development and impaired social skills.
17. An uncontrolled outburst of anger and frustration, typically in a young child.
18. Explain or make (something) clear by using examples, charts, pictures, etc.
19. The ability to see, hear, or become aware of something through the senses.

DOWN

1. Clearly show the existence or truth of (something) by giving proof or evidence.
2. Recognize or treat (someone or something) as different.
4. The condition of being abnormally or extremely active.
5. Place in a particular class or group.
8. Determine (the amount or number of something) mathematically.
9. Influence of external aspects on development.
10. The state of being strikingly different from something else.
12. Adapt a novel or present a particular incident as a play or movie.
13. Indicate the faults of (someone or something) in a disapproving way.

A. Illustrate	B. Distinguish	C. Criticize	D. Calculate
E. Affect	F. Application	G. Compare	H. Exosystem
I. Cellular Respiration	J. Demonstrate	K. Hyperactivity	L. Dramatize
M. Asperger	N. Tantrum	O. Contrast	P. Perception
Q. Cerebral Palsy	R. Biography	S. Categorize	T. Microsystem

23. Using the Across and Down clues, write the correct words in the numbered grid below.

ACROSS

6. Clearly show the existence or truth of (something) by giving proof or evidence.
7. A condition characterized by paralysis, weakness, lack of coordination.
8. The process by which cells use oxygen to produce energy from food.
11. Explain or make (something) clear by using examples, charts, pictures, etc.
14. Leader in field of child psychology and development, outlined 4 types of nested systems.
15. Combine one thing with another so that they become a whole.
16. Recognize or treat (someone or something) as different.
17. Emotion or desire, especially as influencing behavior or action.
18. A scientific procedure undertaken to make a discovery, test a hypothesis, or demonstrate a fact.
19. Influence of external aspects on development.

DOWN

1. Indicate the faults of (someone or something) in a disapproving way.
2. Estimate, measure, or note the similarity or dissimilarity between.
3. Determine (the amount or number of something) mathematically.
4. Place in a particular class or group.
5. Breakdown information into parts and use those parts.
9. The ability to see, hear, or become aware of something through the senses.
10. Assigning human qualities to objects "the sun was mad and burned me".
12. Interaction of two microsystems.
13. The state of being strikingly different from something else.
14. Detailed classification of critical thinking and learning skills and objectives into tiered levels.

A. Compare	B. Distinguish	C. Illustrate	D. Affect
E. Demonstrate	F. Mesosystem	G. Calculate	H. Exosystem
I. Categorize	J. Analysis	K. Cerebral Palsy	L. Cellular Respiration
M. Bloom	N. Contrast	O. Animism	P. Brofenbrenner
Q. Perception	R. Experiment	S. Integration	T. Criticize

24. Using the Across and Down clues, write the correct words in the numbered grid below.

ACROSS

1. A type of autism characterized by normal cognitive and language development and impaired social skills.
3. Breakdown information into parts and use those parts.
4. Explain or make (something) clear by using examples, charts, pictures, etc.
7. Recognize or treat (someone or something) as different.
8. Influence of external aspects on development.
11. Leader in field of child psychology and development, outlined 4 types of nested systems.
13. Reports events about someone's life.
14. The ability to see, hear, or become aware of something through the senses.
15. The process by which cells use oxygen to produce energy from food.
16. Indicate the faults of (someone or something) in a disapproving way.
17. An uncontrolled outburst of anger and frustration, typically in a young child.

DOWN

1. Assigning human qualities to objects "the sun was mad and burned me".
2. Interaction of two microsystems.
5. Bloom's 3rd level, take previous learning and use it in a new way.
6. Recognize or treat (someone or something) as different.
7. Clearly show the existence or truth of (something) by giving proof or evidence.
8. A scientific procedure undertaken to make a discovery, test a hypothesis, or demonstrate a fact.
9. Place in a particular class or group.
10. Adapt a novel or present a particular incident as a play or movie.
12. Estimate, measure, or note the similarity or dissimilarity between.

A. Mesosystem
B. Application
C. Demonstrate
D. Brofenbrenner
E. Compare
F. Biography
G. Asperger
H. Perception
I. Experiment
J. Criticize
K. Illustrate
L. Dramatize
M. Animism
N. Analysis
O. Cellular Respiration
P. Exosystem
Q. Categorize
R. Distinguish
S. Tantrum
T. Distinguish

25. Using the Across and Down clues, write the correct words in the numbered grid below.

ACROSS

1. Family of classroom.
4. Estimate, measure, or note the similarity or dissimilarity between.
6. Reports events about someone's life.
9. A type of autism characterized by normal cognitive and language development and impaired social skills.
13. Emotion or desire, especially as influencing behavior or action.
16. Recognize or treat (someone or something) as different.
17. A comparison of two things based on their being alike in some way.
18. The state of being strikingly different from something else.
19. Assigning human qualities to objects "the sun was mad and burned me".
20. The process by which cells use oxygen to produce energy from food.

DOWN

2. Combine one thing with another so that they become a whole.
3. Leader in field of child psychology and development, outlined 4 types of nested systems.
5. Breakdown information into parts and use those parts.
7. An uncontrolled outburst of anger and frustration, typically in a young child.
8. The whole socio-cultural context.
10. A scientific procedure undertaken to make a discovery, test a hypothesis, or demonstrate a fact.
11. Influence of external aspects on development.
12. Determine (the amount or number of something) mathematically.
14. inspect (someone or something) in detail to determine their nature or condition.
15. Detailed classification of critical thinking and learning skills and objectives into tiered levels.

A. Examine
B. Animism
C. Integration
D. Analysis
E. Biography
F. Analogy
G. Macrosystem
H. Brofenbrenner
I. Asperger
J. Distinguish
K. Bloom
L. Microsystem
M. Cellular Respiration
N. Affect
O. Compare
P. Contrast
Q. Exosystem
R. Calculate
S. Experiment
T. Tantrum

26. Using the Across and Down clues, write the correct words in the numbered grid below.

ACROSS

3. A scientific procedure undertaken to make a discovery, test a hypothesis, or demonstrate a fact.
4. Bloom's 3rd level, take previous learning and use it in a new way.
5. Breakdown information into parts and use those parts.
8. A lack of compatibility or similarity between two or more facts.
9. A comparison of two things based on their being alike in some way.
10. Emotion or desire, especially as influencing behavior or action.
12. Combine one thing with another so that they become a whole.
14. The state of being strikingly different from something else.
15. Determine (the amount or number of something) mathematically.
16. Indicate the faults of (someone or something) in a disapproving way.
17. The whole socio-cultural context.
18. Estimate, measure, or note the similarity or dissimilarity between.
19. Detailed classification of critical thinking and learning skills and objectives into tiered levels.
20. Influence of external aspects on development.

DOWN

1. Clearly show the existence or truth of (something) by giving proof or evidence.
2. Leader in field of child psychology and development, outlined 4 types of nested systems.
6. A type of autism characterized by normal cognitive and language development and impaired social skills.
7. The ability to see, hear, or become aware of something through the senses.
11. inspect (someone or something) in detail to determine their nature or condition.
13. Assigning human qualities to objects "the sun was mad and burned me".

A. Criticize	B. Bloom	C. Integration	D. Demonstrate	E. Perception
F. Affect	G. Analogy	H. Brofenbrenner	I. Analysis	J. Macrosystem
K. Calculate	L. Contrast	M. Examine	N. Application	O. Experiment
P. Compare	Q. Exosystem	R. Animism	S. Discrepancy	T. Asperger

27. Using the Across and Down clues, write the correct words in the numbered grid below.

ACROSS

4. Acting or done without forethought.
6. Emotion or desire, especially as influencing behavior or action.
7. The ability to see, hear, or become aware of something through the senses.
8. Interaction of two microsystems.
10. Leader in field of child psychology and development, outlined 4 types of nested systems.
12. Place in a particular class or group.
14. Breakdown information into parts and use those parts.
15. The process by which cells use oxygen to produce energy from food.
16. Recognize or treat (someone or something) as different.
17. Reports events about someone's life.
18. The whole socio-cultural context.
19. Estimate, measure, or note the similarity or dissimilarity between.

DOWN

1. Recognize or treat (someone or something) as different.
2. Explain or make (something) clear by using examples, charts, pictures, etc.
3. Influence of external aspects on development.
5. A condition characterized by paralysis, weakness, lack of coordination.
9. Detailed classification of critical thinking and learning skills and objectives into tiered levels.
11. A scientific procedure undertaken to make a discovery, test a hypothesis, or demonstrate a fact.
13. A type of autism characterized by normal cognitive and language development and impaired social skills.
14. Assigning human qualities to objects "the sun was mad and burned me".

A. Cellular Respiration	B. Bloom	C. Impulsive	D. Brofenbrenner
E. Affect	F. Animism	G. Analysis	H. Experiment
I. Biography	J. Exosystem	K. Compare	L. Categorize
M. Mesosystem	N. Distinguish	O. Macrosystem	P. Cerebral Palsy
Q. Perception	R. Illustrate	S. Asperger	T. Distinguish

28. Using the Across and Down clues, write the correct words in the numbered grid below.

ACROSS

1. A scientific procedure undertaken to make a discovery, test a hypothesis, or demonstrate a fact.
2. Recognize or treat (someone or something) as different.
6. Assigning human qualities to objects "the sun was mad and burned me".
8. Detailed classification of critical thinking and learning skills and objectives into tiered levels.
9. An uncontrolled outburst of anger and frustration, typically in a young child.
10. Family of classroom.
11. The ability to see, hear, or become aware of something through the senses.
12. A type of autism characterized by normal cognitive and language development and impaired social skills.
13. The state of being strikingly different from something else.
14. Breakdown information into parts and use those parts.
15. The whole socio-cultural context.
16. Indicate the faults of (someone or something) in a disapproving way.
17. The condition of being abnormally or extremely active.

DOWN

1. Influence of external aspects on development.
2. Adapt a novel or present a particular incident as a play or movie.
3. inspect (someone or something) in detail to determine their nature or condition.
4. Explain or make (something) clear by using examples, charts, pictures, etc.
5. Clearly show the existence or truth of (something) by giving proof or evidence.
7. Emotion or desire, especially as influencing behavior or action.
12. A comparison of two things based on their being alike in some way.

A. Perception	B. Exosystem	C. Examine	D. Affect	E. Hyperactivity
F. Microsystem	G. Asperger	H. Animism	I. Analysis	J. Dramatize
K. Tantrum	L. Criticize	M. Contrast	N. Experiment	O. Distinguish
P. Demonstrate	Q. Analogy	R. Bloom	S. Illustrate	T. Macrosystem

29. Using the Across and Down clues, write the correct words in the numbered grid below.

ACROSS

3. Adapt a novel or present a particular incident as a play or movie.
5. A condition characterized by paralysis, weakness, lack of coordination.
6. The condition of being abnormally or extremely active.
10. Recognize or treat (someone or something) as different.
12. inspect (someone or something) in detail to determine their nature or condition.
13. Clearly show the existence or truth of (something) by giving proof or evidence.
15. The whole socio-cultural context.
17. Assigning human qualities to objects "the sun was mad and burned me".
18. The process by which cells use oxygen to produce energy from food.
19. Reports events about someone's life.

DOWN

1. Indicate the faults of (someone or something) in a disapproving way.
2. Determine (the amount or number of something) mathematically.
4. Family of classroom.
7. Leader in field of child psychology and development, outlined 4 types of nested systems.
8. Bloom's 3rd level, take previous learning and use it in a new way.
9. A scientific procedure undertaken to make a discovery, test a hypothesis, or demonstrate a fact.
10. Recognize or treat (someone or something) as different.
11. Detailed classification of critical thinking and learning skills and objectives into tiered levels.
14. Estimate, measure, or note the similarity or dissimilarity between.
16. Emotion or desire, especially as influencing behavior or action.

A. Examine	B. Cellular Respiration	C. Macrosystem	D. Hyperactivity
E. Criticize	F. Microsystem	G. Biography	H. Calculate
I. Bloom	J. Brofenbrenner	K. Distinguish	L. Animism
M. Cerebral Palsy	N. Demonstrate	O. Experiment	P. Compare
Q. Dramatize	R. Affect	S. Distinguish	T. Application

30. Using the Across and Down clues, write the correct words in the numbered grid below.

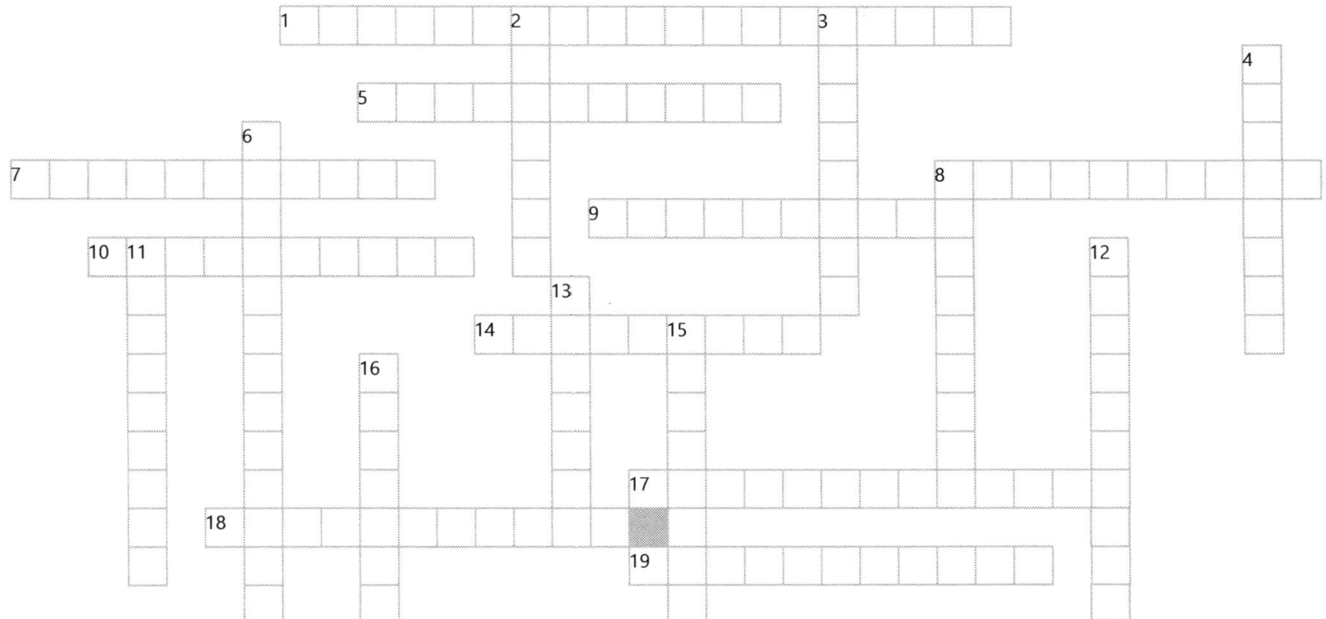

ACROSS

1. The process by which cells use oxygen to produce energy from food.
5. Recognize or treat (someone or something) as different.
7. The whole socio-cultural context.
8. Explain or make (something) clear by using examples, charts, pictures, etc.
9. Interaction of two microsystems.
10. The ability to see, hear, or become aware of something through the senses.
14. Reports events about someone's life.
17. Leader in field of child psychology and development, outlined 4 types of nested systems.
18. Family of classroom.
19. Clearly show the existence or truth of (something) by giving proof or evidence.

DOWN

2. Assigning human qualities to objects "the sun was mad and burned me".
3. Breakdown information into parts and use those parts.
4. The state of being strikingly different from something else.
6. The condition of being abnormally or extremely active.
8. Acting or done without forethought.
11. Influence of external aspects on development.
12. Place in a particular class or group.
13. Estimate, measure, or note the similarity or dissimilarity between.
15. A type of autism characterized by normal cognitive and language development and impaired social skills.
16. A comparison of two things based on their being alike in some way.

A. Cellular Respiration
B. Distinguish
C. Analogy
D. Hyperactivity
E. Demonstrate
F. Brofenbrenner
G. Biography
H. Asperger
I. Compare
J. Categorize
K. Microsystem
L. Illustrate
M. Mesosystem
N. Analysis
O. Impulsive
P. Animism
Q. Perception
R. Exosystem
S. Contrast
T. Macrosystem

1. Using the Across and Down clues, write the correct words in the numbered grid below.

ACROSS

3. Determine (the amount or number of something) mathematically.
5. The process by which cells use oxygen to produce energy from food.
7. The ability to see, hear, or become aware of something through the senses.
9. inspect (someone or something) in detail to determine their nature or condition.
11. Estimate, measure, or note the similarity or dissimilarity between.
12. Place in a particular class or group.
13. Assigning human qualities to objects "the sun was mad and burned me".
15. A comparison of two things based on their being alike in some way.
16. Clearly show the existence or truth of (something) by giving proof or evidence.
17. The state of being strikingly different from something else.
18. Recognize or treat (someone or something) as different.

DOWN

1. Family of classroom.
2. A condition characterized by paralysis, weakness, lack of coordination.
4. A type of autism characterized by normal cognitive and language development and impaired social skills.
6. Combine one thing with another so that they become a whole.
8. Acting or done without forethought.
9. Influence of external aspects on development.
10. Interaction of two microsystems.
13. Breakdown information into parts and use those parts.
14. Emotion or desire, especially as influencing behavior or action.

A. Compare	B. Asperger	C. Examine	D. Contrast
E. Demonstrate	F. Mesosystem	G. Perception	H. Cerebral Palsy
I. Affect	J. Distinguish	K. Microsystem	L. Animism
M. Impulsive	N. Categorize	O. Exosystem	P. Analogy
Q. Calculate	R. Cellular Respiration	S. Integration	T. Analysis

2. Using the Across and Down clues, write the correct words in the numbered grid below.

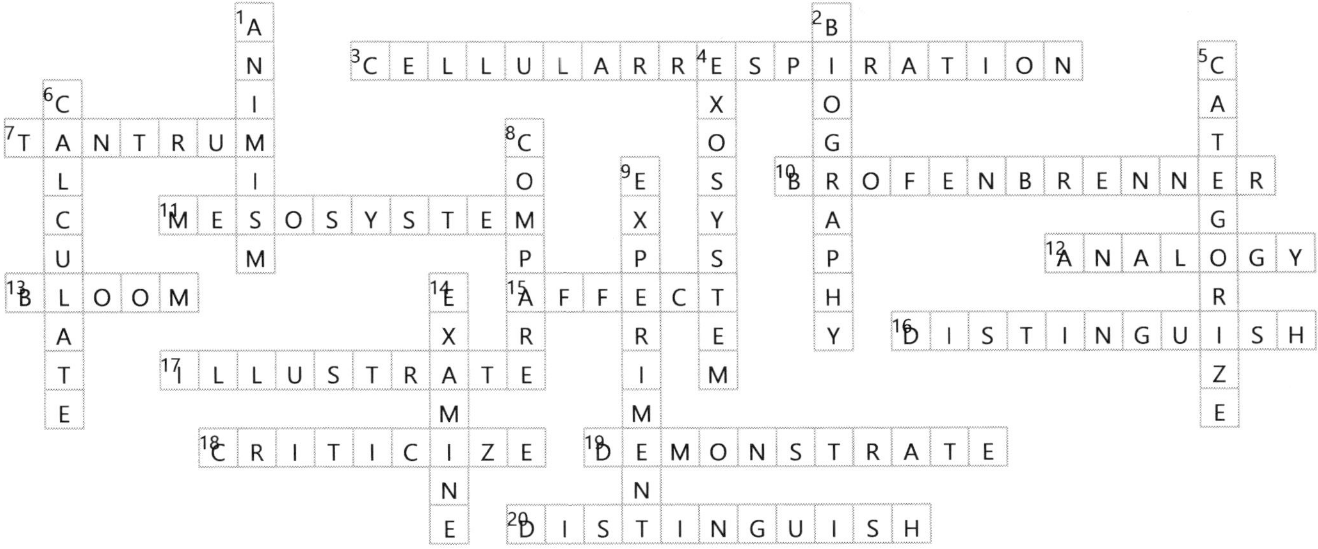

ACROSS

3. The process by which cells use oxygen to produce energy from food.
7. An uncontrolled outburst of anger and frustration, typically in a young child.
10. Leader in field of child psychology and development, outlined 4 types of nested systems.
11. Interaction of two microsystems.
12. A comparison of two things based on their being alike in some way.
13. Detailed classification of critical thinking and learning skills and objectives into tiered levels.
15. Emotion or desire, especially as influencing behavior or action.
16. Recognize or treat (someone or something) as different.
17. Explain or make (something) clear by using examples, charts, pictures, etc.
18. Indicate the faults of (someone or something) in a disapproving way.
19. Clearly show the existence or truth of (something) by giving proof or evidence.
20. Recognize or treat (someone or something) as different.

DOWN

1. Assigning human qualities to objects "the sun was mad and burned me".
2. Reports events about someone's life.
4. Influence of external aspects on development.
5. Place in a particular class or group.
6. Determine (the amount or number of something) mathematically.
8. Estimate, measure, or note the similarity or dissimilarity between.
9. A scientific procedure undertaken to make a discovery, test a hypothesis, or demonstrate a fact.
14. inspect (someone or something) in detail to determine their nature or condition.

A. Cellular Respiration	B. Bloom	C. Analogy	D. Illustrate
E. Tantrum	F. Mesosystem	G. Exosystem	H. Calculate
I. Brofenbrenner	J. Biography	K. Demonstrate	L. Affect
M. Experiment	N. Animism	O. Compare	P. Distinguish
Q. Distinguish	R. Criticize	S. Examine	T. Categorize

3. Using the Across and Down clues, write the correct words in the numbered grid below.

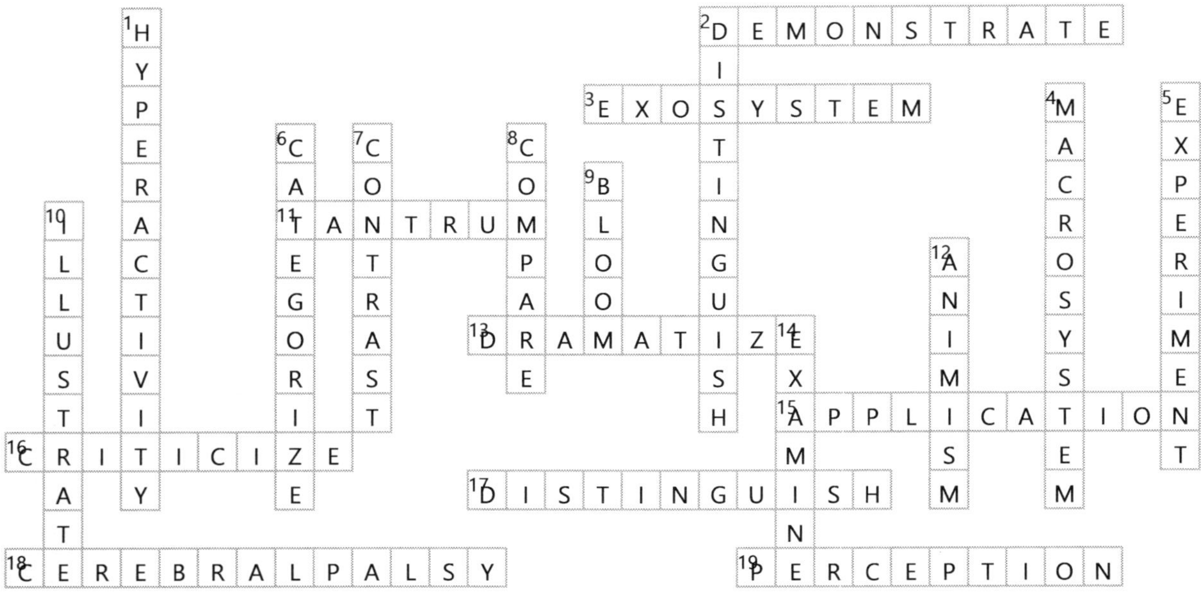

ACROSS

2. Clearly show the existence or truth of (something) by giving proof or evidence.
3. Influence of external aspects on development.
11. An uncontrolled outburst of anger and frustration, typically in a young child.
13. Adapt a novel or present a particular incident as a play or movie.
15. Bloom's 3rd level, take previous learning and use it in a new way.
16. Indicate the faults of (someone or something) in a disapproving way.
17. Recognize or treat (someone or something) as different.
18. A condition characterized by paralysis, weakness, lack of coordination.
19. The ability to see, hear, or become aware of something through the senses.

DOWN

1. The condition of being abnormally or extremely active.
2. Recognize or treat (someone or something) as different.
4. The whole socio-cultural context.
5. A scientific procedure undertaken to make a discovery, test a hypothesis, or demonstrate a fact.
6. Place in a particular class or group.
7. The state of being strikingly different from something else.
8. Estimate, measure, or note the similarity or dissimilarity between.
9. Detailed classification of critical thinking and learning skills and objectives into tiered levels.
10. Explain or make (something) clear by using examples, charts, pictures, etc.
12. Assigning human qualities to objects "the sun was mad and burned me".
14. inspect (someone or something) in detail to determine their nature or condition.

A. Dramatize	B. Hyperactivity	C. Contrast	D. Illustrate	E. Macrosystem
F. Distinguish	G. Animism	H. Criticize	I. Cerebral Palsy	J. Perception
K. Tantrum	L. Exosystem	M. Application	N. Distinguish	O. Bloom
P. Demonstrate	Q. Compare	R. Experiment	S. Categorize	T. Examine

4. Using the Across and Down clues, write the correct words in the numbered grid below.

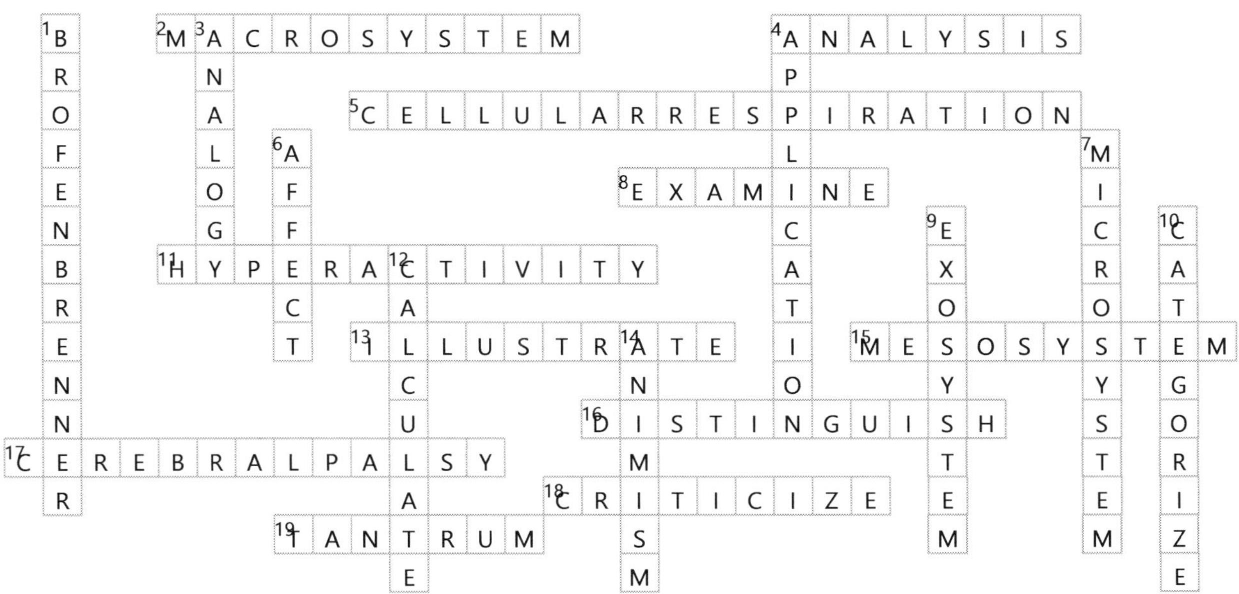

ACROSS

2. The whole socio-cultural context.
4. Breakdown information into parts and use those parts.
5. The process by which cells use oxygen to produce energy from food.
8. inspect (someone or something) in detail to determine their nature or condition.
11. The condition of being abnormally or extremely active.
13. Explain or make (something) clear by using examples, charts, pictures, etc.
15. Interaction of two microsystems.
16. Recognize or treat (someone or something) as different.
17. A condition characterized by paralysis, weakness, lack of coordination.
18. Indicate the faults of (someone or something) in a disapproving way.
19. An uncontrolled outburst of anger and frustration, typically in a young child.

DOWN

1. Leader in field of child psychology and development, outlined 4 types of nested systems.
3. A comparison of two things based on their being alike in some way.
4. Bloom's 3rd level, take previous learning and use it in a new way.
6. Emotion or desire, especially as influencing behavior or action.
7. Family of classroom.
9. Influence of external aspects on development.
10. Place in a particular class or group.
12. Determine (the amount or number of something) mathematically.
14. Assigning human qualities to objects "the sun was mad and burned me".

A. Mesosystem
B. Examine
C. Analogy
D. Animism
E. Criticize
F. Affect
G. Tantrum
H. Distinguish
I. Categorize
J. Cerebral Palsy
K. Analysis
L. Cellular Respiration
M. Macrosystem
N. Calculate
O. Microsystem
P. Hyperactivity
Q. Illustrate
R. Exosystem
S. Brofenbrenner
T. Application

5. Using the Across and Down clues, write the correct words in the numbered grid below.

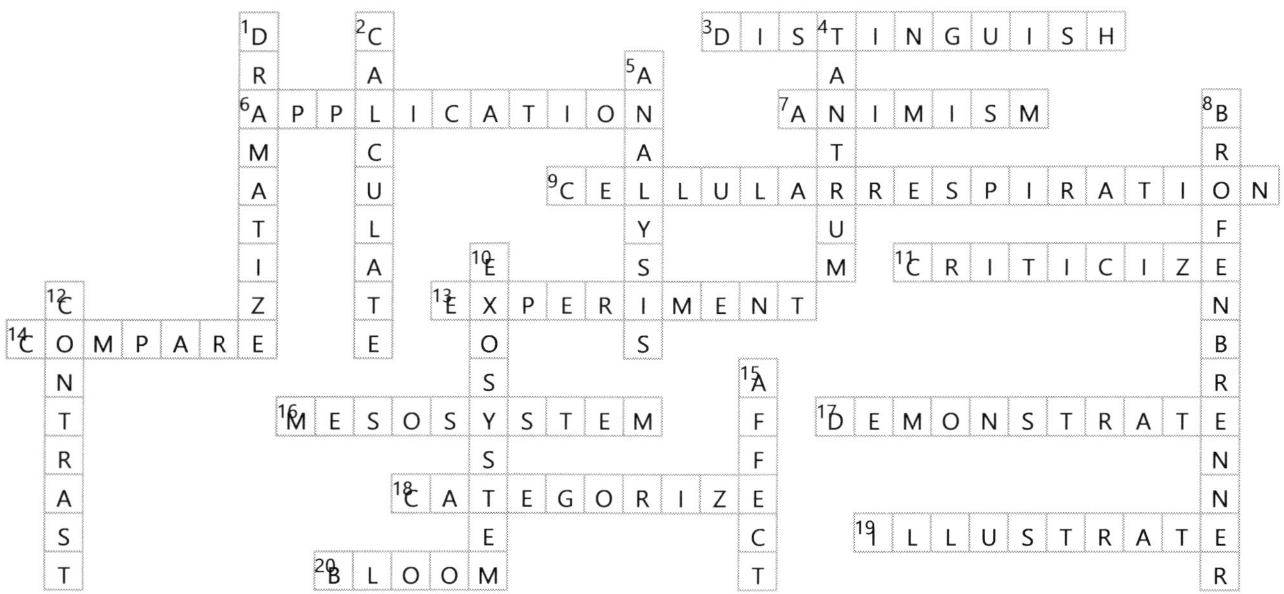

ACROSS

3. Recognize or treat (someone or something) as different.
6. Bloom's 3rd level, take previous learning and use it in a new way.
7. Assigning human qualities to objects "the sun was mad and burned me".
9. The process by which cells use oxygen to produce energy from food.
11. Indicate the faults of (someone or something) in a disapproving way.
13. A scientific procedure undertaken to make a discovery, test a hypothesis, or demonstrate a fact.
14. Estimate, measure, or note the similarity or dissimilarity between.
16. Interaction of two microsystems.
17. Clearly show the existence or truth of (something) by giving proof or evidence.
18. Place in a particular class or group.
19. Explain or make (something) clear by using examples, charts, pictures, etc.
20. Detailed classification of critical thinking and learning skills and objectives into tiered levels.

DOWN

1. Adapt a novel or present a particular incident as a play or movie.
2. Determine (the amount or number of something) mathematically.
4. An uncontrolled outburst of anger and frustration, typically in a young child.
5. Breakdown information into parts and use those parts.
8. Leader in field of child psychology and development, outlined 4 types of nested systems.
10. Influence of external aspects on development.
12. The state of being strikingly different from something else.
15. Emotion or desire, especially as influencing behavior or action.

A. Brofenbrenner	B. Cellular Respiration	C. Bloom	D. Criticize
E. Contrast	F. Application	G. Affect	H. Calculate
I. Demonstrate	J. Exosystem	K. Dramatize	L. Compare
M. Distinguish	N. Animism	O. Illustrate	P. Tantrum
Q. Experiment	R. Analysis	S. Mesosystem	T. Categorize

6. Using the Across and Down clues, write the correct words in the numbered grid below.

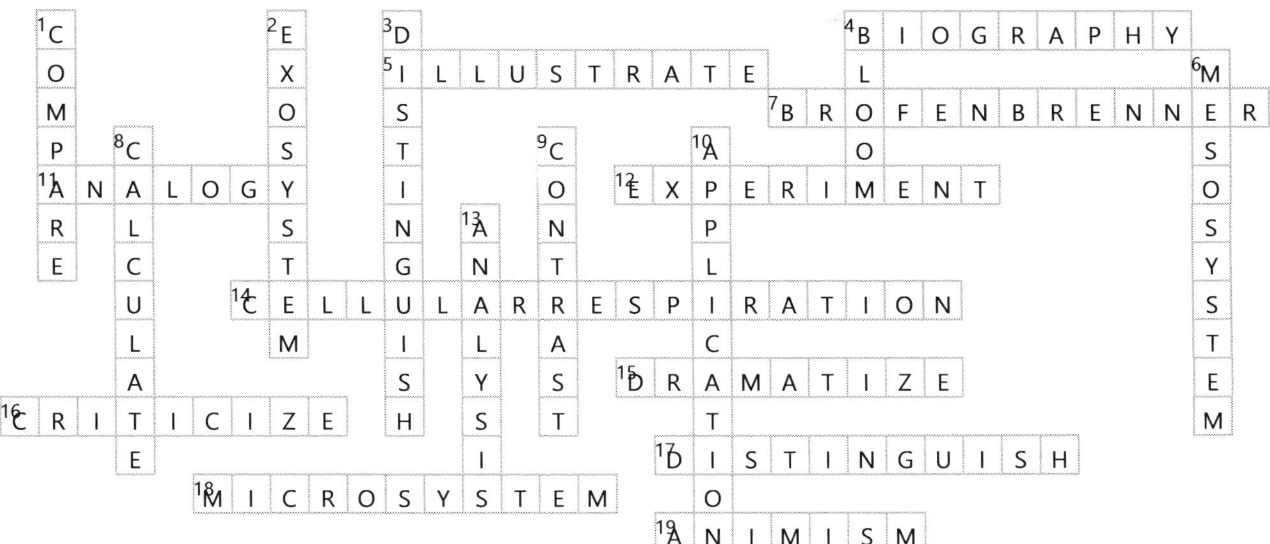

ACROSS

4. Reports events about someone's life.
5. Explain or make (something) clear by using examples, charts, pictures, etc.
7. Leader in field of child psychology and development, outlined 4 types of nested systems.
11. A comparison of two things based on their being alike in some way.
12. A scientific procedure undertaken to make a discovery, test a hypothesis, or demonstrate a fact.
14. The process by which cells use oxygen to produce energy from food.
15. Adapt a novel or present a particular incident as a play or movie.
16. Indicate the faults of (someone or something) in a disapproving way.
17. Recognize or treat (someone or something) as different.
18. Family of classroom.
19. Assigning human qualities to objects "the sun was mad and burned me".

DOWN

1. Estimate, measure, or note the similarity or dissimilarity between.
2. Influence of external aspects on development.
3. Recognize or treat (someone or something) as different.
4. Detailed classification of critical thinking and learning skills and objectives into tiered levels.
6. Interaction of two microsystems.
8. Determine (the amount or number of something) mathematically.
9. The state of being strikingly different from something else.
10. Bloom's 3rd level, take previous learning and use it in a new way.
13. Breakdown information into parts and use those parts.

A. Cellular Respiration	B. Exosystem	C. Illustrate	D. Dramatize
E. Analysis	F. Microsystem	G. Mesosystem	H. Brofenbrenner
I. Contrast	J. Distinguish	K. Calculate	L. Application
M. Experiment	N. Compare	O. Biography	P. Criticize
Q. Animism	R. Distinguish	S. Analogy	T. Bloom

7. Using the Across and Down clues, write the correct words in the numbered grid below.

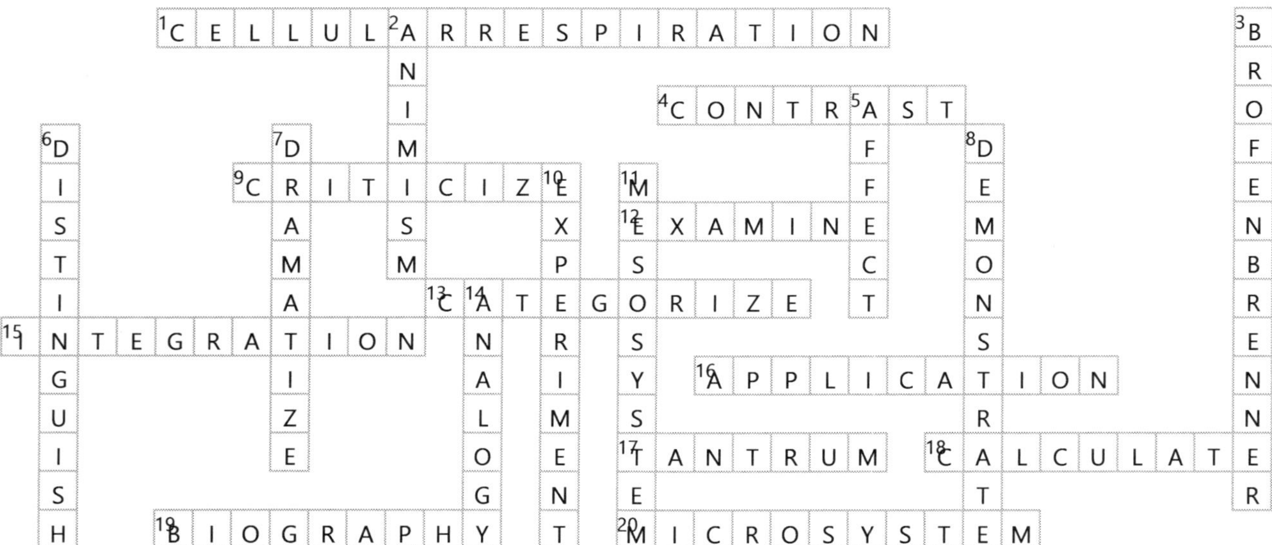

ACROSS

1. The process by which cells use oxygen to produce energy from food.
4. The state of being strikingly different from something else.
9. Indicate the faults of (someone or something) in a disapproving way.
12. inspect (someone or something) in detail to determine their nature or condition.
13. Place in a particular class or group.
15. Combine one thing with another so that they become a whole.
16. Bloom's 3rd level, take previous learning and use it in a new way.
17. An uncontrolled outburst of anger and frustration, typically in a young child.
18. Determine (the amount or number of something) mathematically.
19. Reports events about someone's life.
20. Family of classroom.

DOWN

2. Assigning human qualities to objects "the sun was mad and burned me".
3. Leader in field of child psychology and development, outlined 4 types of nested systems.
5. Emotion or desire, especially as influencing behavior or action.
6. Recognize or treat (someone or something) as different.
7. Adapt a novel or present a particular incident as a play or movie.
8. Clearly show the existence or truth of (something) by giving proof or evidence.
10. A scientific procedure undertaken to make a discovery, test a hypothesis, or demonstrate a fact.
11. Interaction of two microsystems.
14. A comparison of two things based on their being alike in some way.

A. Application	B. Biography	C. Tantrum	D. Brofenbrenner
E. Demonstrate	F. Contrast	G. Dramatize	H. Cellular Respiration
I. Categorize	J. Mesosystem	K. Distinguish	L. Criticize
M. Experiment	N. Animism	O. Calculate	P. Integration
Q. Analogy	R. Microsystem	S. Affect	T. Examine

8. Using the Across and Down clues, write the correct words in the numbered grid below.

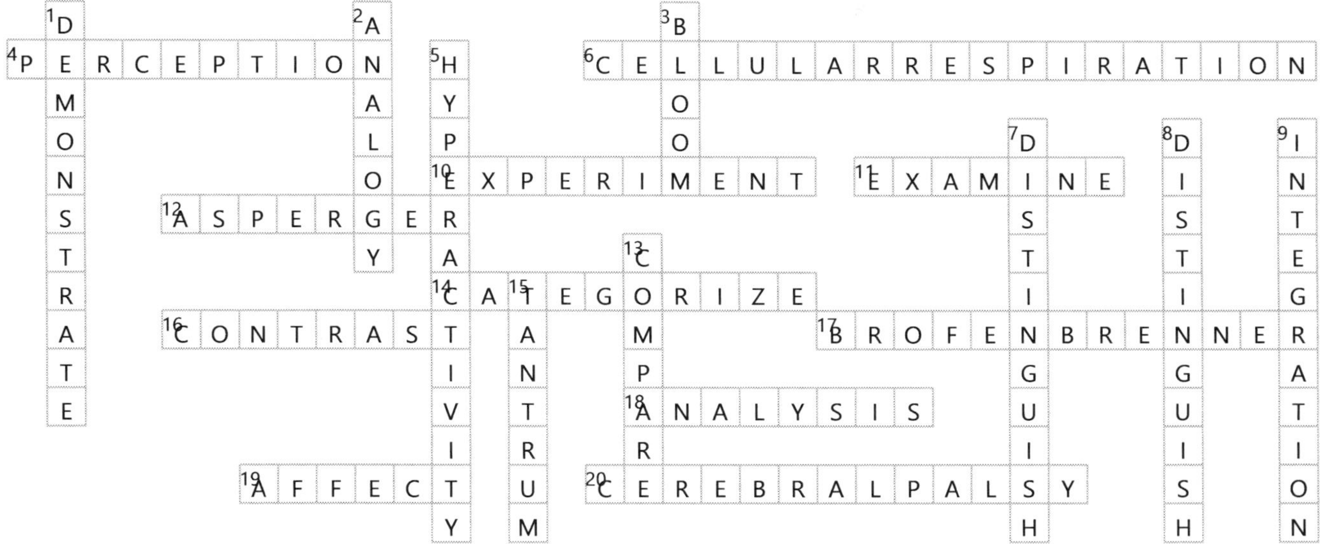

ACROSS

4. The ability to see, hear, or become aware of something through the senses.
6. The process by which cells use oxygen to produce energy from food.
10. A scientific procedure undertaken to make a discovery, test a hypothesis, or demonstrate a fact.
11. inspect (someone or something) in detail to determine their nature or condition.
12. A type of autism characterized by normal cognitive and language development and impaired social skills.
14. Place in a particular class or group.
16. The state of being strikingly different from something else.
17. Leader in field of child psychology and development, outlined 4 types of nested systems.
18. Breakdown information into parts and use those parts.
19. Emotion or desire, especially as influencing behavior or action.
20. A condition characterized by paralysis, weakness, lack of coordination.

DOWN

1. Clearly show the existence or truth of (something) by giving proof or evidence.
2. A comparison of two things based on their being alike in some way.
3. Detailed classification of critical thinking and learning skills and objectives into tiered levels.
5. The condition of being abnormally or extremely active.
7. Recognize or treat (someone or something) as different.
8. Recognize or treat (someone or something) as different.
9. Combine one thing with another so that they become a whole.
13. Estimate, measure, or note the similarity or dissimilarity between.
15. An uncontrolled outburst of anger and frustration, typically in a young child.

A. Analysis	B. Asperger	C. Categorize	D. Perception
E. Cerebral Palsy	F. Affect	G. Compare	H. Demonstrate
I. Brofenbrenner	J. Experiment	K. Distinguish	L. Tantrum
M. Integration	N. Analogy	O. Bloom	P. Distinguish
Q. Examine	R. Contrast	S. Hyperactivity	T. Cellular Respiration

9. Using the Across and Down clues, write the correct words in the numbered grid below.

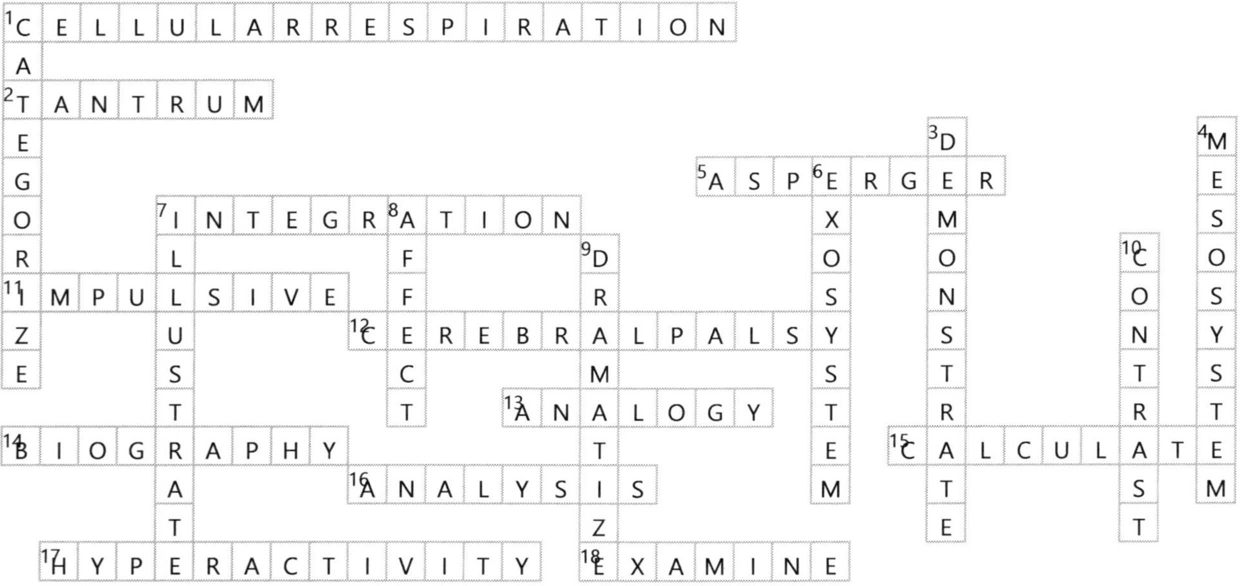

ACROSS

1. The process by which cells use oxygen to produce energy from food.
2. An uncontrolled outburst of anger and frustration, typically in a young child.
5. A type of autism characterized by normal cognitive and language development and impaired social skills.
7. Combine one thing with another so that they become a whole.
11. Acting or done without forethought.
12. A condition characterized by paralysis, weakness, lack of coordination.
13. A comparison of two things based on their being alike in some way.
14. Reports events about someone's life.
15. Determine (the amount or number of something) mathematically.
16. Breakdown information into parts and use those parts.
17. The condition of being abnormally or extremely active.
18. inspect (someone or something) in detail to determine their nature or condition.

DOWN

1. Place in a particular class or group.
3. Clearly show the existence or truth of (something) by giving proof or evidence.
4. Interaction of two microsystems.
6. Influence of external aspects on development.
7. Explain or make (something) clear by using examples, charts, pictures, etc.
8. Emotion or desire, especially as influencing behavior or action.
9. Adapt a novel or present a particular incident as a play or movie.
10. The state of being strikingly different from something else.

A. Demonstrate	B. Impulsive	C. Illustrate	D. Dramatize
E. Examine	F. Categorize	G. Tantrum	H. Calculate
I. Integration	J. Asperger	K. Affect	L. Analogy
M. Contrast	N. Biography	O. Cellular Respiration	P. Cerebral Palsy
Q. Mesosystem	R. Hyperactivity	S. Exosystem	T. Analysis

10. Using the Across and Down clues, write the correct words in the numbered grid below.

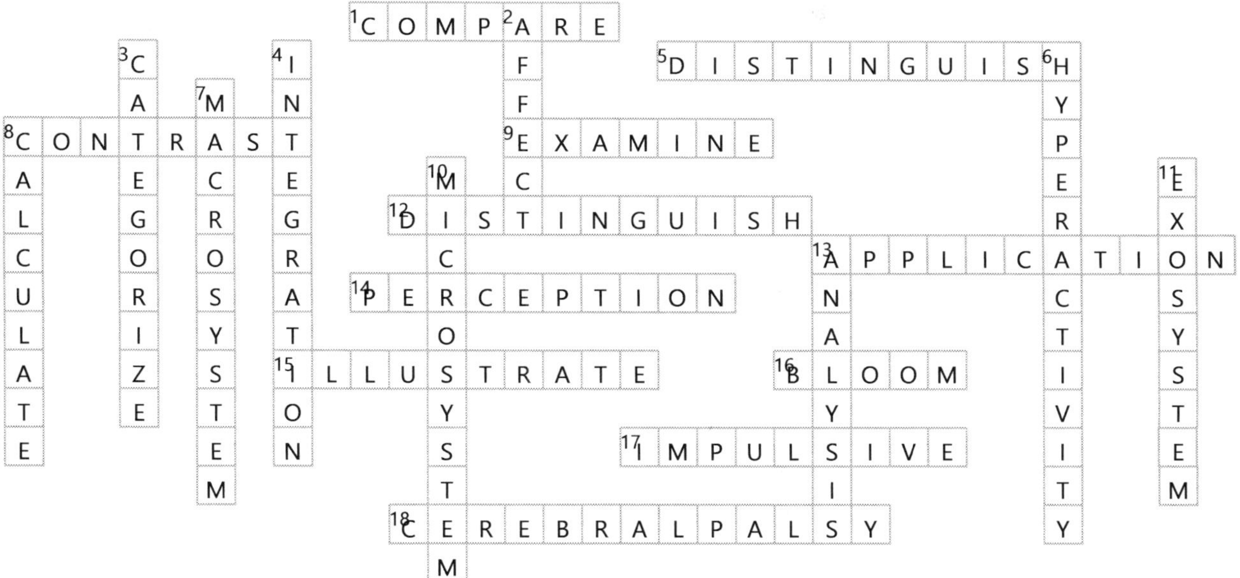

ACROSS

1. Estimate, measure, or note the similarity or dissimilarity between.
5. Recognize or treat (someone or something) as different.
8. The state of being strikingly different from something else.
9. inspect (someone or something) in detail to determine their nature or condition.
12. Recognize or treat (someone or something) as different.
13. Bloom's 3rd level, take previous learning and use it in a new way.
14. The ability to see, hear, or become aware of something through the senses.
15. Explain or make (something) clear by using examples, charts, pictures, etc.
16. Detailed classification of critical thinking and learning skills and objectives into tiered levels.
17. Acting or done without forethought.
18. A condition characterized by paralysis, weakness, lack of coordination.

DOWN

2. Emotion or desire, especially as influencing behavior or action.
3. Place in a particular class or group.
4. Combine one thing with another so that they become a whole.
6. The condition of being abnormally or extremely active.
7. The whole socio-cultural context.
8. Determine (the amount or number of something) mathematically.
10. Family of classroom.
11. Influence of external aspects on development.
13. Breakdown information into parts and use those parts.

A. Compare	B. Calculate	C. Affect	D. Application	E. Impulsive
F. Analysis	G. Examine	H. Integration	I. Hyperactivity	J. Microsystem
K. Perception	L. Macrosystem	M. Distinguish	N. Contrast	O. Categorize
P. Distinguish	Q. Cerebral Palsy	R. Bloom	S. Exosystem	T. Illustrate

11. Using the Across and Down clues, write the correct words in the numbered grid below.

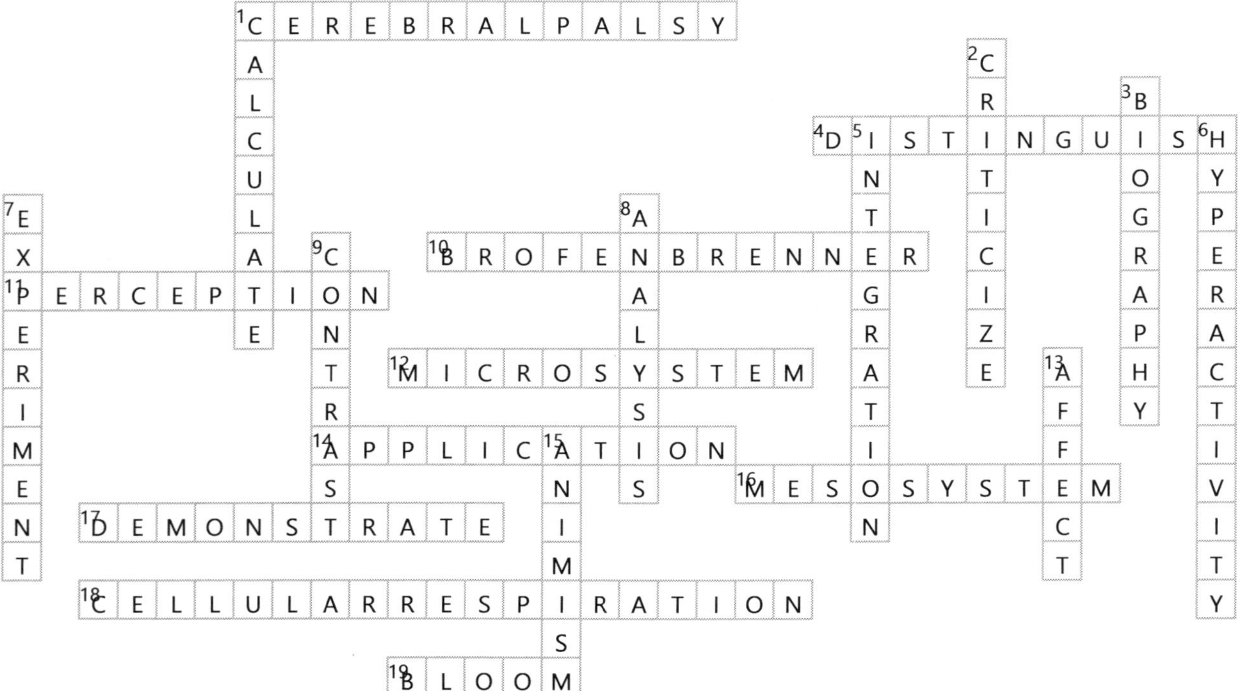

ACROSS

1. A condition characterized by paralysis, weakness, lack of coordination.
4. Recognize or treat (someone or something) as different.
10. Leader in field of child psychology and development, outlined 4 types of nested systems.
11. The ability to see, hear, or become aware of something through the senses.
12. Family of classroom.
14. Bloom's 3rd level, take previous learning and use it in a new way.
16. Interaction of two microsystems.
17. Clearly show the existence or truth of (something) by giving proof or evidence.
18. The process by which cells use oxygen to produce energy from food.
19. Detailed classification of critical thinking and learning skills and objectives into tiered levels.

DOWN

1. Determine (the amount or number of something) mathematically.
2. Indicate the faults of (someone or something) in a disapproving way.
3. Reports events about someone's life.
5. Combine one thing with another so that they become a whole.
6. The condition of being abnormally or extremely active.
7. A scientific procedure undertaken to make a discovery, test a hypothesis, or demonstrate a fact.
8. Breakdown information into parts and use those parts.
9. The state of being strikingly different from something else.
13. Emotion or desire, especially as influencing behavior or action.
15. Assigning human qualities to objects "the sun was mad and burned me".

A. Cerebral Palsy
B. Analysis
C. Distinguish
D. Experiment
E. Criticize
F. Calculate
G. Contrast
H. Biography
I. Brofenbrenner
J. Animism
K. Mesosystem
L. Application
M. Microsystem
N. Perception
O. Hyperactivity
P. Demonstrate
Q. Integration
R. Bloom
S. Affect
T. Cellular Respiration

12. Using the Across and Down clues, write the correct words in the numbered grid below.

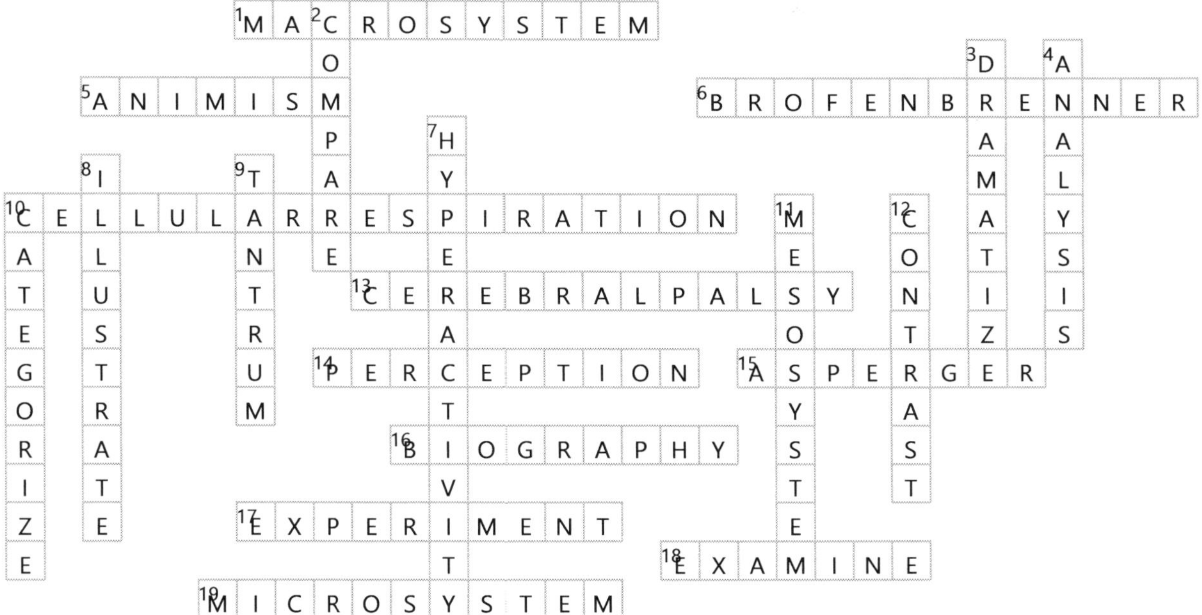

ACROSS

1. The whole socio-cultural context.
5. Assigning human qualities to objects "the sun was mad and burned me".
6. Leader in field of child psychology and development, outlined 4 types of nested systems.
10. The process by which cells use oxygen to produce energy from food.
13. A condition characterized by paralysis, weakness, lack of coordination.
14. The ability to see, hear, or become aware of something through the senses.
15. A type of autism characterized by normal cognitive and language development and impaired social skills.
16. Reports events about someone's life.
17. A scientific procedure undertaken to make a discovery, test a hypothesis, or demonstrate a fact.
18. inspect (someone or something) in detail to determine their nature or condition.
19. Family of classroom.

DOWN

2. Estimate, measure, or note the similarity or dissimilarity between.
3. Adapt a novel or present a particular incident as a play or movie.
4. Breakdown information into parts and use those parts.
7. The condition of being abnormally or extremely active.
8. Explain or make (something) clear by using examples, charts, pictures, etc.
9. An uncontrolled outburst of anger and frustration, typically in a young child.
10. Place in a particular class or group.
11. Interaction of two microsystems.
12. The state of being strikingly different from something else.

A. Experiment	B. Dramatize	C. Cellular Respiration	D. Examine
E. Asperger	F. Mesosystem	G. Analysis	H. Hyperactivity
I. Cerebral Palsy	J. Microsystem	K. Contrast	L. Tantrum
M. Animism	N. Categorize	O. Illustrate	P. Macrosystem
Q. Brofenbrenner	R. Compare	S. Perception	T. Biography

13. Using the Across and Down clues, write the correct words in the numbered grid below.

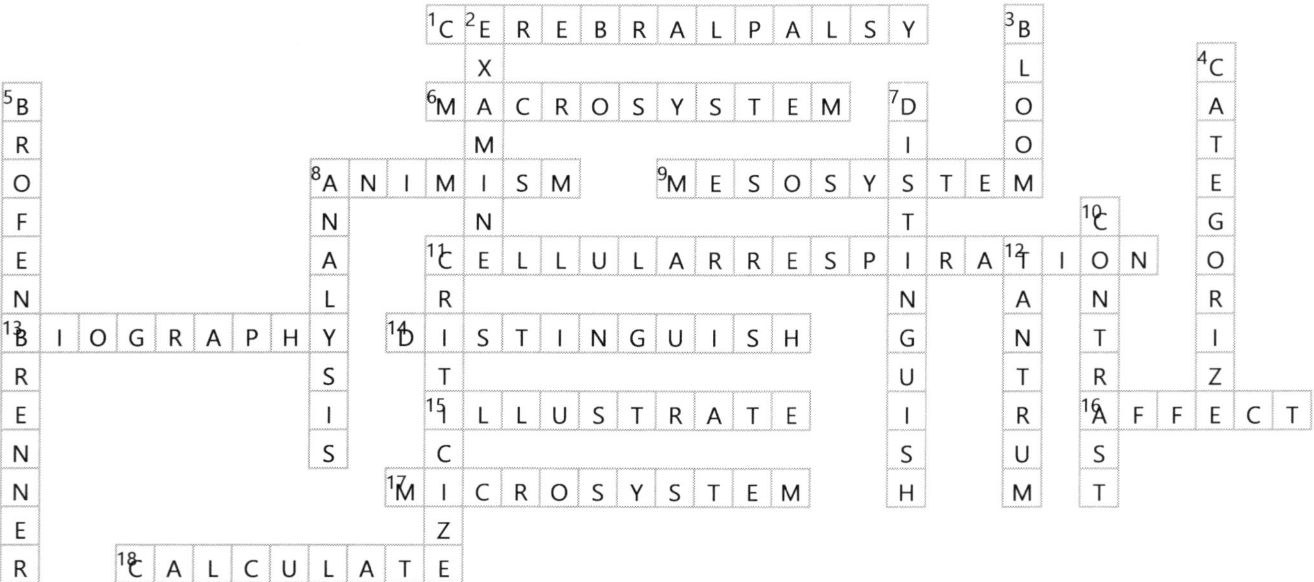

ACROSS

1. A condition characterized by paralysis, weakness, lack of coordination.
6. The whole socio-cultural context.
8. Assigning human qualities to objects "the sun was mad and burned me".
9. Interaction of two microsystems.
11. The process by which cells use oxygen to produce energy from food.
13. Reports events about someone's life.
14. Recognize or treat (someone or something) as different.
15. Explain or make (something) clear by using examples, charts, pictures, etc.
16. Emotion or desire, especially as influencing behavior or action.
17. Family of classroom.
18. Determine (the amount or number of something) mathematically.

DOWN

2. inspect (someone or something) in detail to determine their nature or condition.
3. Detailed classification of critical thinking and learning skills and objectives into tiered levels.
4. Place in a particular class or group.
5. Leader in field of child psychology and development, outlined 4 types of nested systems.
7. Recognize or treat (someone or something) as different.
8. Breakdown information into parts and use those parts.
10. The state of being strikingly different from something else.
11. Indicate the faults of (someone or something) in a disapproving way.
12. An uncontrolled outburst of anger and frustration, typically in a young child.

A. Illustrate	B. Brofenbrenner	C. Calculate	D. Affect
E. Biography	F. Contrast	G. Cerebral Palsy	H. Microsystem
I. Examine	J. Distinguish	K. Bloom	L. Criticize
M. Cellular Respiration	N. Animism	O. Categorize	P. Mesosystem
Q. Distinguish	R. Analysis	S. Tantrum	T. Macrosystem

14. Using the Across and Down clues, write the correct words in the numbered grid below.

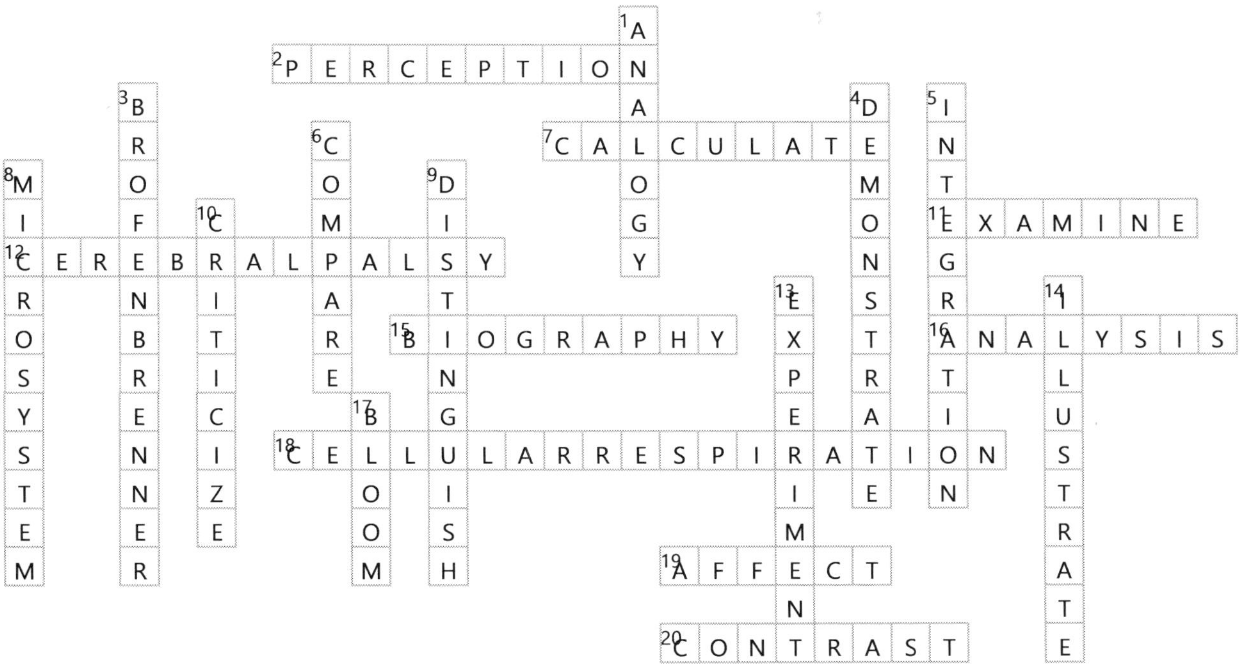

ACROSS

2. The ability to see, hear, or become aware of something through the senses.
7. Determine (the amount or number of something) mathematically.
11. inspect (someone or something) in detail to determine their nature or condition.
12. A condition characterized by paralysis, weakness, lack of coordination.
15. Reports events about someone's life.
16. Breakdown information into parts and use those parts.
18. The process by which cells use oxygen to produce energy from food.
19. Emotion or desire, especially as influencing behavior or action.
20. The state of being strikingly different from something else.

DOWN

1. A comparison of two things based on their being alike in some way.
3. Leader in field of child psychology and development, outlined 4 types of nested systems.
4. Clearly show the existence or truth of (something) by giving proof or evidence.
5. Combine one thing with another so that they become a whole.
6. Estimate, measure, or note the similarity or dissimilarity between.
8. Family of classroom.
9. Recognize or treat (someone or something) as different.
10. Indicate the faults of (someone or something) in a disapproving way.
13. A scientific procedure undertaken to make a discovery, test a hypothesis, or demonstrate a fact.
14. Explain or make (something) clear by using examples, charts, pictures, etc.
17. Detailed classification of critical thinking and learning skills and objectives into tiered levels.

A. Illustrate	B. Distinguish	C. Criticize	D. Biography
E. Cerebral Palsy	F. Compare	G. Integration	H. Examine
I. Brofenbrenner	J. Bloom	K. Demonstrate	L. Analogy
M. Perception	N. Analysis	O. Affect	P. Contrast
Q. Calculate	R. Cellular Respiration	S. Experiment	T. Microsystem

15. Using the Across and Down clues, write the correct words in the numbered grid below.

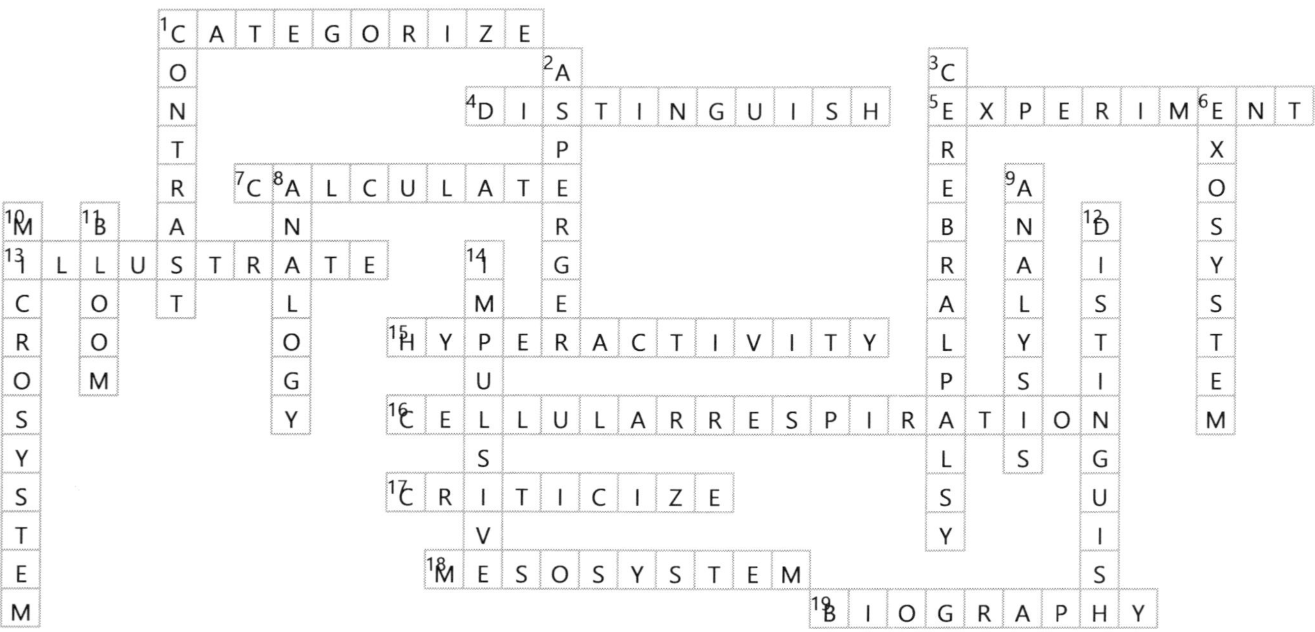

ACROSS

1. Place in a particular class or group.
4. Recognize or treat (someone or something) as different.
5. A scientific procedure undertaken to make a discovery, test a hypothesis, or demonstrate a fact.
7. Determine (the amount or number of something) mathematically.
13. Explain or make (something) clear by using examples, charts, pictures, etc.
15. The condition of being abnormally or extremely active.
16. The process by which cells use oxygen to produce energy from food.
17. Indicate the faults of (someone or something) in a disapproving way.
18. Interaction of two microsystems.
19. Reports events about someone's life.

DOWN

1. The state of being strikingly different from something else.
2. A type of autism characterized by normal cognitive and language development and impaired social skills.
3. A condition characterized by paralysis, weakness, lack of coordination.
6. Influence of external aspects on development.
8. A comparison of two things based on their being alike in some way.
9. Breakdown information into parts and use those parts.
10. Family of classroom.
11. Detailed classification of critical thinking and learning skills and objectives into tiered levels.
12. Recognize or treat (someone or something) as different.
14. Acting or done without forethought.

A. Categorize
E. Contrast
I. Asperger
M. Exosystem
Q. Impulsive

B. Criticize
F. Microsystem
J. Mesosystem
N. Analogy
R. Distinguish

C. Cellular Respiration
G. Hyperactivity
K. Distinguish
O. Calculate
S. Cerebral Palsy

D. Illustrate
H. Experiment
L. Analysis
P. Bloom
T. Biography

16. Using the Across and Down clues, write the correct words in the numbered grid below.

ACROSS

3. A condition characterized by paralysis, weakness, lack of coordination.
5. Adapt a novel or present a particular incident as a play or movie.
6. Determine (the amount or number of something) mathematically.
10. inspect (someone or something) in detail to determine their nature or condition.
12. Detailed classification of critical thinking and learning skills and objectives into tiered levels.
14. Bloom's 3rd level, take previous learning and use it in a new way.
17. Interaction of two microsystems.
18. The process by which cells use oxygen to produce energy from food.
19. Estimate, measure, or note the similarity or dissimilarity between.

DOWN

1. Leader in field of child psychology and development, outlined 4 types of nested systems.
2. Recognize or treat (someone or something) as different.
4. A scientific procedure undertaken to make a discovery, test a hypothesis, or demonstrate a fact.
7. The whole socio-cultural context.
8. Clearly show the existence or truth of (something) by giving proof or evidence.
9. Family of classroom.
11. Explain or make (something) clear by using examples, charts, pictures, etc.
13. A comparison of two things based on their being alike in some way.
14. Assigning human qualities to objects "the sun was mad and burned me".
15. Emotion or desire, especially as influencing behavior or action.
16. An uncontrolled outburst of anger and frustration, typically in a young child.

A. Calculate	B. Illustrate	C. Tantrum	D. Examine
E. Compare	F. Affect	G. Bloom	H. Application
I. Demonstrate	J. Cellular Respiration	K. Mesosystem	L. Brofenbrenner
M. Analogy	N. Cerebral Palsy	O. Dramatize	P. Macrosystem
Q. Microsystem	R. Animism	S. Experiment	T. Distinguish

17. Using the Across and Down clues, write the correct words in the numbered grid below.

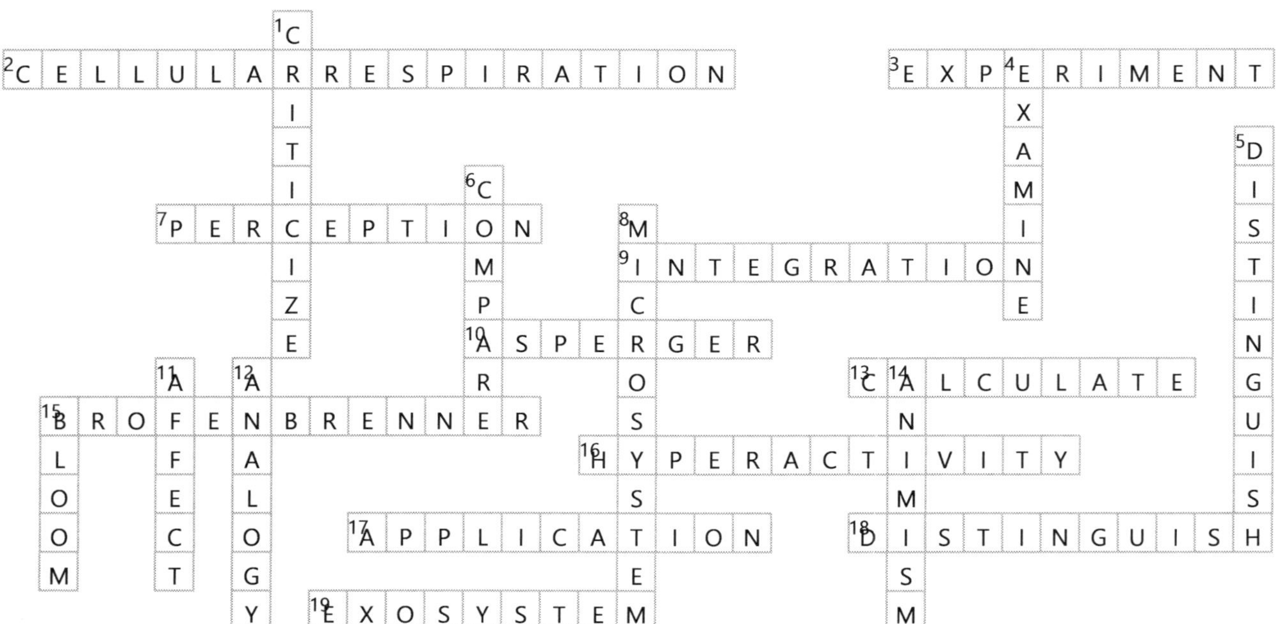

ACROSS

2. The process by which cells use oxygen to produce energy from food.
3. A scientific procedure undertaken to make a discovery, test a hypothesis, or demonstrate a fact.
7. The ability to see, hear, or become aware of something through the senses.
9. Combine one thing with another so that they become a whole.
10. A type of autism characterized by normal cognitive and language development and impaired social skills.
13. Determine (the amount or number of something) mathematically.
15. Leader in field of child psychology and development, outlined 4 types of nested systems.
16. The condition of being abnormally or extremely active.
17. Bloom's 3rd level, take previous learning and use it in a new way.
18. Recognize or treat (someone or something) as different.
19. Influence of external aspects on development.

DOWN

1. Indicate the faults of (someone or something) in a disapproving way.
4. inspect (someone or something) in detail to determine their nature or condition.
5. Recognize or treat (someone or something) as different.
6. Estimate, measure, or note the similarity or dissimilarity between.
8. Family of classroom.
11. Emotion or desire, especially as influencing behavior or action.
12. A comparison of two things based on their being alike in some way.
14. Assigning human qualities to objects "the sun was mad and burned me".
15. Detailed classification of critical thinking and learning skills and objectives into tiered levels.

A. Integration	B. Calculate	C. Animism	D. Exosystem
E. Asperger	F. Affect	G. Examine	H. Compare
I. Experiment	J. Distinguish	K. Brofenbrenner	L. Application
M. Bloom	N. Perception	O. Analogy	P. Hyperactivity
Q. Distinguish	R. Cellular Respiration	S. Criticize	T. Microsystem

18. Using the Across and Down clues, write the correct words in the numbered grid below.

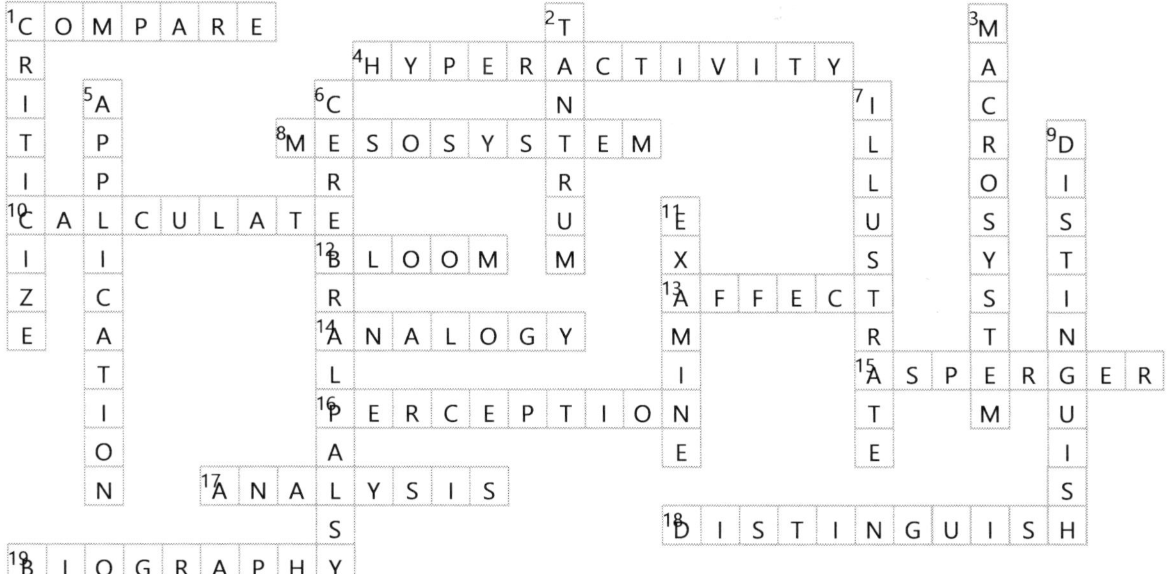

ACROSS

1. Estimate, measure, or note the similarity or dissimilarity between.
4. The condition of being abnormally or extremely active.
8. Interaction of two microsystems.
10. Determine (the amount or number of something) mathematically.
12. Detailed classification of critical thinking and learning skills and objectives into tiered levels.
13. Emotion or desire, especially as influencing behavior or action.
14. A comparison of two things based on their being alike in some way.
15. A type of autism characterized by normal cognitive and language development and impaired social skills.
16. The ability to see, hear, or become aware of something through the senses.
17. Breakdown information into parts and use those parts.
18. Recognize or treat (someone or something) as different.
19. Reports events about someone's life.

DOWN

1. Indicate the faults of (someone or something) in a disapproving way.
2. An uncontrolled outburst of anger and frustration, typically in a young child.
3. The whole socio-cultural context.
5. Bloom's 3rd level, take previous learning and use it in a new way.
6. A condition characterized by paralysis, weakness, lack of coordination.
7. Explain or make (something) clear by using examples, charts, pictures, etc.
9. Recognize or treat (someone or something) as different.
11. inspect (someone or something) in detail to determine their nature or condition.

A. Bloom	B. Distinguish	C. Compare	D. Macrosystem	E. Mesosystem
F. Affect	G. Criticize	H. Hyperactivity	I. Application	J. Perception
K. Analysis	L. Distinguish	M. Analogy	N. Asperger	O. Tantrum
P. Examine	Q. Cerebral Palsy	R. Calculate	S. Biography	T. Illustrate

19. Using the Across and Down clues, write the correct words in the numbered grid below.

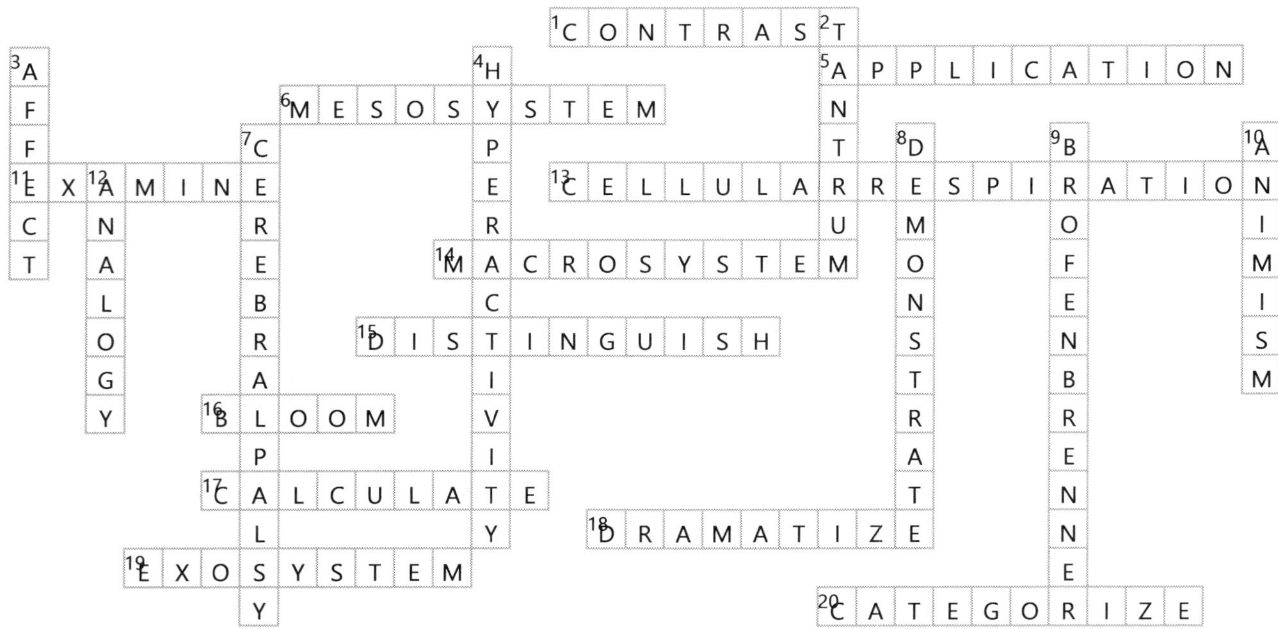

ACROSS

1. The state of being strikingly different from something else.
5. Bloom's 3rd level, take previous learning and use it in a new way.
6. Interaction of two microsystems.
11. inspect (someone or something) in detail to determine their nature or condition.
13. The process by which cells use oxygen to produce energy from food.
14. The whole socio-cultural context.
15. Recognize or treat (someone or something) as different.
16. Detailed classification of critical thinking and learning skills and objectives into tiered levels.
17. Determine (the amount or number of something) mathematically.
18. Adapt a novel or present a particular incident as a play or movie.
19. Influence of external aspects on development.
20. Place in a particular class or group.

DOWN

2. An uncontrolled outburst of anger and frustration, typically in a young child.
3. Emotion or desire, especially as influencing behavior or action.
4. The condition of being abnormally or extremely active.
7. A condition characterized by paralysis, weakness, lack of coordination.
8. Clearly show the existence or truth of (something) by giving proof or evidence.
9. Leader in field of child psychology and development, outlined 4 types of nested systems.
10. Assigning human qualities to objects "the sun was mad and burned me".
12. A comparison of two things based on their being alike in some way.

A. Bloom	B. Animism	C. Hyperactivity	D. Categorize
E. Brofenbrenner	F. Tantrum	G. Mesosystem	H. Contrast
I. Analogy	J. Examine	K. Affect	L. Cellular Respiration
M. Calculate	N. Distinguish	O. Cerebral Palsy	P. Demonstrate
Q. Exosystem	R. Dramatize	S. Macrosystem	T. Application

20. Using the Across and Down clues, write the correct words in the numbered grid below.

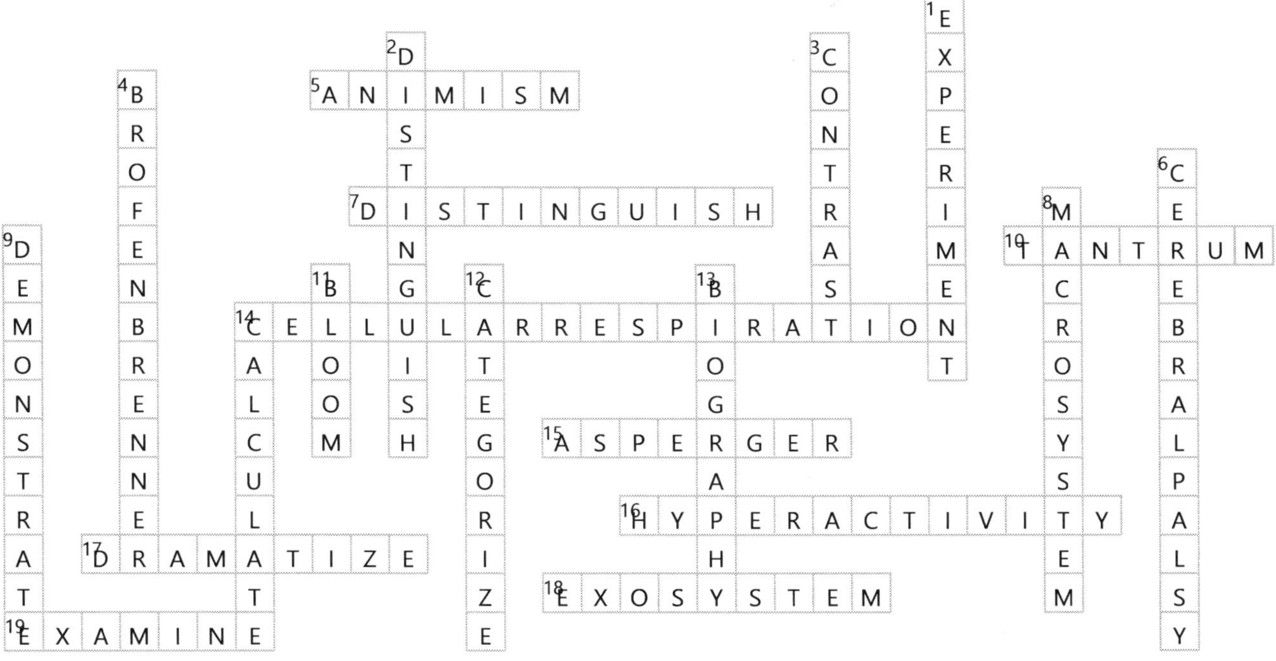

ACROSS

5. Assigning human qualities to objects "the sun was mad and burned me".
7. Recognize or treat (someone or something) as different.
10. An uncontrolled outburst of anger and frustration, typically in a young child.
14. The process by which cells use oxygen to produce energy from food.
15. A type of autism characterized by normal cognitive and language development and impaired social skills.
16. The condition of being abnormally or extremely active.
17. Adapt a novel or present a particular incident as a play or movie.
18. Influence of external aspects on development.
19. inspect (someone or something) in detail to determine their nature or condition.

DOWN

1. A scientific procedure undertaken to make a discovery, test a hypothesis, or demonstrate a fact.
2. Recognize or treat (someone or something) as different.
3. The state of being strikingly different from something else.
4. Leader in field of child psychology and development, outlined 4 types of nested systems.
6. A condition characterized by paralysis, weakness, lack of coordination.
8. The whole socio-cultural context.
9. Clearly show the existence or truth of (something) by giving proof or evidence.
11. Detailed classification of critical thinking and learning skills and objectives into tiered levels.
12. Place in a particular class or group.
13. Reports events about someone's life.
14. Determine (the amount or number of something) mathematically.

A. Animism	B. Hyperactivity	C. Examine	D. Calculate
E. Brofenbrenner	F. Dramatize	G. Asperger	H. Bloom
I. Macrosystem	J. Distinguish	K. Distinguish	L. Biography
M. Categorize	N. Experiment	O. Cellular Respiration	P. Exosystem
Q. Contrast	R. Tantrum	S. Cerebral Palsy	T. Demonstrate

21. Using the Across and Down clues, write the correct words in the numbered grid below.

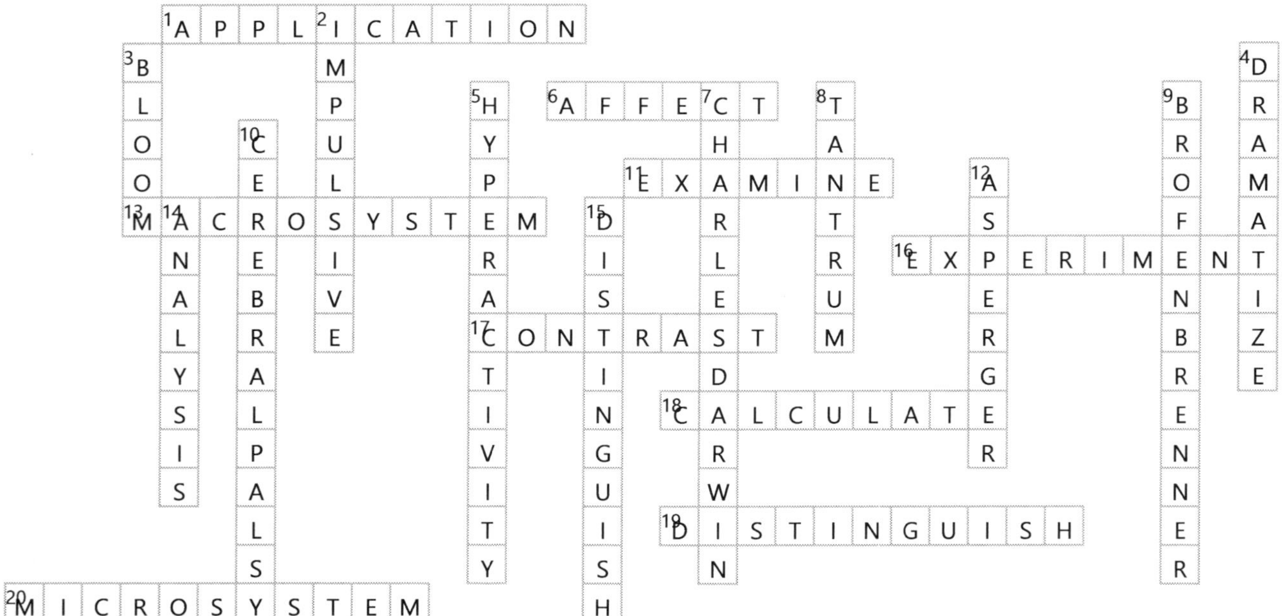

ACROSS

1. Bloom's 3rd level, take previous learning and use it in a new way.
6. Emotion or desire, especially as influencing behavior or action.
11. inspect (someone or something) in detail to determine their nature or condition.
13. The whole socio-cultural context.
16. A scientific procedure undertaken to make a discovery, test a hypothesis, or demonstrate a fact.
17. The state of being strikingly different from something else.
18. Determine (the amount or number of something) mathematically.
19. Recognize or treat (someone or something) as different.
20. Family of classroom.

DOWN

2. Acting or done without forethought.
3. Detailed classification of critical thinking and learning skills and objectives into tiered levels.
4. Adapt a novel or present a particular incident as a play or movie.
5. The condition of being abnormally or extremely active.
7. English natural scientist who formulated a theory of evolution by natural selection.
8. An uncontrolled outburst of anger and frustration, typically in a young child.
9. Leader in field of child psychology and development, outlined 4 types of nested systems.
10. A condition characterized by paralysis, weakness, lack of coordination.
12. A type of autism characterized by normal cognitive and language development and impaired social skills.
14. Breakdown information into parts and use those parts.
15. Recognize or treat (someone or something) as different.

A. Macrosystem	B. Hyperactivity	C. Impulsive	D. Asperger	E. Distinguish
F. Tantrum	G. Experiment	H. Distinguish	I. Affect	J. Examine
K. Bloom	L. Microsystem	M. Calculate	N. Analysis	O. Application
P. Dramatize	Q. Brofenbrenner	R. Cerebral Palsy	S. Contrast	T. Charles Darwin

22. Using the Across and Down clues, write the correct words in the numbered grid below.

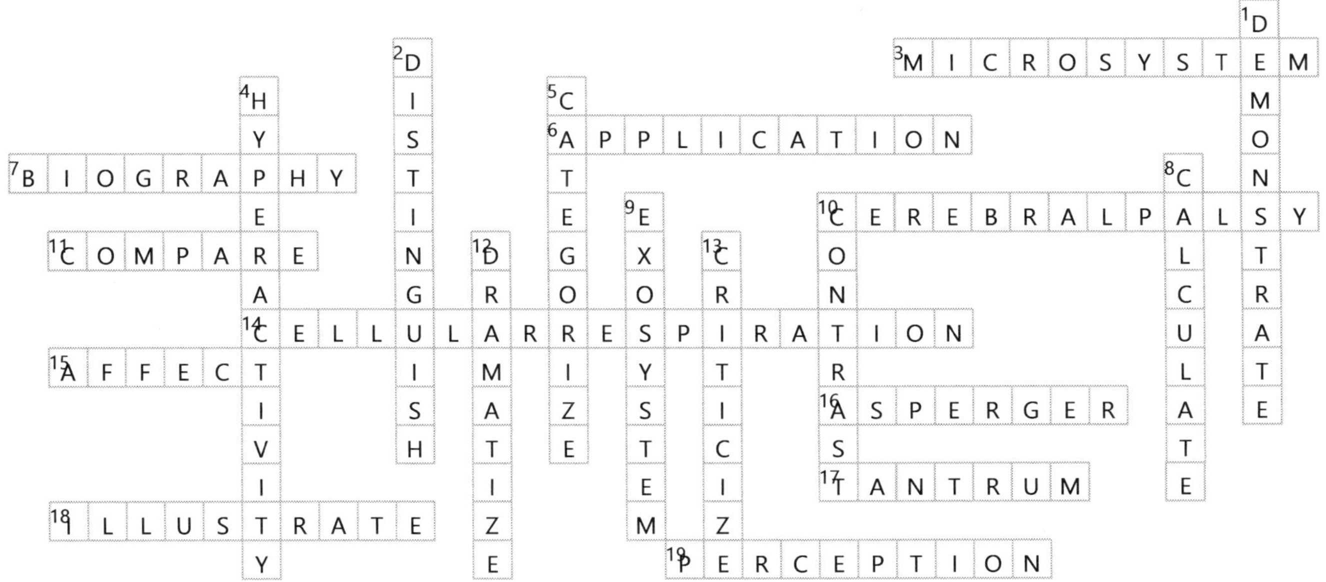

ACROSS

3. Family of classroom.
6. Bloom's 3rd level, take previous learning and use it in a new way.
7. Reports events about someone's life.
10. A condition characterized by paralysis, weakness, lack of coordination.
11. Estimate, measure, or note the similarity or dissimilarity between.
14. The process by which cells use oxygen to produce energy from food.
15. Emotion or desire, especially as influencing behavior or action.
16. A type of autism characterized by normal cognitive and language development and impaired social skills.
17. An uncontrolled outburst of anger and frustration, typically in a young child.
18. Explain or make (something) clear by using examples, charts, pictures, etc.
19. The ability to see, hear, or become aware of something through the senses.

DOWN

1. Clearly show the existence or truth of (something) by giving proof or evidence.
2. Recognize or treat (someone or something) as different.
4. The condition of being abnormally or extremely active.
5. Place in a particular class or group.
8. Determine (the amount or number of something) mathematically.
9. Influence of external aspects on development.
10. The state of being strikingly different from something else.
12. Adapt a novel or present a particular incident as a play or movie.
13. Indicate the faults of (someone or something) in a disapproving way.

A. Illustrate	B. Distinguish	C. Criticize	D. Calculate
E. Affect	F. Application	G. Compare	H. Exosystem
I. Cellular Respiration	J. Demonstrate	K. Hyperactivity	L. Dramatize
M. Asperger	N. Tantrum	O. Contrast	P. Perception
Q. Cerebral Palsy	R. Biography	S. Categorize	T. Microsystem

23. Using the Across and Down clues, write the correct words in the numbered grid below.

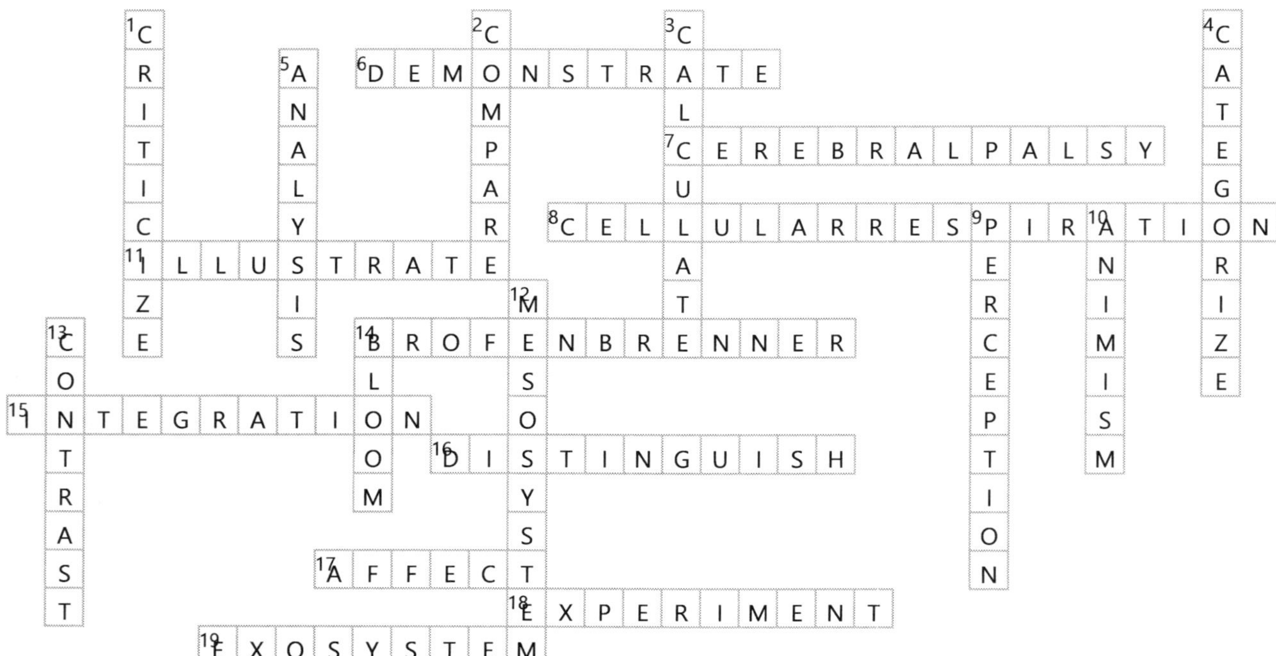

ACROSS

6. Clearly show the existence or truth of (something) by giving proof or evidence.
7. A condition characterized by paralysis, weakness, lack of coordination.
8. The process by which cells use oxygen to produce energy from food.
11. Explain or make (something) clear by using examples, charts, pictures, etc.
14. Leader in field of child psychology and development, outlined 4 types of nested systems.
15. Combine one thing with another so that they become a whole.
16. Recognize or treat (someone or something) as different.
17. Emotion or desire, especially as influencing behavior or action.
18. A scientific procedure undertaken to make a discovery, test a hypothesis, or demonstrate a fact.
19. Influence of external aspects on development.

DOWN

1. Indicate the faults of (someone or something) in a disapproving way.
2. Estimate, measure, or note the similarity or dissimilarity between.
3. Determine (the amount or number of something) mathematically.
4. Place in a particular class or group.
5. Breakdown information into parts and use those parts.
9. The ability to see, hear, or become aware of something through the senses.
10. Assigning human qualities to objects "the sun was mad and burned me".
12. Interaction of two microsystems.
13. The state of being strikingly different from something else.
14. Detailed classification of critical thinking and learning skills and objectives into tiered levels.

A. Compare	B. Distinguish	C. Illustrate	D. Affect
E. Demonstrate	F. Mesosystem	G. Calculate	H. Exosystem
I. Categorize	J. Analysis	K. Cerebral Palsy	L. Cellular Respiration
M. Bloom	N. Contrast	O. Animism	P. Brofenbrenner
Q. Perception	R. Experiment	S. Integration	T. Criticize

24. Using the Across and Down clues, write the correct words in the numbered grid below.

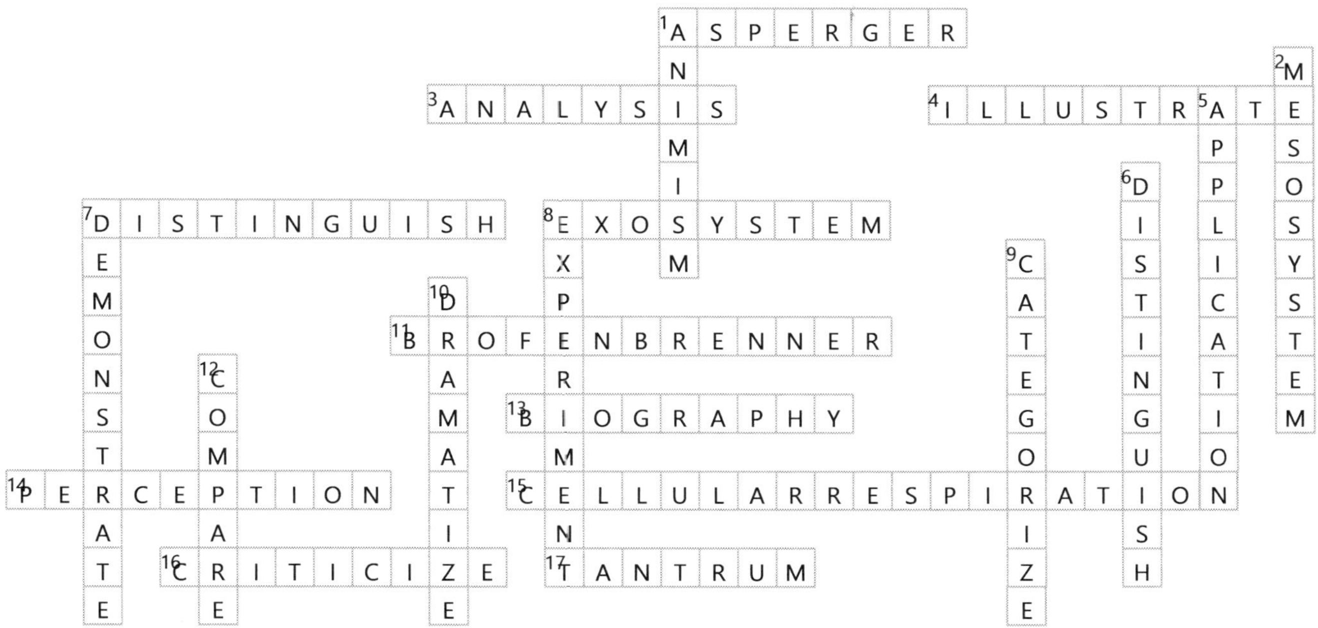

ACROSS

1. A type of autism characterized by normal cognitive and language development and impaired social skills.
3. Breakdown information into parts and use those parts.
4. Explain or make (something) clear by using examples, charts, pictures, etc.
7. Recognize or treat (someone or something) as different.
8. Influence of external aspects on development.
11. Leader in field of child psychology and development, outlined 4 types of nested systems.
13. Reports events about someone's life.
14. The ability to see, hear, or become aware of something through the senses.
15. The process by which cells use oxygen to produce energy from food.
16. Indicate the faults of (someone or something) in a disapproving way.
17. An uncontrolled outburst of anger and frustration, typically in a young child.

DOWN

1. Assigning human qualities to objects "the sun was mad and burned me".
2. Interaction of two microsystems.
5. Bloom's 3rd level, take previous learning and use it in a new way.
6. Recognize or treat (someone or something) as different.
7. Clearly show the existence or truth of (something) by giving proof or evidence.
8. A scientific procedure undertaken to make a discovery, test a hypothesis, or demonstrate a fact.
9. Place in a particular class or group.
10. Adapt a novel or present a particular incident as a play or movie.
12. Estimate, measure, or note the similarity or dissimilarity between.

A. Mesosystem
B. Application
C. Demonstrate
D. Brofenbrenner
E. Compare
F. Biography
G. Asperger
H. Perception
I. Experiment
J. Criticize
K. Illustrate
L. Dramatize
M. Animism
N. Analysis
O. Cellular Respiration
P. Exosystem
Q. Categorize
R. Distinguish
S. Tantrum
T. Distinguish

25. Using the Across and Down clues, write the correct words in the numbered grid below.

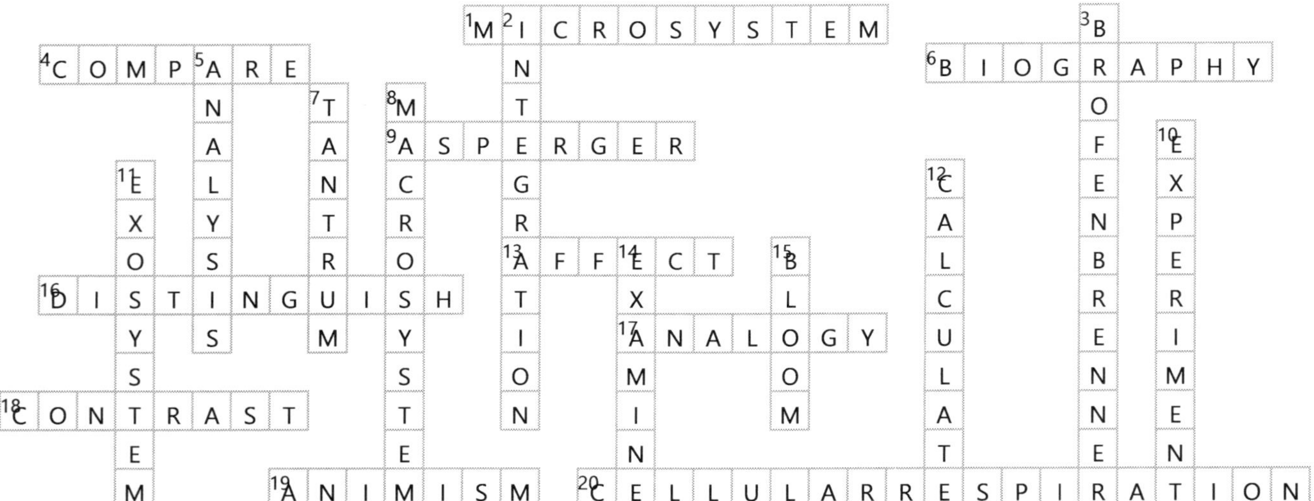

ACROSS

1. Family of classroom.
4. Estimate, measure, or note the similarity or dissimilarity between.
6. Reports events about someone's life.
9. A type of autism characterized by normal cognitive and language development and impaired social skills.
13. Emotion or desire, especially as influencing behavior or action.
16. Recognize or treat (someone or something) as different.
17. A comparison of two things based on their being alike in some way.
18. The state of being strikingly different from something else.
19. Assigning human qualities to objects "the sun was mad and burned me".
20. The process by which cells use oxygen to produce energy from food.

DOWN

2. Combine one thing with another so that they become a whole.
3. Leader in field of child psychology and development, outlined 4 types of nested systems.
5. Breakdown information into parts and use those parts.
7. An uncontrolled outburst of anger and frustration, typically in a young child.
8. The whole socio-cultural context.
10. A scientific procedure undertaken to make a discovery, test a hypothesis, or demonstrate a fact.
11. Influence of external aspects on development.
12. Determine (the amount or number of something) mathematically.
14. inspect (someone or something) in detail to determine their nature or condition.
15. Detailed classification of critical thinking and learning skills and objectives into tiered levels.

A. Examine
B. Animism
C. Integration
D. Analysis
E. Biography
F. Analogy
G. Macrosystem
H. Brofenbrenner
I. Asperger
J. Distinguish
K. Bloom
L. Microsystem
M. Cellular Respiration
N. Affect
O. Compare
P. Contrast
Q. Exosystem
R. Calculate
S. Experiment
T. Tantrum

26. Using the Across and Down clues, write the correct words in the numbered grid below.

ACROSS

3. A scientific procedure undertaken to make a discovery, test a hypothesis, or demonstrate a fact.
4. Bloom's 3rd level, take previous learning and use it in a new way.
5. Breakdown information into parts and use those parts.
8. A lack of compatibility or similarity between two or more facts.
9. A comparison of two things based on their being alike in some way.
10. Emotion or desire, especially as influencing behavior or action.
12. Combine one thing with another so that they become a whole.
14. The state of being strikingly different from something else.
15. Determine (the amount or number of something) mathematically.
16. Indicate the faults of (someone or something) in a disapproving way.
17. The whole socio-cultural context.
18. Estimate, measure, or note the similarity or dissimilarity between.
19. Detailed classification of critical thinking and learning skills and objectives into tiered levels.
20. Influence of external aspects on development.

DOWN

1. Clearly show the existence or truth of (something) by giving proof or evidence.
2. Leader in field of child psychology and development, outlined 4 types of nested systems.
6. A type of autism characterized by normal cognitive and language development and impaired social skills.
7. The ability to see, hear, or become aware of something through the senses.
11. inspect (someone or something) in detail to determine their nature or condition.
13. Assigning human qualities to objects "the sun was mad and burned me".

A. Criticize	B. Bloom	C. Integration	D. Demonstrate	E. Perception
F. Affect	G. Analogy	H. Brofenbrenner	I. Analysis	J. Macrosystem
K. Calculate	L. Contrast	M. Examine	N. Application	O. Experiment
P. Compare	Q. Exosystem	R. Animism	S. Discrepancy	T. Asperger

27. Using the Across and Down clues, write the correct words in the numbered grid below.

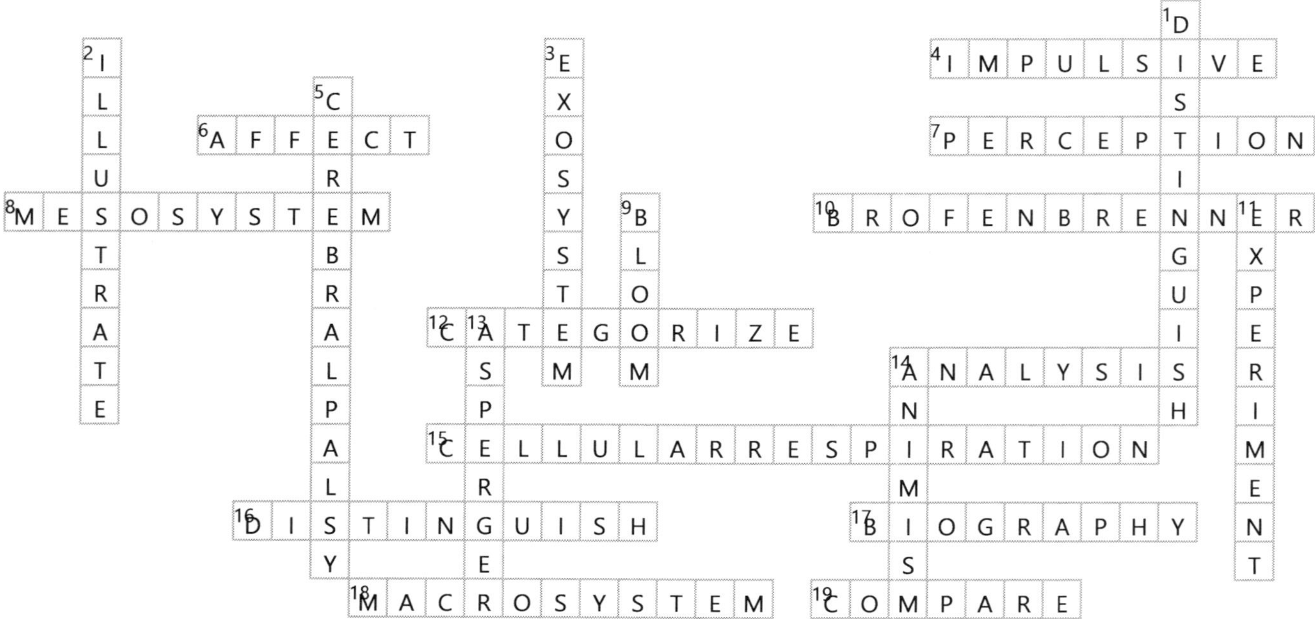

ACROSS

4. Acting or done without forethought.
6. Emotion or desire, especially as influencing behavior or action.
7. The ability to see, hear, or become aware of something through the senses.
8. Interaction of two microsystems.
10. Leader in field of child psychology and development, outlined 4 types of nested systems.
12. Place in a particular class or group.
14. Breakdown information into parts and use those parts.
15. The process by which cells use oxygen to produce energy from food.
16. Recognize or treat (someone or something) as different.
17. Reports events about someone's life.
18. The whole socio-cultural context.
19. Estimate, measure, or note the similarity or dissimilarity between.

DOWN

1. Recognize or treat (someone or something) as different.
2. Explain or make (something) clear by using examples, charts, pictures, etc.
3. Influence of external aspects on development.
5. A condition characterized by paralysis, weakness, lack of coordination.
9. Detailed classification of critical thinking and learning skills and objectives into tiered levels.
11. A scientific procedure undertaken to make a discovery, test a hypothesis, or demonstrate a fact.
13. A type of autism characterized by normal cognitive and language development and impaired social skills.
14. Assigning human qualities to objects "the sun was mad and burned me".

A. Cellular Respiration
B. Bloom
C. Impulsive
D. Brofenbrenner
E. Affect
F. Animism
G. Analysis
H. Experiment
I. Biography
J. Exosystem
K. Compare
L. Categorize
M. Mesosystem
N. Distinguish
O. Macrosystem
P. Cerebral Palsy
Q. Perception
R. Illustrate
S. Asperger
T. Distinguish

28. Using the Across and Down clues, write the correct words in the numbered grid below.

ACROSS

1. A scientific procedure undertaken to make a discovery, test a hypothesis, or demonstrate a fact.
2. Recognize or treat (someone or something) as different.
6. Assigning human qualities to objects "the sun was mad and burned me".
8. Detailed classification of critical thinking and learning skills and objectives into tiered levels.
9. An uncontrolled outburst of anger and frustration, typically in a young child.
10. Family of classroom.
11. The ability to see, hear, or become aware of something through the senses.
12. A type of autism characterized by normal cognitive and language development and impaired social skills.
13. The state of being strikingly different from something else.
14. Breakdown information into parts and use those parts.
15. The whole socio-cultural context.
16. Indicate the faults of (someone or something) in a disapproving way.
17. The condition of being abnormally or extremely active.

DOWN

1. Influence of external aspects on development.
2. Adapt a novel or present a particular incident as a play or movie.
3. inspect (someone or something) in detail to determine their nature or condition.
4. Explain or make (something) clear by using examples, charts, pictures, etc.
5. Clearly show the existence or truth of (something) by giving proof or evidence.
7. Emotion or desire, especially as influencing behavior or action.
12. A comparison of two things based on their being alike in some way.

A. Perception	B. Exosystem	C. Examine	D. Affect	E. Hyperactivity
F. Microsystem	G. Asperger	H. Animism	I. Analysis	J. Dramatize
K. Tantrum	L. Criticize	M. Contrast	N. Experiment	O. Distinguish
P. Demonstrate	Q. Analogy	R. Bloom	S. Illustrate	T. Macrosystem

29. Using the Across and Down clues, write the correct words in the numbered grid below.

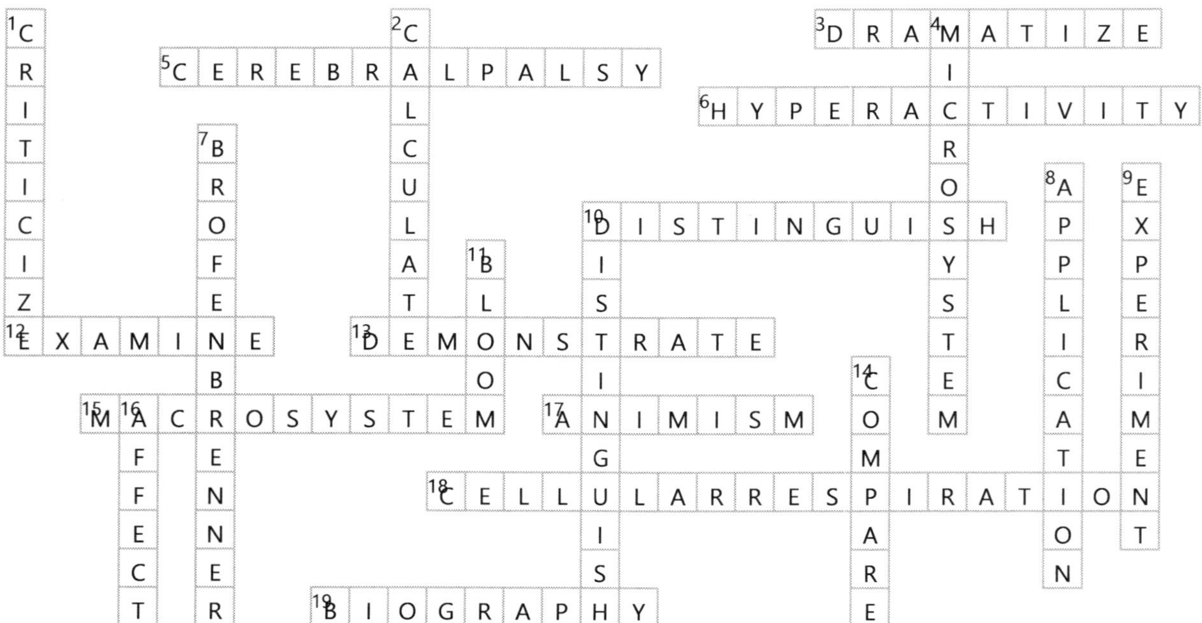

ACROSS

3. Adapt a novel or present a particular incident as a play or movie.
5. A condition characterized by paralysis, weakness, lack of coordination.
6. The condition of being abnormally or extremely active.
10. Recognize or treat (someone or something) as different.
12. inspect (someone or something) in detail to determine their nature or condition.
13. Clearly show the existence or truth of (something) by giving proof or evidence.
15. The whole socio-cultural context.
17. Assigning human qualities to objects "the sun was mad and burned me".
18. The process by which cells use oxygen to produce energy from food.
19. Reports events about someone's life.

DOWN

1. Indicate the faults of (someone or something) in a disapproving way.
2. Determine (the amount or number of something) mathematically.
4. Family of classroom.
7. Leader in field of child psychology and development, outlined 4 types of nested systems.
8. Bloom's 3rd level, take previous learning and use it in a new way.
9. A scientific procedure undertaken to make a discovery, test a hypothesis, or demonstrate a fact.
10. Recognize or treat (someone or something) as different.
11. Detailed classification of critical thinking and learning skills and objectives into tiered levels.
14. Estimate, measure, or note the similarity or dissimilarity between.
16. Emotion or desire, especially as influencing behavior or action.

A. Examine	B. Cellular Respiration	C. Macrosystem	D. Hyperactivity
E. Criticize	F. Microsystem	G. Biography	H. Calculate
I. Bloom	J. Brofenbrenner	K. Distinguish	L. Animism
M. Cerebral Palsy	N. Demonstrate	O. Experiment	P. Compare
Q. Dramatize	R. Affect	S. Distinguish	T. Application

30. Using the Across and Down clues, write the correct words in the numbered grid below.

ACROSS

1. The process by which cells use oxygen to produce energy from food.
5. Recognize or treat (someone or something) as different.
7. The whole socio-cultural context.
8. Explain or make (something) clear by using examples, charts, pictures, etc.
9. Interaction of two microsystems.
10. The ability to see, hear, or become aware of sometning through the senses.
14. Reports events about someone's life.
17. Leader in field of child psychology and development, outlined 4 types of nested systems.
18. Family of classroom.
19. Clearly show the existence or truth of (something) by giving proof or evidence.

DOWN

2. Assigning human qualities to objects "the sun was mad and burned me".
3. Breakdown information into parts and use those parts.
4. The state of being strikingly different from something else.
6. The condition of being abnormally or extremely active.
8. Acting or done without forethought.
11. Influence of external aspects on development.
12. Place in a particular class or group.
13. Estimate, measure, or note the similarity or dissimilarity between.
15. A type of autism characterized by normal cognitive and language development and impaired social skills.
16. A comparison of two things based on their being alike in some way.

A. Cellular Respiration	B. Distinguish	C. Analogy	D. Hyperactivity
E. Demonstrate	F. Brofenbrenner	G. Biography	H. Asperger
I. Compare	J. Categorize	K. Microsystem	L. Illustrate
M. Mesosystem	N. Analysis	O. Impulsive	P. Animism
Q. Perception	R. Exosystem	S. Contrast	T. Macrosystem

Multiple Choice

From the words provided for each clue, provide the letter of the word which best matches the clue.

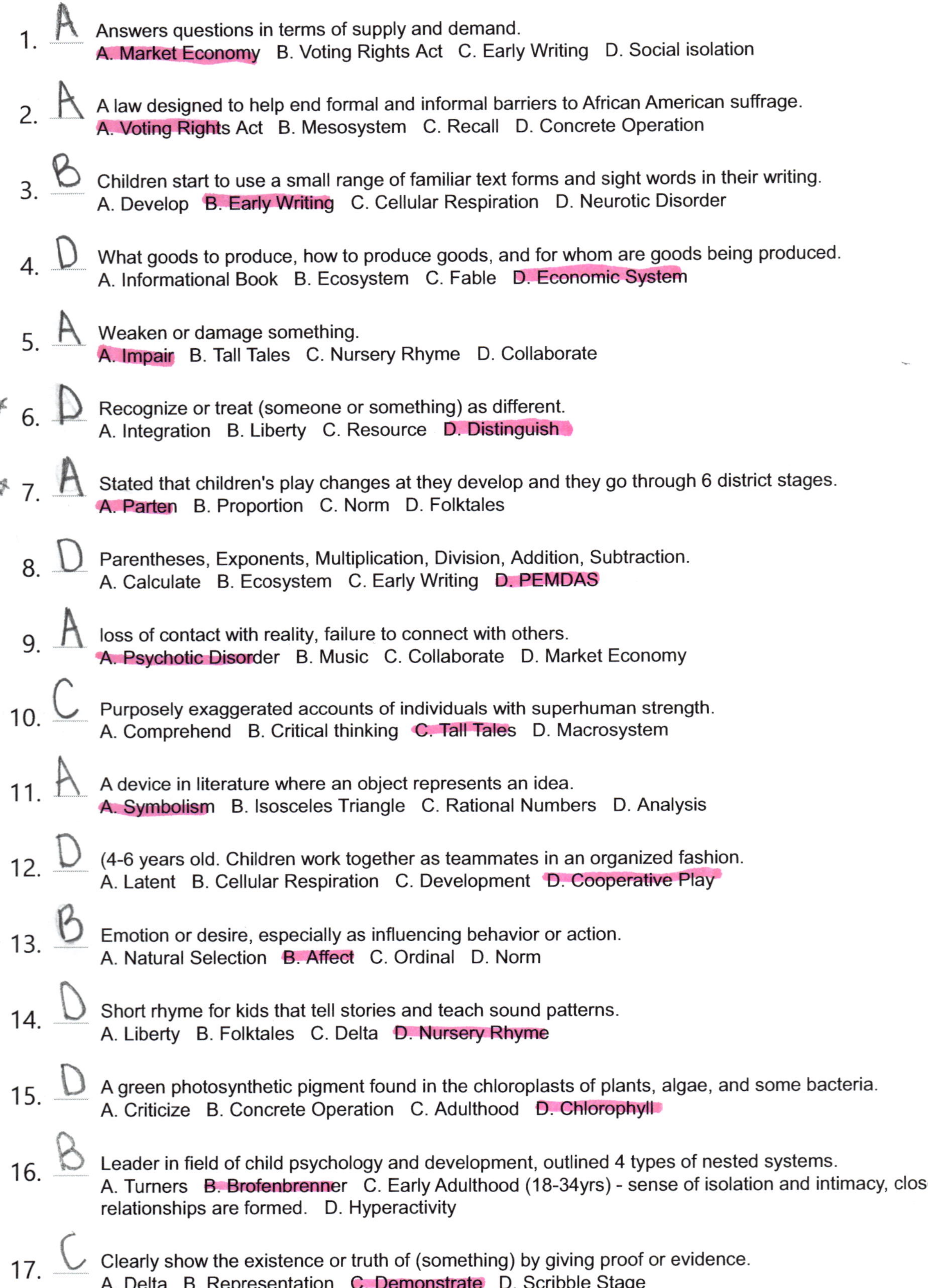

1. A Answers questions in terms of supply and demand.
   A. Market Economy B. Voting Rights Act C. Early Writing D. Social isolation
2. A A law designed to help end formal and informal barriers to African American suffrage.
   A. Voting Rights Act B. Mesosystem C. Recall D. Concrete Operation
3. B Children start to use a small range of familiar text forms and sight words in their writing.
   A. Develop B. Early Writing C. Cellular Respiration D. Neurotic Disorder
4. D What goods to produce, how to produce goods, and for whom are goods being produced.
   A. Informational Book B. Ecosystem C. Fable D. Economic System
5. A Weaken or damage something.
   A. Impair B. Tall Tales C. Nursery Rhyme D. Collaborate
6. D Recognize or treat (someone or something) as different.
   A. Integration B. Liberty C. Resource D. Distinguish
7. A Stated that children's play changes at they develop and they go through 6 district stages.
   A. Parten B. Proportion C. Norm D. Folktales
8. D Parentheses, Exponents, Multiplication, Division, Addition, Subtraction.
   A. Calculate B. Ecosystem C. Early Writing D. PEMDAS
9. A loss of contact with reality, failure to connect with others.
   A. Psychotic Disorder B. Music C. Collaborate D. Market Economy
10. C Purposely exaggerated accounts of individuals with superhuman strength.
    A. Comprehend B. Critical thinking C. Tall Tales D. Macrosystem
11. A A device in literature where an object represents an idea.
    A. Symbolism B. Isosceles Triangle C. Rational Numbers D. Analysis
12. D (4-6 years old. Children work together as teammates in an organized fashion.
    A. Latent B. Cellular Respiration C. Development D. Cooperative Play
13. B Emotion or desire, especially as influencing behavior or action.
    A. Natural Selection B. Affect C. Ordinal D. Norm
14. D Short rhyme for kids that tell stories and teach sound patterns.
    A. Liberty B. Folktales C. Delta D. Nursery Rhyme
15. D A green photosynthetic pigment found in the chloroplasts of plants, algae, and some bacteria.
    A. Criticize B. Concrete Operation C. Adulthood D. Chlorophyll
16. B Leader in field of child psychology and development, outlined 4 types of nested systems.
    A. Turners B. Brofenbrenner C. Early Adulthood (18-34yrs) - sense of isolation and intimacy, close relationships are formed. D. Hyperactivity
17. C Clearly show the existence or truth of (something) by giving proof or evidence.
    A. Delta B. Representation C. Demonstrate D. Scribble Stage

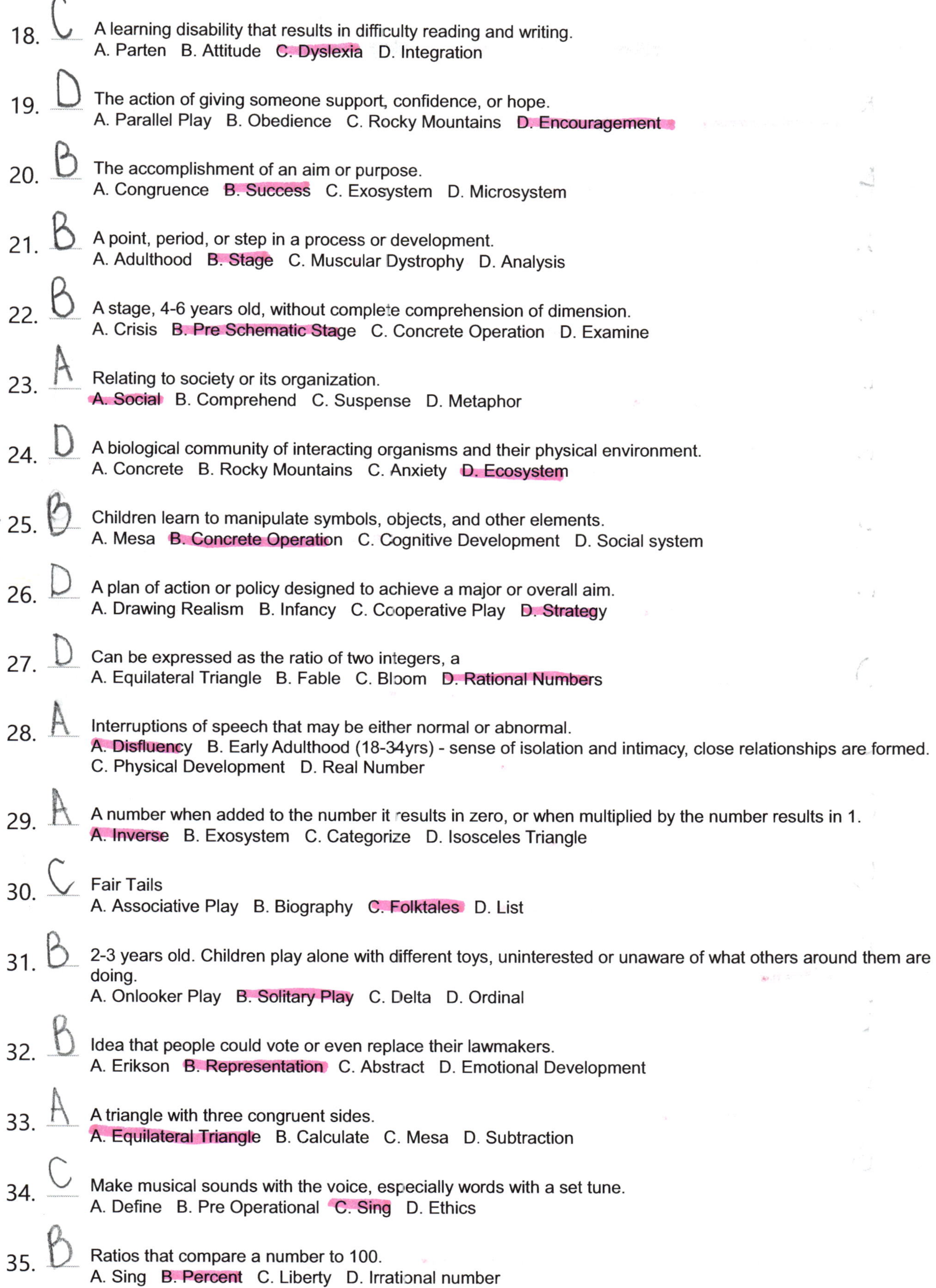

18. C A learning disability that results in difficulty reading and writing.
A. Parten B. Attitude C. Dyslexia D. Integration

19. D The action of giving someone support, confidence, or hope.
A. Parallel Play B. Obedience C. Rocky Mountains D. Encouragement

20. B The accomplishment of an aim or purpose.
A. Congruence B. Success C. Exosystem D. Microsystem

21. B A point, period, or step in a process or development.
A. Adulthood B. Stage C. Muscular Dystrophy D. Analysis

22. B A stage, 4-6 years old, without complete comprehension of dimension.
A. Crisis B. Pre Schematic Stage C. Concrete Operation D. Examine

23. A Relating to society or its organization.
A. Social B. Comprehend C. Suspense D. Metaphor

24. D A biological community of interacting organisms and their physical environment.
A. Concrete B. Rocky Mountains C. Anxiety D. Ecosystem

25. B Children learn to manipulate symbols, objects, and other elements.
A. Mesa B. Concrete Operation C. Cognitive Development D. Social system

26. D A plan of action or policy designed to achieve a major or overall aim.
A. Drawing Realism B. Infancy C. Cooperative Play D. Strategy

27. D Can be expressed as the ratio of two integers, a
A. Equilateral Triangle B. Fable C. Bloom D. Rational Numbers

28. A Interruptions of speech that may be either normal or abnormal.
A. Disfluency B. Early Adulthood (18-34yrs) - sense of isolation and intimacy, close relationships are formed.
C. Physical Development D. Real Number

29. A A number when added to the number it results in zero, or when multiplied by the number results in 1.
A. Inverse B. Exosystem C. Categorize D. Isosceles Triangle

30. C Fair Tails
A. Associative Play B. Biography C. Folktales D. List

31. B 2-3 years old. Children play alone with different toys, uninterested or unaware of what others around them are doing.
A. Onlooker Play B. Solitary Play C. Delta D. Ordinal

32. B Idea that people could vote or even replace their lawmakers.
A. Erikson B. Representation C. Abstract D. Emotional Development

33. A A triangle with three congruent sides.
A. Equilateral Triangle B. Calculate C. Mesa D. Subtraction

34. C Make musical sounds with the voice, especially words with a set tune.
A. Define B. Pre Operational C. Sing D. Ethics

35. B Ratios that compare a number to 100.
A. Sing B. Percent C. Liberty D. Irrational number

36. C Individuals have developed their own personal set of ethics and morals.
A. Illustrate B. Charles Darwin C. Post Conventional D. Suspense

37. A 3-4 years old. Children begin to play with each other but not focused on the same common goal.
A. Associative Play B. Cooperative Play C. Brofenbrenner D. Contrast

38. B Kohlberg's stage. Egocentric. Up to age nine.
A. Adolescence B. Pre-Conventional C. Symbolism D. Sing

39. D Grasp mentally; understand.
A. Calculate B. Pre Operational C. Criticize D. Comprehend

40. C A genetic disorder characterized by an excessive secretion of mucus and vulnerability to infection.
A. Morality B. Impair C. Cystic Fibrosis D. Multiplication

41. B Relating to or in the form of words.
A. Hyperactivity B. Verbal C. Distinguish D. Natural Selection

42. B A comparison of two things based on their being alike in some way.
A. Emotional Development B. Analogy C. Stage D. Solitary Play

43. C The process by which cells use oxygen to produce energy from food.
A. Metaphor B. Psychotic Disorder C. Cellular Respiration D. Strategy

44. B Indicate the faults of (someone or something) in a disapproving way.
A. Distinguish B. Criticize C. Early Adulthood (18-34yrs) - sense of isolation and intimacy, close relationships are formed. D. Irrational number

45. D Sounds combined in such a way as to produce form, harmony, and expression of emotion.
A. Addition B. Dramatize C. Historical Fiction D. Music

46. C Studied the importance of play.
A. Functional Play B. Infancy C. Vygotsky D. Young Childhood

47. C Stories about events from earliest times, and are considered to be true in their societies.
A. Parallel Play B. Ethics C. Myth D. Trapezoid

48. C Compliance with an order, request, or law or submission to another's authority.
A. Compare B. Distinguish C. Obedience D. Dyslexia

49. A Breakdown information into parts and use those parts.
A. Analysis B. Bloom C. Impair D. Ecosystem

50. C Make an action or process easier.
A. Dramatic play B. Knowledge C. Facilitate D. Formal Operation

51. B Explain or make (something) clear by using examples, charts, pictures, etc.
A. Legends B. Illustrate C. Onlooker Play D. Brofenbrenner

52. D Talk with continued involuntary repetition of sounds, especially initial consonants.
A. Examine B. Social C. Irrational number D. Stuttering

53. D Commit to memory; learn by heart.
A. Failure B. Examine C. Proportion D. Memorize

54. C Ages 9-11, drawing become increasingly representational.
A. Representation B. Erikson C. Drawing Realism D. Repetition

55. C Ages 6-10 years. Take pride in work and sense of achievement, develop friendships.
A. Distinguish B. Criticize C. Middle childhood D. Success

56. D A figure of speech using deliberate exaggeration or overstatement.
A. Scalene Triangle B. Simile C. Intellect D. Hyperbole

57. C Bloom's 3rd level, take previous learning and use it in a new way.
A. Rational Numbers B. Ozone Layer C. Application D. Recall

58. C A time of intense difficulty, trouble, or danger.
A. Market Economy B. Photosynthesis C. Crisis D. Liberty

59. C Describing concepts, animals, or objects by endowing them with human attributes.
A. Social B. Comprehend C. Personification D. Principles

60. D Adapt a novel or present a particular incident as a play or movie.
A. Historical Fiction B. Disfluency C. Multiplication D. Dramatize

61. A Lack of contact between an individual and society.
A. Social isolation B. Ecosystem C. Supply D. Irrational number

62. D Up to 12 months. Develops trust and mistrust.
A. Impair B. Stimuli C. Middle Adulthood D. Infancy

63. C Existing in thought or as an idea but not having a physical or concrete existence.
A. Great Plains B. Rocky Mountains C. Abstract D. Perception

64. A A type of autism characterized by normal cognitive and language development and impaired social skills.
A. Asperger B. Norm C. Analogy D. Analysis

65. B A quality or state existing but not yet developed or manifest; hidden; concealed.
A. Examine B. Latent C. Mesa D. Experiment

66. A The condition of being abnormally or extremely active.
A. Hyperactivity B. Senate C. Pre Schematic Stage D. Post Conventional

67. C When a child pretends to take on a role of someone else, imitating actions and speech.
A. Muscular Dystrophy B. Fractions C. Dramatic play D. Illustrate

68. C Similar to myths, but tend to deal with events that happened more recently.
A. Develop B. Social C. Legends D. Ozone Layer

69. D Something that is usual, typical, or standard.
A. Morality B. Sensory Motor C. Mojave Desert D. Norm

70. A Idea that people should be free to pursue their own course.
A. Liberty B. Resource C. Emotional Development D. Functional Play

71. A Assigning human qualities to objects "the sun was mad and burned me".
A. Animism B. Tessellation C. Modern Fantasy D. Interpersonal

72. D Ages 11-18 years. Starts to wonder how they appear to others, maturity.
A. Market Economy B. Equality C. Down Syndrome D. Adolescence

73. C Detailed classification of critical thinking and learning skills and objectives into tiered levels.
A. Division B. Foothills C. Bloom D. Early Writing

74. C The action or process of adding something to something else.
A. Cognitive Development B. Scalene Triangle C. Addition D. Collaborate

75. C Conversion of light energy from the sun into chemical energy.
A. Science Fiction B. Onlooker Play C. Photosynthesis D. Early Writing

76. C Estimate, measure, or note the similarity or dissimilarity between.
A. Exosystem B. Symbolism C. Compare D. Music

77. D Bring back into one's mind, especially so as to recount it to others; remember.
A. Fractions B. Pseudo realistic C. Symbolism D. Recall

78. C Animals that act like humans are featured and reveal human foibles or teach a lesson.
A. Post Conventional B. Macrosystem C. Fable D. Perception

79. B The whole socio-cultural context.
A. Solitary Play B. Macrosystem C. Formal Operation D. Emotional Development

80. D Land area found between hills or mountains.
A. Scribble Stage B. Cellular Respiration C. Tall Tales D. Valley

81. C 0-2 years old. Not engaged or actively playing with others at all.
A. Simile B. Myth C. Unoccupied Play D. Social isolation

82. A Reports events about someone's life.
A. Biography B. Application C. Charles Darwin D. Longitude

83. D A physical or mental condition that limits a person's movements, senses, or activities.
A. Simile B. Voting Rights Act C. Period of Decision D. Disability

84. C Characterized by constant change, activity, or progress.
A. Foothills B. Attitude C. Dynamic D. Onlooker Play

85. C A feeling of uncertainty and curiosity about what will happen next in a story.
A. Integration B. Abstract C. Suspense D. Knowledge

86. A A thing that rouses activity or energy in someone or something; a spur or incentive.
A. Stimuli B. Mesosystem C. Schematic Stage D. Associative Play

87. C Belief that students create their own reality of knowledge.
A. Interpersonal B. Majority Rule C. Constructivist Learning D. Chlorophyll

88. B The faculty of reasoning and understanding objectively.
A. Success B. Intellect C. Psychotic Disorder D. Supreme Court

89. C The infliction or imposition of a penalty as retribution for an offense.
A. Solitary Play B. Tantrum C. Punishment D. Distinguish

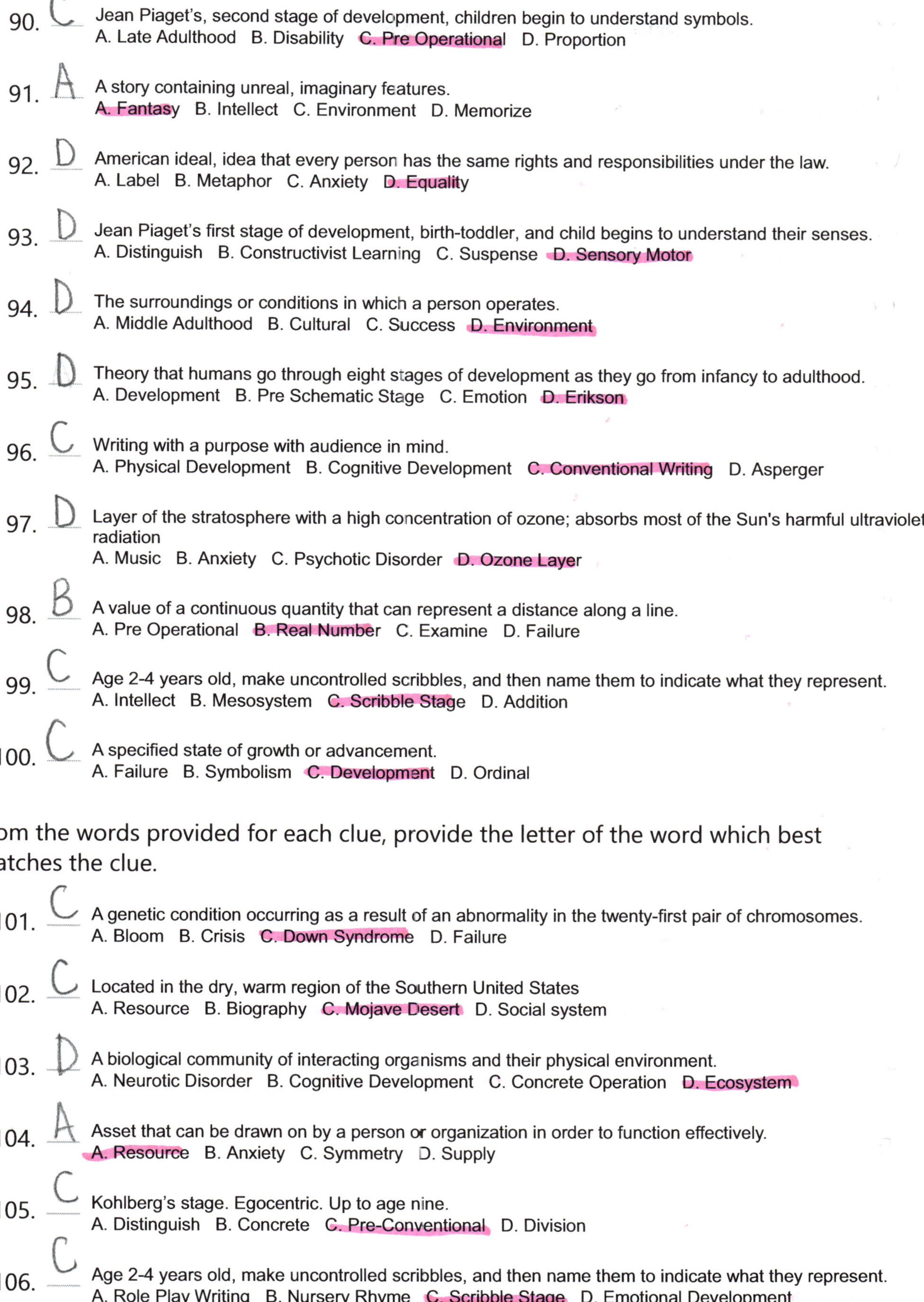

90. C Jean Piaget's, second stage of development, children begin to understand symbols.
A. Late Adulthood B. Disability C. Pre Operational D. Proportion

91. A A story containing unreal, imaginary features.
A. Fantasy B. Intellect C. Environment D. Memorize

92. D American ideal, idea that every person has the same rights and responsibilities under the law.
A. Label B. Metaphor C. Anxiety D. Equality

93. D Jean Piaget's first stage of development, birth-toddler, and child begins to understand their senses.
A. Distinguish B. Constructivist Learning C. Suspense D. Sensory Motor

94. D The surroundings or conditions in which a person operates.
A. Middle Adulthood B. Cultural C. Success D. Environment

95. D Theory that humans go through eight stages of development as they go from infancy to adulthood.
A. Development B. Pre Schematic Stage C. Emotion D. Erikson

96. C Writing with a purpose with audience in mind.
A. Physical Development B. Cognitive Development C. Conventional Writing D. Asperger

97. D Layer of the stratosphere with a high concentration of ozone; absorbs most of the Sun's harmful ultraviolet radiation
A. Music B. Anxiety C. Psychotic Disorder D. Ozone Layer

98. B A value of a continuous quantity that can represent a distance along a line.
A. Pre Operational B. Real Number C. Examine D. Failure

99. C Age 2-4 years old, make uncontrolled scribbles, and then name them to indicate what they represent.
A. Intellect B. Mesosystem C. Scribble Stage D. Addition

100. C A specified state of growth or advancement.
A. Failure B. Symbolism C. Development D. Ordinal

From the words provided for each clue, provide the letter of the word which best matches the clue.

101. C A genetic condition occurring as a result of an abnormality in the twenty-first pair of chromosomes.
A. Bloom B. Crisis C. Down Syndrome D. Failure

102. C Located in the dry, warm region of the Southern United States
A. Resource B. Biography C. Mojave Desert D. Social system

103. D A biological community of interacting organisms and their physical environment.
A. Neurotic Disorder B. Cognitive Development C. Concrete Operation D. Ecosystem

104. A Asset that can be drawn on by a person or organization in order to function effectively.
A. Resource B. Anxiety C. Symmetry D. Supply

105. C Kohlberg's stage. Egocentric. Up to age nine.
A. Distinguish B. Concrete C. Pre-Conventional D. Division

106. C Age 2-4 years old, make uncontrolled scribbles, and then name them to indicate what they represent.
A. Role Play Writing B. Nursery Rhyme C. Scribble Stage D. Emotional Development

107. C Increasingly sophisticated understandings of other people and of society as a whole.
A. Erikson B. Unoccupied Play C. Social Development D. Irrational number

108. A The correspondence in size and shape, of parts on opposite sides of a median line.
A. Symmetry B. Rational Numbers C. Inverse D. Supreme Court

109. C The amount by which something, especially a sum of money, is too small.
A. Examine B. Contrast C. Deficit D. Valley

110. A Interaction of two microsystems.
A. Mesosystem B. Intellect C. Attitude D. Fractions

111. A Up to 12 months. Develops trust and mistrust.
A. Infancy B. Period of Decision C. Constructivist Learning D. Early Adulthood (18-34yrs) - sense of isolation and intimacy, close relationships are formed.

112. B The accomplishment of an aim or purpose.
A. Neurotic Disorder B. Success C. Division D. Legends

113. B Recognize or treat (someone or something) as different.
A. Formal Operation B. Distinguish C. Understand D. Cystic Fibrosis

114. B A triangle with no congruent sides.
A. Proportion B. Scalene Triangle C. Great Plains D. Application

115. A Arrangement of closed shapes that completely cover a plan without overlapping.
A. Tessellation B. Down Syndrome C. Pre Operational D. Physical Development

116. A The faculty of reasoning and understanding objectively.
A. Intellect B. Rhombus C. Rule of Law D. Constructive Play

117. D Stated that children's play changes at they develop and they go through 6 district stages.
A. Perception B. Pseudo realistic C. Tantrum D. Parten

118. A A comparison of two unlike things without using the word like or as.
A. Metaphor B. Drawing Realism C. Formal Operation D. Develop

119. D Grow or cause to grow and become more mature, advanced, or elaborate.
A. Early Adulthood (18-34yrs) - sense of isolation and intimacy, close relationships are formed. B. Recall C. Anxiety D. Develop

120. C A figure of speech using deliberate exaggeration or overstatement.
A. Develop B. Valley C. Hyperbole D. Rhombus

121. D Writing with a purpose with audience in mind.
A. Stuttering B. Understand C. Foothills D. Conventional Writing

122. D Children begin to understand that good behavior is expected, and achieving those expectations is moral.
A. Social isolation B. Knowledge C. Compare D. Interpersonal

123. B Condition seen in individuals carrying single X chromosome but no other sex chromosome.
A. Legends B. Turners C. Recall D. Vygotsky

124. A State or describe exactly the nature, scope, or meaning of.
A. Define B. Formal Operation C. Science Fiction D. Evaluation

125. ______ A fundamental democratic principle requiring that the majority's view be respected.
A. Onlooker Play B. Majority Rule C. Unoccupied Play D. Evaluation

126. ______ 1st, 2nd, 10th, show position not quantity.
A. Ordinal B. Ecosystem C. Due Process D. Critical thinking

127. ______ The condition of being abnormally or extremely active.
A. Mesosystem B. Hyperactivity C. Fractions D. Equality

128. ______ Age 7-9 years old, drawings reflect actual physical proportions and colors.
A. Discrepancy B. Role Play Writing C. Failure D. Schematic Stage

different stages

129. ______ A quadrilateral with exactly one pair of parallel sides.
A. Constructivist Learning B. Ecosystem C. Erikson D. Trapezoid

130. ______ loss of contact with reality, failure to connect with others.
A. Recall B. Parallel Play C. Disfluency D. Psychotic Disorder

131. ______ A classifying phrase applied to a person or thing, especially one that is inaccurate or restrictive.
A. Discrepancy B. Scientific Revolution C. Label D. Microsystem

132. ______ Stories about events from earliest times, and are considered to be true in their societies.
A. Scientific Revolution B. Develop C. Supply D. Myth

133. ______ A real number that cannot be written as a simple fraction.
A. Schematic Stage B. Emotional Development C. Irrational number D. Sing

134. ______ 0-2 years old. Not engaged or actively playing with others at all.
A. Schematic Stage B. Addition C. Unoccupied Play D. Discrepancy

135. ______ Children learn to manipulate symbols, objects, and other elements.
A. Dramatic play B. Concrete Operation C. Rocky Mountains D. Experiment

136. ______ A number of connected items or names written or printed consecutively.
A. Liberty B. List C. Nursery Rhyme D. Erikson

137. ______ Idea that people could vote or even replace their lawmakers.
A. Fantasy B. Cystic Fibrosis C. Representation D. Mesa

138. ______ The action or process of adding something to something else.
A. Addition B. Valley C. Multiplication D. Social Development

139. ______ Compliance with an order, request, or law or submission to another's authority.
A. Percent B. Obedience C. Verbal D. Dramatic Play

140. ______ Short rhyme for kids that tell stories and teach sound patterns.
A. Ordinal B. Cognitive Development C. Legends D. Nursery Rhyme

141. ______ A condition characterized by paralysis, weakness, lack of coordination.
A. Cerebral Palsy B. Strategy C. Drawing Realism D. Representation

142. ______ Robots, spacecraft, mystery, civilizations from other ages. A "what if" aspect to the story.
A. Science Fiction B. Solitary Play C. Pre-Conventional D. Ethics

143. Characterized by constant change, activity, or progress.
A. Latitude B. Natural Selection C. Dynamic D. Dyslexia

144. Explain or make (something) clear by using examples, charts, pictures, etc.
A. Exosystem B. Physical Development C. Illustrate D. Mojave Desert

145. Adolescents understand that there is a need for them to fulfill obligations and expectations.
A. Social system B. Categorize C. Fable D. Cooperative Play

146. Sounds combined in such a way as to produce form, harmony, and expression of emotion.
A. Dyslexia B. Music C. Emotion D. Period of Decision

147. Involves changes in how an individual experiences and expresses different feelings.
A. Calculate B. Animism C. Fractions D. Emotional Development

148. Family of classroom.
A. Microsystem B. Norm C. Perception D. Analogy

149. Development of processes of knowing, perceiving, reasoning, and problem solving.
A. Calculate B. Mojave Desert C. Crisis D. Cognitive Development

150. Relating to or in the form of words.
A. Tall Tales B. Legends C. Chlorophyll D. Verbal

151. The state of being strikingly different from something else.
A. Valley B. Voting Rights Act C. Contrast D. Early Writing

152. Relating to society or its organization.
A. Rational Numbers B. Social C. Metaphor D. Sensory Motor

153. Play in which children manipulate objects to produce or build something.
A. Constructive Play B. Longitude C. Integration D. Scientific Revolution

154. Ages 9-11, drawing become increasingly representational.
A. Drawing Realism B. Success C. Informational Book D. Perception

155. A learning disability that results in difficulty reading and writing.
A. Impulsive B. Drawing Realism C. Dyslexia D. Due Process

156. Survival of the fittest.
A. Memoirs B. Dyslexia C. Natural Selection D. Pre-Conventional

157. Talk with continued involuntary repetition of sounds, especially initial consonants.
A. Proportion B. Norm C. Stuttering D. Label

158. No clue.
A. Drawing Realism B. Infancy C. Early Adulthood (18-34yrs) - sense of isolation and intimacy, close relationships are formed. D. Repetition

159. Extend from New Mexico in the south through the Canadian border on the North.
A. Multiplication B. Rocky Mountains C. Ozone Layer D. Evaluation

160. A law designed to help end formal and informal barriers to African American suffrage.
A. Development B. Fable C. Voting Rights Act D. Proportion

161. A value of a continuous quantity that can represent a distance along a line.
A. Real Number B. Mesosystem C. Perception D. Legends

162. Parentheses, Exponents, Multiplication, Division, Addition, Subtraction.
A. PEMDAS B. Microsystem C. Foothills D. Analysis

163. Large, grassy region drained by the Mississippi River.
A. Encouragement B. PEMDAS C. Great Plains D. Parallel Play

164. Principles concerning the distinction between right and wrong or good and bad behavior.
A. Irrational number B. Morality C. Scientific Revolution D. Tall Tales

165. Used to underscore the importance of a work to point to the central theme.
A. Natural Selection B. Photosynthesis C. Repetition D. Evaluation

166. Existing in thought or as an idea but not having a physical or concrete existence.
A. Concrete Operation B. Pre-Conventional C. Abstract D. Down Syndrome

167. A kind of writing that tells someone's memories.
A. PEMDAS B. Affect C. Memoirs D. Constructive Play

168. A type of autism characterized by normal cognitive and language development and impaired social skills.
A. Impair B. Solitary Play C. Asperger D. Voting Rights Act

169. Indicate the faults of (someone or something) in a disapproving way.
A. Encouragement B. Criticize C. Majority Rule D. Functional Play

170. Detailed classification of critical thinking and learning skills and objectives into tiered levels.
A. Cystic Fibrosis B. Constructive Play C. Bloom D. Rule of Law

171. A triangle with three congruent sides.
A. Equilateral Triangle B. Ethics C. Dramatic play D. Tessellation

172. Adapt a novel or present a particular incident as a play or movie.
A. Folktales B. Chlorophyll C. Emotional Development D. Dramatize

173. A stage, 11-13 years old, reflecting child's ability to reason.
A. Down Syndrome B. Norm C. Vygotsky D. Pseudo realistic

174. Consists of nine justices, each appointed by the President and confirmed by Congress.
A. Fable B. Percent C. Supreme Court D. Illustrate

175. Existing in a material or physical form; real or solid; not abstract.
A. Social isolation B. Modern Fantasy C. Concrete D. Conventional Writing

176. (4-6 years old. Children work together as teammates in an organized fashion.
A. Nursery Rhyme B. Early Childhood C. Cooperative Play D. List

177. Ages 3-5 years. Child learns to initiate tasks and carry them out, guilt when task not completed.
A. Early Childhood B. Symmetry C. Impair D. Calculate

178. Age 35-60. Commitment to family and career.
A. Middle Adulthood B. Morality C. Economic System D. Disability

179. The process of dividing a matrix, vector, or other quantity by another under specific rules to obtain a quotient.
A. Fractions B. Critical thinking C. Division D. Knowledge

180. The ability to see, hear, or become aware of something through the senses.
A. Exosystem B. List C. Biography D. Perception

181. A number when added to the number it results in zero, or when multiplied by the number results in 1.
A. Period of Decision B. Inverse C. Develop D. Examine

182. Jean Piaget's first stage of development, birth-toddler, and child begins to understand their senses.
A. Social system B. Sensory Motor C. Examine D. Unoccupied Play

183. A feeling of worry, nervousness, or unease, typically about an imminent event.
A. Critical thinking B. Isosceles Triangle C. Demonstrate D. Anxiety

184. A plan of action or policy designed to achieve a major or overall aim.
A. Hyperactivity B. Brofenbrenner C. Strategy D. Distinguish

185. Agreement, harmony, or correspondence.
A. Illustrate B. Congruence C. Understand D. PEMDAS

186. English natural scientist who formulated a theory of evolution by natural selection.
A. Liberty B. Chlorophyll C. Equilateral Triangle D. Charles Darwin

187. Combination or composition, in particular.
A. Muscular Dystrophy B. Fantasy C. Synthesis D. Stimuli

188. Perceive the intended meaning of.
A. Emotional Development B. Understand C. Recall D. Informational Book

189. Children start to use a small range of familiar text forms and sight words in their writing.
A. Emotion B. Fable C. Anxiety D. Early Writing

190. Something that is usual, typical, or standard.
A. Contrast B. Resource C. Norm D. Cognitive Development

191. The state or condition of being fully grown or mature.
A. Early Adulthood (18-34yrs) - sense of isolation and intimacy, close relationships are formed. B. Adulthood
C. Norm D. Analogy

192. Facts, information, and skills acquired by a person through experience or education.
A. Formal Operation B. Delta C. Subtraction D. Knowledge

193. A settled way of thinking or feeling about something that is reflected in a person's behavior.
A. Hyperactivity B. Calculate C. Attitude D. Period of Decision

194. Conversion of light energy from the sun into chemical energy.
A. Synthesis B. Photosynthesis C. Early Childhood D. Rational Numbers

195. Age 60-death.
A. Late Adulthood B. Concrete Operation C. Categorize D. Norm

196. A physical or mental condition that limits a person's movements, senses, or activities.
A. Hyperbole B. Disability C. Illustrate D. Legends

197. ______ Interruptions of speech that may be either normal or abnormal.
A. Evaluation B. Mojave Desert C. Disfluency D. Failure

198. ______ Inherited disease characterized by progressive weakness and degeneration of muscle fibers.
A. Suspense B. Lowenfeld C. Bloom D. Muscular Dystrophy

199. ______ A triangle that has 2 equal sides.
A. Dyslexia B. Isosceles Triangle C. Equilateral Triangle D. Music

200. ______ A thing that rouses activity or energy in someone or something; a spur or incentive.
A. Perception B. Memoirs C. Stimuli D. Animism

From the words provided for each clue, provide the letter of the word which best matches the clue.

1. A Answers questions in terms of supply and demand.
A. Market Economy B. Voting Rights Act C. Early Writing D. Social isolation

2. A A law designed to help end formal and informal barriers to African American suffrage.
A. Voting Rights Act B. Mesosystem C. Recall D. Concrete Operation

3. B Children start to use a small range of familiar text forms and sight words in their writing.
A. Develop B. Early Writing C. Cellular Respiration D. Neurotic Disorder

4. D What goods to produce, how to produce goods, and for whom are goods being produced.
A. Informational Book B. Ecosystem C. Fable D. Economic System

5. A Weaken or damage something.
A. Impair B. Tall Tales C. Nursery Rhyme D. Collaborate

6. D Recognize or treat (someone or something) as different.
A. Integration B. Liberty C. Resource D. Distinguish

7. A Stated that children's play changes at they develop and they go through 6 district stages.
A. Parten B. Proportion C. Norm D. Folktales

8. D Parentheses, Exponents, Multiplication, Division, Addition, Subtraction.
A. Calculate B. Ecosystem C. Early Writing D. PEMDAS

9. A loss of contact with reality, failure to connect with others.
A. Psychotic Disorder B. Music C. Collaborate D. Market Economy

10. C Purposely exaggerated accounts of individuals with superhuman strength.
A. Comprehend B. Critical thinking C. Tall Tales D. Macrosystem

11. A A device in literature where an object represents an idea.
A. Symbolism B. Isosceles Triangle C. Rational Numbers D. Analysis

12. D (4-6 years old. Children work together as teammates in an organized fashion.
A. Latent B. Cellular Respiration C. Development D. Cooperative Play

13. B Emotion or desire, especially as influencing behavior or action.
A. Natural Selection B. Affect C. Ordinal D. Norm

14. D Short rhyme for kids that tell stories and teach sound patterns.
A. Liberty B. Folktales C. Delta D. Nursery Rhyme

15. D A green photosynthetic pigment found in the chloroplasts of plants, algae, and some bacteria.
A. Criticize B. Concrete Operation C. Adulthood D. Chlorophyll

16. B Leader in field of child psychology and development, outlined 4 types of nested systems.
A. Turners B. Brofenbrenner C. Early Adulthood (18-34yrs) - sense of isolation and intimacy, close relationships are formed. D. Hyperactivity

17. C Clearly show the existence or truth of (something) by giving proof or evidence.
A. Delta B. Representation C. Demonstrate D. Scribble Stage

18. C A learning disability that results in difficulty reading and writing.
A. Parten B. Attitude C. Dyslexia D. Integration

19. D The action of giving someone support, confidence, or hope.
A. Parallel Play B. Obedience C. Rocky Mountains D. Encouragement

20. B The accomplishment of an aim or purpose.
A. Congruence B. Success C. Exosystem D. Microsystem

21. B A point, period, or step in a process or development.
A. Adulthood B. Stage C. Muscular Dystrophy D. Analysis

22. B A stage, 4-6 years old, without complete comprehension of dimension.
A. Crisis B. Pre Schematic Stage C. Concrete Operation D. Examine

23. A Relating to society or its organization.
A. Social B. Comprehend C. Suspense D. Metaphor

24. D A biological community of interacting organisms and their physical environment.
A. Concrete B. Rocky Mountains C. Anxiety D. Ecosystem

25. B Children learn to manipulate symbols, objects, and other elements.
A. Mesa B. Concrete Operation C. Cognitive Development D. Social system

26. D A plan of action or policy designed to achieve a major or overall aim.
A. Drawing Realism B. Infancy C. Cooperative Play D. Strategy

27. D Can be expressed as the ratio of two integers, a
A. Equilateral Triangle B. Fable C. Bloom D. Rational Numbers

28. A Interruptions of speech that may be either normal or abnormal.
A. Disfluency B. Early Adulthood (18-34yrs) - sense of isolation and intimacy, close relationships are formed.
C. Physical Development D. Real Number

29. A A number when added to the number it results in zero, or when multiplied by the number results in 1.
A. Inverse B. Exosystem C. Categorize D. Isosceles Triangle

30. C Fair Tails
A. Associative Play B. Biography C. Folktales D. List

31. B 2-3 years old. Children play alone with different toys, uninterested or unaware of what others around them are doing.
A. Onlooker Play B. Solitary Play C. Delta D. Ordinal

32. B Idea that people could vote or even replace their lawmakers.
A. Erikson B. Representation C. Abstract D. Emotional Development

33. A A triangle with three congruent sides.
A. Equilateral Triangle B. Calculate C. Mesa D. Subtraction

34. C Make musical sounds with the voice, especially words with a set tune.
A. Define B. Pre Operational C. Sing D. Ethics

35. B Ratios that compare a number to 100.
A. Sing B. Percent C. Liberty D. Irrational number

36. C Individuals have developed their own personal set of ethics and morals.
A. Illustrate B. Charles Darwin C. Post Conventional D. Suspense

37. A 3-4 years old. Children begin to play with each other but not focused on the same common goal.
A. Associative Play B. Cooperative Play C. Brofenbrenner D. Contrast

38. B Kohlberg's stage. Egocentric. Up to age nine.
A. Adolescence B. Pre-Conventional C. Symbolism D. Sing

39. D Grasp mentally; understand.
A. Calculate B. Pre Operational C. Criticize D. Comprehend

40. C A genetic disorder characterized by an excessive secretion of mucus and vulnerability to infection.
A. Morality B. Impair C. Cystic Fibrosis D. Multiplication

41. B Relating to or in the form of words.
A. Hyperactivity B. Verbal C. Distinguish D. Natural Selection

42. B A comparison of two things based on their being alike in some way.
A. Emotional Development B. Analogy C. Stage D. Solitary Play

43. C The process by which cells use oxygen to produce energy from food.
A. Metaphor B. Psychotic Disorder C. Cellular Respiration D. Strategy

44. B Indicate the faults of (someone or something) in a disapproving way.
A. Distinguish B. Criticize C. Early Adulthood (18-34yrs) - sense of isolation and intimacy, close relationships are formed. D. Irrational number

45. D Sounds combined in such a way as to produce form, harmony, and expression of emotion.
A. Addition B. Dramatize C. Historical Fiction D. Music

46. C Studied the importance of play.
A. Functional Play B. Infancy C. Vygotsky D. Young Childhood

47. C Stories about events from earliest times, and are considered to be true in their societies.
A. Parallel Play B. Ethics C. Myth D. Trapezoid

48. C Compliance with an order, request, or law or submission to another's authority.
A. Compare B. Distinguish C. Obedience D. Dyslexia

49. A Breakdown information into parts and use those parts.
A. Analysis B. Bloom C. Impair D. Ecosystem

50. C Make an action or process easier.
A. Dramatic play B. Knowledge C. Facilitate D. Formal Operation

51. B Explain or make (something) clear by using examples, charts, pictures, etc.
A. Legends B. Illustrate C. Onlooker Play D. Brofenbrenner

52. D Talk with continued involuntary repetition of sounds, especially initial consonants.
A. Examine B. Social C. Irrational number D. Stuttering

53. D Commit to memory; learn by heart.
A. Failure B. Examine C. Proportion D. Memorize

54. C Ages 9-11, drawing become increasingly representational.
A. Representation B. Erikson C. Drawing Realism D. Repetition

55. C Ages 6-10 years. Take pride in work and sense of achievement, develop friendships.
A. Distinguish B. Criticize C. Middle childhood D. Success

56. D A figure of speech using deliberate exaggeration or overstatement.
A. Scalene Triangle B. Simile C. Intellect D. Hyperbole

57. C Bloom's 3rd level, take previous learning and use it in a new way.
A. Rational Numbers B. Ozone Layer C. Application D. Recall

58. C A time of intense difficulty, trouble, or danger.
A. Market Economy B. Photosynthesis C. Crisis D. Liberty

59. C Describing concepts, animals, or objects by endowing them with human attributes.
A. Social B. Comprehend C. Personification D. Principles

60. D Adapt a novel or present a particular incident as a play or movie.
A. Historical Fiction B. Disfluency C. Multiplication D. Dramatize

61. A Lack of contact between an individual and society.
A. Social isolation B. Ecosystem C. Supply D. Irrational number

62. D Up to 12 months. Develops trust and mistrust.
A. Impair B. Stimuli C. Middle Adulthood D. Infancy

63. C Existing in thought or as an idea but not having a physical or concrete existence.
A. Great Plains B. Rocky Mountains C. Abstract D. Perception

64. A A type of autism characterized by normal cognitive and language development and impaired social skills.
A. Asperger B. Norm C. Analogy D. Analysis

65. B A quality or state existing but not yet developed or manifest; hidden; concealed.
A. Examine B. Latent C. Mesa D. Experiment

66. A The condition of being abnormally or extremely active.
A. Hyperactivity B. Senate C. Pre Schematic Stage D. Post Conventional

67. C When a child pretends to take on a role of someone else, imitating actions and speech.
A. Muscular Dystrophy B. Fractions C. Dramatic play D. Illustrate

68. C Similar to myths, but tend to deal with events that happened more recently.
A. Develop B. Social C. Legends D. Ozone Layer

69. D Something that is usual, typical, or standard.
A. Morality B. Sensory Motor C. Mojave Desert D. Norm

70. A Idea that people should be free to pursue their own course.
A. Liberty B. Resource C. Emotional Development D. Functional Play

71. A Assigning human qualities to objects "the sun was mad and burned me".
A. Animism B. Tessellation C. Modern Fantasy D. Interpersonal

72. D Ages 11-18 years. Starts to wonder how they appear to others, maturity.
A. Market Economy B. Equality C. Down Syndrome D. Adolescence

73. C Detailed classification of critical thinking and learning skills and objectives into tiered levels.
A. Division B. Foothills C. Bloom D. Early Writing

74. C The action or process of adding something to something else.
A. Cognitive Development B. Scalene Triangle C. Addition D. Collaborate

75. C Conversion of light energy from the sun into chemical energy.
A. Science Fiction B. Onlooker Play C. Photosynthesis D. Early Writing

76. C Estimate, measure, or note the similarity or dissimilarity between.
A. Exosystem B. Symbolism C. Compare D. Music

77. D Bring back into one's mind, especially so as to recount it to others; remember.
A. Fractions B. Pseudo realistic C. Symbolism D. Recall

78. C Animals that act like humans are featured and reveal human foibles or teach a lesson.
A. Post Conventional B. Macrosystem C. Fable D. Perception

79. B The whole socio-cultural context.
A. Solitary Play B. Macrosystem C. Formal Operation D. Emotional Development

80. D Land area found between hills or mountains.
A. Scribble Stage B. Cellular Respiration C. Tall Tales D. Valley

81. C 0-2 years old. Not engaged or actively playing with others at all.
A. Simile B. Myth C. Unoccupied Play D. Social isolation

82. A Reports events about someone's life.
A. Biography B. Application C. Charles Darwin D. Longitude

83. D A physical or mental condition that limits a person's movements, senses, or activities.
A. Simile B. Voting Rights Act C. Period of Decision D. Disability

84. C Characterized by constant change, activity, or progress.
A. Foothills B. Attitude C. Dynamic D. Onlooker Play

85. C A feeling of uncertainty and curiosity about what will happen next in a story.
A. Integration B. Abstract C. Suspense D. Knowledge

86. A A thing that rouses activity or energy in someone or something; a spur or incentive.
A. Stimuli B. Mesosystem C. Schematic Stage D. Associative Play

87. C Belief that students create their own reality of knowledge.
A. Interpersonal B. Majority Rule C. Constructivist Learning D. Chlorophyll

88. B The faculty of reasoning and understanding objectively.
A. Success B. Intellect C. Psychotic Disorder D. Supreme Court

89. C The infliction or imposition of a penalty as retribution for an offense.
A. Solitary Play B. Tantrum C. Punishment D. Distinguish

90. C Jean Piaget's, second stage of development, children begin to understand symbols.
A. Late Adulthood B. Disability C. Pre Operational D. Proportion

91. A A story containing unreal, imaginary features.
A. Fantasy B. Intellect C. Environment D. Memorize

92. D American ideal, idea that every person has the same rights and responsibilities under the law.
A. Label B. Metaphor C. Anxiety D. Equality

93. D Jean Piaget's first stage of development, birth-toddler, and child begins to understand their senses.
A. Distinguish B. Constructivist Learning C. Suspense D. Sensory Motor

94. D The surroundings or conditions in which a person operates.
A. Middle Adulthood B. Cultural C. Success D. Environment

95. D Theory that humans go through eight stages of development as they go from infancy to adulthood.
A. Development B. Pre Schematic Stage C. Emotion D. Erikson

96. C Writing with a purpose with audience in mind.
A. Physical Development B. Cognitive Development C. Conventional Writing D. Asperger

97. D Layer of the stratosphere with a high concentration of ozone; absorbs most of the Sun's harmful ultraviolet radiation
A. Music B. Anxiety C. Psychotic Disorder D. Ozone Layer

98. B A value of a continuous quantity that can represent a distance along a line.
A. Pre Operational B. Real Number C. Examine D. Failure

99. C Age 2-4 years old, make uncontrolled scribbles, and then name them to indicate what they represent.
A. Intellect B. Mesosystem C. Scribble Stage D. Addition

100. C A specified state of growth or advancement.
A. Failure B. Symbolism C. Development D. Ordinal

From the words provided for each clue, provide the letter of the word which best matches the clue.

101. C A genetic condition occurring as a result of an abnormality in the twenty-first pair of chromosomes.
A. Bloom B. Crisis C. Down Syndrome D. Failure

102. C Located in the dry, warm region of the Southern United States
A. Resource B. Biography C. Mojave Desert D. Social system

103. D A biological community of interacting organisms and their physical environment.
A. Neurotic Disorder B. Cognitive Development C. Concrete Operation D. Ecosystem

104. A Asset that can be drawn on by a person or organization in order to function effectively.
A. Resource B. Anxiety C. Symmetry D. Supply

105. C Kohlberg's stage. Egocentric. Up to age nine.
A. Distinguish B. Concrete C. Pre-Conventional D. Division

106. C Age 2-4 years old, make uncontrolled scribbles, and then name them to indicate what they represent.
A. Role Play Writing B. Nursery Rhyme C. Scribble Stage D. Emotional Development

107. C Increasingly sophisticated understandings of other people and of society as a whole.
A. Erikson B. Unoccupied Play C. Social Development D. Irrational number

108. A The correspondence in size and shape, of parts on opposite sides of a median line.
A. Symmetry B. Rational Numbers C. Inverse D. Supreme Court

109. C The amount by which something, especially a sum of money, is too small.
A. Examine B. Contrast C. Deficit D. Valley

110. A Interaction of two microsystems.
A. Mesosystem B. Intellect C. Attitude D. Fractions

111. A Up to 12 months. Develops trust and mistrust.
A. Infancy B. Period of Decision C. Constructivist Learning D. Early Adulthood (18-34yrs) - sense of isolation and intimacy, close relationships are formed.

112. B The accomplishment of an aim or purpose.
A. Neurotic Disorder B. Success C. Division D. Legends

113. B Recognize or treat (someone or something) as different.
A. Formal Operation B. Distinguish C. Understand D. Cystic Fibrosis

114. B A triangle with no congruent sides.
A. Proportion B. Scalene Triangle C. Great Plains D. Application

115. A Arrangement of closed shapes that completely cover a plan without overlapping.
A. Tessellation B. Down Syndrome C. Pre Operational D. Physical Development

116. A The faculty of reasoning and understanding objectively.
A. Intellect B. Rhombus C. Rule of Law D. Constructive Play

117. D Stated that children's play changes at they develop and they go through 6 district stages.
A. Perception B. Pseudo realistic C. Tantrum D. Parten

118. A A comparison of two unlike things without using the word like or as.
A. Metaphor B. Drawing Realism C. Formal Operation D. Develop

119. D Grow or cause to grow and become more mature, advanced, or elaborate.
A. Early Adulthood (18-34yrs) - sense of isolation and intimacy, close relationships are formed. B. Recall C. Anxiety D. Develop

120. C A figure of speech using deliberate exaggeration or overstatement.
A. Develop B. Valley C. Hyperbole D. Rhombus

121. D Writing with a purpose with audience in mind.
A. Stuttering B. Understand C. Foothills D. Conventional Writing

122. D Children begin to understand that good behavior is expected, and achieving those expectations is moral.
A. Social isolation B. Knowledge C. Compare D. Interpersonal

123. B Condition seen in individuals carrying single X chromosome but no other sex chromosome.
A. Legends B. Turners C. Recall D. Vygotsky

124. A State or describe exactly the nature, scope, or meaning of.
A. Define B. Formal Operation C. Science Fiction D. Evaluation

125. B A fundamental democratic principle requiring that the majority's view be respected.
A. Onlooker Play B. Majority Rule C. Unoccupied Play D. Evaluation

126. A 1st, 2nd, 10th, show position not quantity.
A. Ordinal B. Ecosystem C. Due Process D. Critical thinking

127. B The condition of being abnormally or extremely active.
A. Mesosystem B. Hyperactivity C. Fractions D. Equality

128. D Age 7-9 years old, drawings reflect actual physical proportions and colors.
A. Discrepancy B. Role Play Writing C. Failure D. Schematic Stage

129. D A quadrilateral with exactly one pair of parallel sides.
A. Constructivist Learning B. Ecosystem C. Erikson D. Trapezoid

130. D loss of contact with reality, failure to connect with others.
A. Recall B. Parallel Play C. Disfluency D. Psychotic Disorder

131. C A classifying phrase applied to a person or thing, especially one that is inaccurate or restrictive.
A. Discrepancy B. Scientific Revolution C. Label D. Microsystem

132. D Stories about events from earliest times, and are considered to be true in their societies.
A. Scientific Revolution B. Develop C. Supply D. Myth

133. C A real number that cannot be written as a simple fraction.
A. Schematic Stage B. Emotional Development C. Irrational number D. Sing

134. C 0-2 years old. Not engaged or actively playing with others at all.
A. Schematic Stage B. Addition C. Unoccupied Play D. Discrepancy

135. B Children learn to manipulate symbols, objects, and other elements.
A. Dramatic play B. Concrete Operation C. Rocky Mountains D. Experiment

136. B A number of connected items or names written or printed consecutively.
A. Liberty B. List C. Nursery Rhyme D. Erikson

137. C Idea that people could vote or even replace their lawmakers.
A. Fantasy B. Cystic Fibrosis C. Representation D. Mesa

138. A The action or process of adding something to something else.
A. Addition B. Valley C. Multiplication D. Social Development

139. B Compliance with an order, request, or law or submission to another's authority.
A. Percent B. Obedience C. Verbal D. Dramatic Play

140. D Short rhyme for kids that tell stories and teach sound patterns.
A. Ordinal B. Cognitive Development C. Legends D. Nursery Rhyme

141. A A condition characterized by paralysis, weakness, lack of coordination.
A. Cerebral Palsy B. Strategy C. Drawing Realism D. Representation

142. A Robots, spacecraft, mystery, civilizations from other ages. A "what if" aspect to the story.
A. Science Fiction B. Solitary Play C. Pre-Conventional D. Ethics

143. C Characterized by constant change, activity, or progress.
A. Latitude B. Natural Selection C. Dynamic D. Dyslexia

144. C Explain or make (something) clear by using examples, charts, pictures, etc.
A. Exosystem B. Physical Development C. Illustrate D. Mojave Desert

145. A Adolescents understand that there is a need for them to fulfill obligations and expectations.
A. Social system B. Categorize C. Fable D. Cooperative Play

146. B Sounds combined in such a way as to produce form, harmony, and expression of emotion.
A. Dyslexia B. Music C. Emotion D. Period of Decision

147. D Involves changes in how an individual experiences and expresses different feelings.
A. Calculate B. Animism C. Fractions D. Emotional Development

148. A Family of classroom.
A. Microsystem B. Norm C. Perception D. Analogy

149. D Development of processes of knowing, perceiving, reasoning, and problem solving.
A. Calculate B. Mojave Desert C. Crisis D. Cognitive Development

150. D Relating to or in the form of words.
A. Tall Tales B. Legends C. Chlorophyll D. Verbal

151. C The state of being strikingly different from something else.
A. Valley B. Voting Rights Act C. Contrast D. Early Writing

152. B Relating to society or its organization.
A. Rational Numbers B. Social C. Metaphor D. Sensory Motor

153. A Play in which children manipulate objects to produce or build something.
A. Constructive Play B. Longitude C. Integration D. Scientific Revolution

154. A Ages 9-11, drawing become increasingly representational.
A. Drawing Realism B. Success C. Informational Book D. Perception

155. C A learning disability that results in difficulty reading and writing.
A. Impulsive B. Drawing Realism C. Dyslexia D. Due Process

156. C Survival of the fittest.
A. Memoirs B. Dyslexia C. Natural Selection D. Pre-Conventional

157. C Talk with continued involuntary repetition of sounds, especially initial consonants.
A. Proportion B. Norm C. Stuttering D. Label

158. C No clue.
A. Drawing Realism B. Infancy C. Early Adulthood (18-34yrs) - sense of isolation and intimacy, close relationships are formed. D. Repetition

159. B Extend from New Mexico in the south through the Canadian border on the North.
A. Multiplication B. Rocky Mountains C. Ozone Layer D. Evaluation

160. C A law designed to help end formal and informal barriers to African American suffrage.
A. Development B. Fable C. Voting Rights Act D. Proportion

161. A A value of a continuous quantity that can represent a distance along a line.
A. Real Number B. Mesosystem C. Perception D. Legends

162. A Parentheses, Exponents, Multiplication, Division, Addition, Subtraction.
A. PEMDAS B. Microsystem C. Foothills D. Analysis

163. C Large, grassy region drained by the Mississippi River.
A. Encouragement B. PEMDAS C. Great Plains D. Parallel Play

164. B Principles concerning the distinction between right and wrong or good and bad behavior.
A. Irrational number B. Morality C. Scientific Revolution D. Tall Tales

165. C Used to underscore the importance of a work to point to the central theme.
A. Natural Selection B. Photosynthesis C. Repetition D. Evaluation

166. C Existing in thought or as an idea but not having a physical or concrete existence.
A. Concrete Operation B. Pre-Conventional C. Abstract D. Down Syndrome

167. C A kind of writing that tells someone's memories.
A. PEMDAS B. Affect C. Memoirs D. Constructive Play

168. C A type of autism characterized by normal cognitive and language development and impaired social skills.
A. Impair B. Solitary Play C. Asperger D. Voting Rights Act

169. B Indicate the faults of (someone or something) in a disapproving way.
A. Encouragement B. Criticize C. Majority Rule D. Functional Play

170. C Detailed classification of critical thinking and learning skills and objectives into tiered levels.
A. Cystic Fibrosis B. Constructive Play C. Bloom D. Rule of Law

171. A A triangle with three congruent sides.
A. Equilateral Triangle B. Ethics C. Dramatic play D. Tessellation

172. D Adapt a novel or present a particular incident as a play or movie.
A. Folktales B. Chlorophyll C. Emotional Development D. Dramatize

173. D A stage, 11-13 years old, reflecting child's ability to reason.
A. Down Syndrome B. Norm C. Vygotsky D. Pseudo realistic

174. C Consists of nine justices, each appointed by the President and confirmed by Congress.
A. Fable B. Percent C. Supreme Court D. Illustrate

175. C Existing in a material or physical form; real or solid; not abstract.
A. Social isolation B. Modern Fantasy C. Concrete D. Conventional Writing

176. C (4-6 years old. Children work together as teammates in an organized fashion.
A. Nursery Rhyme B. Early Childhood C. Cooperative Play D. List

177. A Ages 3-5 years. Child learns to initiate tasks and carry them out, guilt when task not completed.
A. Early Childhood B. Symmetry C. Impair D. Calculate

178. A Age 35-60. Commitment to family and career.
A. Middle Adulthood B. Morality C. Economic System D. Disability

179. C The process of dividing a matrix, vector, or other quantity by another under specific rules to obtain a quotient.
A. Fractions B. Critical thinking C. Division D. Knowledge

180. D The ability to see, hear, or become aware of something through the senses.
A. Exosystem B. List C. Biography D. Perception

181. B A number when added to the number it results in zero, or when multiplied by the number results in 1.
A. Period of Decision B. Inverse C. Develop D. Examine

182. B Jean Piaget's first stage of development, birth-toddler, and child begins to understand their senses.
A. Social system B. Sensory Motor C. Examine D. Unoccupied Play

183. D A feeling of worry, nervousness, or unease, typically about an imminent event.
A. Critical thinking B. Isosceles Triangle C. Demonstrate D. Anxiety

184. C A plan of action or policy designed to achieve a major or overall aim.
A. Hyperactivity B. Brofenbrenner C. Strategy D. Distinguish

185. B Agreement, harmony, or correspondence.
A. Illustrate B. Congruence C. Understand D. PEMDAS

186. D English natural scientist who formulated a theory of evolution by natural selection.
A. Liberty B. Chlorophyll C. Equilateral Triangle D. Charles Darwin

187. C Combination or composition, in particular.
A. Muscular Dystrophy B. Fantasy C. Synthesis D. Stimuli

188. B Perceive the intended meaning of.
A. Emotional Development B. Understand C. Recall D. Informational Book

189. D Children start to use a small range of familiar text forms and sight words in their writing.
A. Emotion B. Fable C. Anxiety D. Early Writing

190. C Something that is usual, typical, or standard.
A. Contrast B. Resource C. Norm D. Cognitive Development

191. B The state or condition of being fully grown or mature.
A. Early Adulthood (18-34yrs) - sense of isolation and intimacy, close relationships are formed. B. Adulthood
C. Norm D. Analogy

192. D Facts, information, and skills acquired by a person through experience or education.
A. Formal Operation B. Delta C. Subtraction D. Knowledge

193. C A settled way of thinking or feeling about something that is reflected in a person's behavior.
A. Hyperactivity B. Calculate C. Attitude D. Period of Decision

194. B Conversion of light energy from the sun into chemical energy.
A. Synthesis B. Photosynthesis C. Early Childhood D. Rational Numbers

195. A Age 60-death.
A. Late Adulthood B. Concrete Operation C. Categorize D. Norm

196. B A physical or mental condition that limits a person's movements, senses, or activities.
A. Hyperbole B. Disability C. Illustrate D. Legends

197. C Interruptions of speech that may be either normal or abnormal.
A. Evaluation B. Mojave Desert C. Disfluency D. Failure

198. D Inherited disease characterized by progressive weakness and degeneration of muscle fibers.
A. Suspense B. Lowenfeld C. Bloom D. Muscular Dystrophy

199. B A triangle that has 2 equal sides.
A. Dyslexia B. Isosceles Triangle C. Equilateral Triangle D. Music

200. C A thing that rouses activity or energy in someone or something; a spur or incentive.
A. Perception B. Memoirs C. Stimuli D. Animism

Matching

Provide the word that best matches each clue.

1. contrast — The state of being strikingly different from something else.
2. tantrum — An uncontrolled outburst of anger and frustration, typically in a young child.
3. ______ — The objective analysis and evaluation of an issue in order to form a judgment.
4. analysis — Breakdown information into parts and use those parts.
5. experiment — A scientific procedure undertaken to make a discovery, test a hypothesis, or demonstrate a fact.
6. animism — Influence of external aspects on development.
7. cell. resp. — The process by which cells use oxygen to produce energy from food.
8. categorize — Place in a particular class or group.
9. criticize — Indicate the faults of (someone or something) in a disapproving way.
10. perception — The ability to see, hear, or become aware of something through the senses.
11. CT — Clearly show the existence or truth of (something) by giving proof or evidence.
12. application — Bloom's 3rd level, take previous learning and use it in a new way.
13. mesosys — Interaction of two microsystems.
14. analogy — Assigning human qualities to objects "the sun was mad and burned me".
15. chlorophyll — A green photosynthetic pigment found in the chloroplasts of plants, algae, and some bacteria.
16. ______ — Recognize or treat (someone or something) as different.
17. dramatize — Adapt a novel or present a particular incident as a play or movie.
18. illustrate — Explain or make (something) clear by using examples, charts, pictures, etc.
19. integration — Combine one thing with another so that they become a whole.
20. biography — Reports events about someone's life.

21. examine — inspect (someone or something) in detail to determine their nature or condition.

22. distingish — A comparison of two things based on their being alike in some way.

23. calcuate — Determine (the amount or number of something) mathematically.

24. hyperactivity — The condition of being abnormally or extremely active.

25. CP — A condition characterized by paralysis, weakness, lack of coordination.

A. Analogy
D. Analysis
G. Integration
J. Hyperactivity
M. Application
P. Cerebral Palsy
S. Animism
V. Perception
Y. Exosystem
B. Contrast
E. Examine
H. Categorize
K. Calculate
N. Distinguish
Q. Criticize
T. Tantrum
W. Demonstrate
C. Dramatize
F. Mesosystem
I. Chlorophyll
L. Critical thinking
O. Illustrate
R. Biography
U. Cellular Respiration
X. Experiment

Provide the word that best matches each clue.

26. ____________ Assigning human qualities to objects "the sun was mad and burned me".

27. ____________ A condition characterized by paralysis, weakness, lack of coordination.

28. ____________ inspect (someone or something) in detail to determine their nature or condition.

29. ____________ Explain or make (something) clear by using examples, charts, pictures, etc.

30. ____________ Estimate, measure, or note the similarity or dissimilarity between.

31. ____________ Family of classroom.

32. ____________ Interaction of two microsystems.

33. ____________ Bloom's 3rd level, take previous learning and use it in a new way.

34. ____________ The condition of being abnormally or extremely active.

35. ____________ Place in a particular class or group.

36. ____________ Combine one thing with another so that they become a whole.

37. ____________ Reports events about someone's life.

38. ______ The whole socio-cultural context.

39. ______ Detailed classification of critical thinking and learning skills and objectives into tiered levels.

40. ______ Emotion or desire, especially as influencing behavior or action.

41. ______ An uncontrolled outburst of anger and frustration, typically in a young child.

42. ______ A type of autism characterized by normal cognitive and language development and impaired social skills.

43. ______ Breakdown information into parts and use those parts.

44. ______ Influence of external aspects on development.

45. ______ Adapt a novel or present a particular incident as a play or movie.

46. ______ The ability to see, hear, or become aware of something through the senses.

47. ______ A green photosynthetic pigment found in the chloroplasts of plants, algae, and some bacteria.

48. ______ A comparison of two things based on their being alike in some way.

49. ______ A scientific procedure undertaken to make a discovery, test a hypothesis, or demonstrate a fact.

50. ______ Acting or done without forethought.

A. Cerebral Palsy	B. Analogy	C. Macrosystem	D. Application
E. Impulsive	F. Mesosystem	G. Dramatize	H. Examine
I. Experiment	J. Affect	K. Chlorophyll	L. Exosystem
M. Perception	N. Biography	O. Bloom	P. Integration
Q. Categorize	R. Analysis	S. Microsystem	T. Illustrate
U. Asperger	V. Hyperactivity	W. Animism	X. Compare
Y. Tantrum			

Provide the word that best matches each clue.

51. ______ Estimate, measure, or note the similarity or dissimilarity between.

52. ______ Leader in field of child psychology and development, outlined 4 types of nested systems.

53. ______ The state of being strikingly different from something else.

54. ______________________ Assigning human qualities to objects "the sun was mad and burned me".

55. ______________________ A lack of compatibility or similarity between two or more facts.

56. ______________________ Combine one thing with another so that they become a whole.

57. ______________________ Place in a particular class or group.

58. ______________________ A green photosynthetic pigment found in the chloroplasts of plants, algae, and some bacteria.

59. ______________________ Explain or make (something) clear by using examples, charts, pictures, etc.

60. ______________________ Adapt a novel or present a particular incident as a play or movie.

61. ______________________ The condition of being abnormally or extremely active.

62. ______________________ Reports events about someone's life.

63. ______________________ A condition characterized by paralysis, weakness, lack of coordination.

64. ______________________ Recognize or treat (someone or something) as different.

65. ______________________ The ability to see, hear, or become aware of something through the senses.

66. ______________________ Detailed classification of critical thinking and learning skills and objectives into tiered levels.

67. ______________________ The whole socio-cultural context.

68. ______________________ Recognize or treat (someone or something) as different.

69. ______________________ Acting or done without forethought.

70. ______________________ Family of classroom.

71. ______________________ Determine (the amount or number of something) mathematically.

72. ______________________ Assignment of objects or people to categories on the basis of shared characteristics.

73. ______________________ The process by which cells use oxygen to produce energy from food.

74. ______________________ Breakdown information into parts and use those parts.

75. ______________________ Clearly show the existence or truth of (something) by giving proof or evidence.

A. Biography
B. Perception
C. Compare
D. Distinguish
E. Animism
F. Hyperactivity
G. Analysis
H. Classification
I. Demonstrate
J. Bloom
K. Macrosystem
L. Categorize
M. Contrast
N. Cerebral Palsy
O. Illustrate
P. Microsystem
Q. Dramatize
R. Discrepancy
S. Integration
T. Chlorophyll
U. Calculate
V. Distinguish
W. Brofenbrenner
X. Cellular Respiration
Y. Impulsive

Provide the word that best matches each clue.

76. ____________ The whole socio-cultural context.

77. ____________ A lack of compatibility or similarity between two or more facts.

78. ____________ Family of classroom.

79. ____________ Assigning human qualities to objects "the sun was mad and burned me".

80. ____________ Reports events about someone's life.

81. ____________ English natural scientist who formulated a theory of evolution by natural selection.

82. ____________ An uncontrolled outburst of anger and frustration, typically in a young child.

83. ____________ Emotion or desire, especially as influencing behavior or action.

84. ____________ The condition of being abnormally or extremely active.

85. ____________ Interaction of two microsystems.

86. ____________ A comparison of two things based on their being alike in some way.

87. ____________ Influence of external aspects on development.

88. ____________ Explain or make (something) clear by using examples, charts, pictures, etc.

89. ____________ Estimate, measure, or note the similarity or dissimilarity between.

90. ____________ Acting or done without forethought.

91. ____________ The state of being strikingly different from something else.

92. ____________ Clearly show the existence or truth of (something) by giving proof or evidence.

93. ________ Indicate the faults of (someone or something) in a disapproving way.

94. ________ Detailed classification of critical thinking and learning skills and objectives into tiered levels.

95. ________ Determine (the amount or number of something) mathematically.

96. ________ Place in a particular class or group.

97. ________ Assignment of objects or people to categories on the basis of shared characteristics.

98. ________ Combine one thing with another so that they become a whole.

99. ________ The ability to see, hear, or become aware of something through the senses.

100. ________ Recognize or treat (someone or something) as different.

A. Charles Darwin
B. Affect
C. Bloom
D. Macrosystem
E. Exosystem
F. Criticize
G. Illustrate
H. Animism
I. Categorize
J. Calculate
K. Contrast
L. Discrepancy
M. Analogy
N. Integration
O. Biography
P. Perception
Q. Impulsive
R. Microsystem
S. Demonstrate
T. Distinguish
U. Hyperactivity
V. Compare
W. Classification
X. Mesosystem
Y. Tantrum

Provide the word that best matches each clue.

101. ________ Detailed classification of critical thinking and learning skills and objectives into tiered levels.

102. ________ Reports events about someone's life.

103. ________ inspect (someone or something) in detail to determine their nature or condition.

104. ________ Indicate the faults of (someone or something) in a disapproving way.

105. ________ Emotion or desire, especially as influencing behavior or action.

106. ________ Combine one thing with another so that they become a whole.

107. ________ A comparison of two things based on their being alike in some way.

108. ________ Estimate, measure, or note the similarity or dissimilarity between.

109. ______________ Assignment of objects or people to categories on the basis of shared characteristics.

110. ______________ Interaction of two microsystems.

111. ______________ Place in a particular class or group.

112. ______________ English natural scientist who formulated a theory of evolution by natural selection.

113. ______________ Assigning human qualities to objects "the sun was mad and burned me".

114. ______________ The state of being strikingly different from something else.

115. ______________ The whole socio-cultural context.

116. ______________ Explain or make (something) clear by using examples, charts, pictures, etc.

117. ______________ Family of classroom.

118. ______________ Recognize or treat (someone or something) as different.

119. ______________ A condition characterized by paralysis, weakness, lack of coordination.

120. ______________ Influence of external aspects on development.

121. ______________ Recognize or treat (someone or something) as different.

122. ______________ Clearly show the existence or truth of (something) by giving proof or evidence.

123. ______________ Determine (the amount or number of something) mathematically.

124. ______________ Adapt a novel or present a particular incident as a play or movie.

125. ______________ Bloom's 3rd level, take previous learning and use it in a new way.

A. Bloom
B. Distinguish
C. Integration
D. Mesosystem
E. Affect
F. Biography
G. Animism
H. Criticize
I. Contrast
J. Exosystem
K. Calculate
L. Application
M. Analogy
N. Macrosystem
O. Distinguish
P. Illustrate
Q. Examine
R. Categorize
S. Compare
T. Classification
U. Microsystem
V. Cerebral Palsy
W. Charles Darwin
X. Demonstrate
Y. Dramatize

Provide the word that best matches each clue.

126. ______________ Indicate the faults of (someone or something) in a disapproving way.

127. ______________ Detailed classification of critical thinking and learning skills and objectives into tiered levels.

128. ______________ inspect (someone or something) in detail to determine their nature or condition.

129. ______________ Estimate, measure, or note the similarity or dissimilarity between.

130. ______________ Assigning human qualities to objects "the sun was mad and burned me".

131. ______________ Leader in field of child psychology and development, outlined 4 types of nested systems.

132. ______________ Reports events about someone's life.

133. ______________ Combine one thing with another so that they become a whole.

134. ______________ An uncontrolled outburst of anger and frustration, typically in a young child.

135. ______________ Acting or done without forethought.

136. ______________ A scientific procedure undertaken to make a discovery, test a hypothesis, or demonstrate a fact.

137. ______________ Breakdown information into parts and use those parts.

138. ______________ Clearly show the existence or truth of (something) by giving proof or evidence.

139. ______________ The process by which cells use oxygen to produce energy from food.

140. ______________ The whole socio-cultural context.

141. ______________ Interaction of two microsystems.

142. ______________ A comparison of two things based on their being alike in some way.

143. ______________ Family of classroom.

144. ______________ A green photosynthetic pigment found in the chloroplasts of plants, algae, and some bacteria.

145. ______________ A condition characterized by paralysis, weakness, lack of coordination.

146. ______________ Recognize or treat (someone or something) as different.

147. ______________ Recognize or treat (someone or something) as different.

148. ______ The ability to see, hear, or become aware of something through the senses.

149. ______ The state of being strikingly different from something else.

150. ______ The condition of being abnormally or extremely active.

A. Distinguish
B. Animism
C. Chlorophyll
D. Microsystem
E. Cerebral Palsy
F. Analysis
G. Integration
H. Biography
I. Hyperactivity
J. Cellular Respiration
K. Tantrum
L. Macrosystem
M. Experiment
N. Contrast
O. Criticize
P. Compare
Q. Examine
R. Mesosystem
S. Perception
T. Analogy
U. Demonstrate
V. Impulsive
W. Distinguish
X. Bloom
Y. Brofenbrenner

Provide the word that best matches each clue.

151. ______ Explain or make (something) clear by using examples, charts, pictures, etc.

152. ______ The state of being strikingly different from something else.

153. ______ Bloom's 3rd level, take previous learning and use it in a new way.

154. ______ A type of autism characterized by normal cognitive and language development and impaired social skills.

155. ______ Clearly show the existence or truth of (something) by giving proof or evidence.

156. ______ An uncontrolled outburst of anger and frustration, typically in a young child.

157. ______ A comparison of two things based on their being alike in some way.

158. ______ The condition of being abnormally or extremely active.

159. ______ The whole socio-cultural context.

160. ______ Recognize or treat (someone or something) as different.

161. ______ The process by which cells use oxygen to produce energy from food.

162. ______ Determine (the amount or number of something) mathematically.

163. ______________ A lack of compatibility or similarity between two or more facts.

164. ______________ Combine one thing with another so that they become a whole.

165. ______________ Family of classroom.

166. ______________ Estimate, measure, or note the similarity or dissimilarity between.

167. ______________ Influence of external aspects on development.

168. ______________ A condition characterized by paralysis, weakness, lack of coordination.

169. ______________ Interaction of two microsystems.

170. ______________ Emotion or desire, especially as influencing behavior or action.

171. ______________ Acting or done without forethought.

172. ______________ Detailed classification of critical thinking and learning skills and objectives into tiered levels.

173. ______________ Adapt a novel or present a particular incident as a play or movie.

174. ______________ Assigning human qualities to objects "the sun was mad and burned me".

175. ______________ A green photosynthetic pigment found in the chloroplasts of plants, algae, and some bacteria.

A. Demonstrate
B. Microsystem
C. Impulsive
D. Analogy
E. Tantrum
F. Asperger
G. Cerebral Palsy
H. Dramatize
I. Cellular Respiration
J. Bloom
K. Contrast
L. Application
M. Affect
N. Macrosystem
O. Distinguish
P. Exosystem
Q. Chlorophyll
R. Compare
S. Calculate
T. Illustrate
U. Integration
V. Animism
W. Discrepancy
X. Hyperactivity
Y. Mesosystem

Provide the word that best matches each clue.

176. ______________ Estimate, measure, or note the similarity or dissimilarity between.

177. ______________ Assignment of objects or people to categories on the basis of shared characteristics.

178. ______________ Influence of external aspects on development.

179. ______________ Place in a particular class or group.

180. ______________ The state of being strikingly different from something else.

181. ______________ Acting or done without forethought.

182. ______________ Interaction of two microsystems.

183. ______________ A lack of compatibility or similarity between two or more facts.

184. ______________ Assigning human qualities to objects "the sun was mad and burned me".

185. ______________ Breakdown information into parts and use those parts.

186. ______________ Family of classroom.

187. ______________ The objective analysis and evaluation of an issue in order to form a judgment.

188. ______________ The condition of being abnormally or extremely active.

189. ______________ Detailed classification of critical thinking and learning skills and objectives into tiered levels.

190. ______________ A condition characterized by paralysis, weakness, lack of coordination.

191. ______________ Indicate the faults of (someone or something) in a disapproving way.

192. ______________ Reports events about someone's life.

193. ______________ Combine one thing with another so that they become a whole.

194. ______________ English natural scientist who formulated a theory of evolution by natural selection.

195. ______________ A scientific procedure undertaken to make a discovery, test a hypothesis, or demonstrate a fact.

196. ______________ Bloom's 3rd level, take previous learning and use it in a new way.

197. ______________ A type of autism characterized by normal cognitive and language development and impaired social skills.

198. ______________ The whole socio-cultural context.

199. ______________ Determine (the amount or number of something) mathematically.

200. ______________ Adapt a novel or present a particular incident as a play or movie.

A. Microsystem
B. Critical thinking
C. Integration
D. Contrast
E. Calculate
F. Bloom
G. Criticize
H. Compare
I. Dramatize
J. Cerebral Palsy
K. Categorize
L. Exosystem
M. Impulsive
N. Charles Darwin
O. Discrepancy
P. Biography
Q. Animism
R. Experiment
S. Macrosystem
T. Classification
U. Analysis
V. Asperger
W. Application
X. Mesosystem
Y. Hyperactivity

Provide the word that best matches each clue.

1. CONTRAST — The state of being strikingly different from something else.
2. TANTRUM — An uncontrolled outburst of anger and frustration, typically in a young child.
3. CRITICAL THINKING — The objective analysis and evaluation of an issue in order to form a judgment.
4. ANALYSIS — Breakdown information into parts and use those parts.
5. EXPERIMENT — A scientific procedure undertaken to make a discovery, test a hypothesis, or demonstrate a fact.
6. EXOSYSTEM — Influence of external aspects on development.
7. CELLULAR RESPIRATION — The process by which cells use oxygen to produce energy from food.
8. CATEGORIZE — Place in a particular class or group.
9. CRITICIZE — Indicate the faults of (someone or something) in a disapproving way.
10. PERCEPTION — The ability to see, hear, or become aware of something through the senses.
11. DEMONSTRATE — Clearly show the existence or truth of (something) by giving proof or evidence.
12. APPLICATION — Bloom's 3rd level, take previous learning and use it in a new way.
13. MESOSYSTEM — Interaction of two microsystems.
14. ANIMISM — Assigning human qualities to objects "the sun was mad and burned me".
15. CHLOROPHYLL — A green photosynthetic pigment found in the chloroplasts of plants, algae, and some bacteria.
16. DISTINGUISH — Recognize or treat (someone or something) as different.
17. DRAMATIZE — Adapt a novel or present a particular incident as a play or movie.
18. ILLUSTRATE — Explain or make (something) clear by using examples, charts, pictures, etc.
19. INTEGRATION — Combine one thing with another so that they become a whole.
20. BIOGRAPHY — Reports events about someone's life.

21. EXAMINE — inspect (someone or something) in detail to determine their nature or condition.

22. ANALOGY — A comparison of two things based on their being alike in some way.

23. CALCULATE — Determine (the amount or number of something) mathematically.

24. HYPERACTIVITY — The condition of being abnormally or extremely active.

25. CEREBRAL PALSY — A condition characterized by paralysis, weakness, lack of coordination.

A. Analogy
B. Contrast
C. Dramatize
D. Analysis
E. Examine
F. Mesosystem
G. Integration
H. Categorize
I. Chlorophyll
J. Hyperactivity
K. Calculate
L. Critical thinking
M. Application
N. Distinguish
O. Illustrate
P. Cerebral Palsy
Q. Criticize
R. Biography
S. Animism
T. Tantrum
U. Cellular Respiration
V. Perception
W. Demonstrate
X. Experiment
Y. Exosystem

Provide the word that best matches each clue.

26. ANIMISM — Assigning human qualities to objects "the sun was mad and burned me".

27. CEREBRAL PALSY — A condition characterized by paralysis, weakness, lack of coordination.

28. EXAMINE — inspect (someone or something) in detail to determine their nature or condition.

29. ILLUSTRATE — Explain or make (something) clear by using examples, charts, pictures, etc.

30. COMPARE — Estimate, measure, or note the similarity or dissimilarity between.

31. MICROSYSTEM — Family of classroom.

32. MESOSYSTEM — Interaction of two microsystems.

33. APPLICATION — Bloom's 3rd level, take previous learning and use it in a new way.

34. HYPERACTIVITY — The condition of being abnormally or extremely active.

35. CATEGORIZE — Place in a particular class or group.

36. INTEGRATION — Combine one thing with another so that they become a whole.

37. BIOGRAPHY — Reports events about someone's life.

38. MACROSYSTEM — The whole socio-cultural context.

39. BLOOM — Detailed classification of critical thinking and learning skills and objectives into tiered levels.

40. AFFECT — Emotion or desire, especially as influencing behavior or action.

41. TANTRUM — An uncontrolled outburst of anger and frustration, typically in a young child.

42. ASPERGER — A type of autism characterized by normal cognitive and language development and impaired social skills.

43. ANALYSIS — Breakdown information into parts and use those parts.

44. EXOSYSTEM — Influence of external aspects on development.

45. DRAMATIZE — Adapt a novel or present a particular incident as a play or movie.

46. PERCEPTION — The ability to see, hear, or become aware of something through the senses.

47. CHLOROPHYLL — A green photosynthetic pigment found in the chloroplasts of plants, algae, and some bacteria.

48. ANALOGY — A comparison of two things based on their being alike in some way.

49. EXPERIMENT — A scientific procedure undertaken to make a discovery, test a hypothesis, or demonstrate a fact.

50. IMPULSIVE — Acting or done without forethought.

A. Cerebral Palsy	B. Analogy	C. Macrosystem	D. Application
E. Impulsive	F. Mesosystem	G. Dramatize	H. Examine
I. Experiment	J. Affect	K. Chlorophyll	L. Exosystem
M. Perception	N. Biography	O. Bloom	P. Integration
Q. Categorize	R. Analysis	S. Microsystem	T. Illustrate
U. Asperger	V. Hyperactivity	W. Animism	X. Compare
Y. Tantrum			

Provide the word that best matches each clue.

51. COMPARE — Estimate, measure, or note the similarity or dissimilarity between.

52. BROFENBRENNER — Leader in field of child psychology and development, outlined 4 types of nested systems.

53. CONTRAST — The state of being strikingly different from something else.

54. ANIMISM — Assigning human qualities to objects "the sun was mad and burned me".

55. DISCREPANCY — A lack of compatibility or similarity between two or more facts.

56. INTEGRATION — Combine one thing with another so that they become a whole.

57. CATEGORIZE — Place in a particular class or group.

58. CHLOROPHYLL — A green photosynthetic pigment found in the chloroplasts of plants, algae, and some bacteria.

59. ILLUSTRATE — Explain or make (something) clear by using examples, charts, pictures, etc.

60. DRAMATIZE — Adapt a novel or present a particular incident as a play or movie.

61. HYPERACTIVITY — The condition of being abnormally or extremely active.

62. BIOGRAPHY — Reports events about someone's life.

63. CEREBRAL PALSY — A condition characterized by paralysis, weakness, lack of coordination.

64. DISTINGUISH — Recognize or treat (someone or something) as different.

65. PERCEPTION — The ability to see, hear, or become aware of something through the senses.

66. BLOOM — Detailed classification of critical thinking and learning skills and objectives into tiered levels.

67. MACROSYSTEM — The whole socio-cultural context.

68. DISTINGUISH — Recognize or treat (someone or something) as different.

69. IMPULSIVE — Acting or done without forethought.

70. MICROSYSTEM — Family of classroom.

71. CALCULATE — Determine (the amount or number of something) mathematically.

72. CLASSIFICATION — Assignment of objects or people to categories on the basis of shared characteristics.

73. CELLULAR RESPIRATION — The process by which cells use oxygen to produce energy from food.

74. ANALYSIS — Breakdown information into parts and use those parts.

75. DEMONSTRATE — Clearly show the existence or truth of (something) by giving proof or evidence.

A. Biography
B. Perception
C. Compare
D. Distinguish
E. Animism
F. Hyperactivity
G. Analysis
H. Classification
I. Demonstrate
J. Bloom
K. Macrosystem
L. Categorize
M. Contrast
N. Cerebral Palsy
O. Illustrate
P. Microsystem
Q. Dramatize
R. Discrepancy
S. Integration
T. Chlorophyll
U. Calculate
V. Distinguish
W. Brofenbrenner
X. Cellular Respiration
Y. Impulsive

Provide the word that best matches each clue.

76. MACROSYSTEM The whole socio-cultural context.

77. DISCREPANCY A lack of compatibility or similarity between two or more facts.

78. MICROSYSTEM Family of classroom.

79. ANIMISM Assigning human qualities to objects "the sun was mad and burned me".

80. BIOGRAPHY Reports events about someone's life.

81. CHARLES DARWIN English natural scientist who formulated a theory of evolution by natural selection.

82. TANTRUM An uncontrolled outburst of anger and frustration, typically in a young child.

83. AFFECT Emotion or desire, especially as influencing behavior or action.

84. HYPERACTIVITY The condition of being abnormally or extremely active.

85. MESOSYSTEM Interaction of two microsystems.

86. ANALOGY A comparison of two things based on their being alike in some way.

87. EXOSYSTEM Influence of external aspects on development.

88. ILLUSTRATE Explain or make (something) clear by using examples, charts, pictures, etc.

89. COMPARE Estimate, measure, or note the similarity or dissimilarity between.

90. IMPULSIVE Acting or done without forethought.

91. CONTRAST The state of being strikingly different from something else.

92. DEMONSTRATE Clearly show the existence or truth of (something) by giving proof or evidence.

93. CRITICIZE — Indicate the faults of (someone or something) in a disapproving way.

94. BLOOM — Detailed classification of critical thinking and learning skills and objectives into tiered levels.

95. CALCULATE — Determine (the amount or number of something) mathematically.

96. CATEGORIZE — Place in a particular class or group.

97. CLASSIFICATION — Assignment of objects or people to categories on the basis of shared characteristics.

98. INTEGRATION — Combine one thing with another so that they become a whole.

99. PERCEPTION — The ability to see, hear, or become aware of something through the senses.

100. DISTINGUISH — Recognize or treat (someone or something) as different.

A. Charles Darwin
B. Affect
C. Bloom
D. Macrosystem
E. Exosystem
F. Criticize
G. Illustrate
H. Animism
I. Categorize
J. Calculate
K. Contrast
L. Discrepancy
M. Analogy
N. Integration
O. Biography
P. Perception
Q. Impulsive
R. Microsystem
S. Demonstrate
T. Distinguish
U. Hyperactivity
V. Compare
W. Classification
X. Mesosystem
Y. Tantrum

Provide the word that best matches each clue.

101. BLOOM — Detailed classification of critical thinking and learning skills and objectives into tiered levels.

102. BIOGRAPHY — Reports events about someone's life.

103. EXAMINE — inspect (someone or something) in detail to determine their nature or condition.

104. CRITICIZE — Indicate the faults of (someone or something) in a disapproving way.

105. AFFECT — Emotion or desire, especially as influencing behavior or action.

106. INTEGRATION — Combine one thing with another so that they become a whole.

107. ANALOGY — A comparison of two things based on their being alike in some way.

108. COMPARE — Estimate, measure, or note the similarity or dissimilarity between.

109. CLASSIFICATION — Assignment of objects or people to categories on the basis of shared characteristics.

110. MESOSYSTEM — Interaction of two microsystems.

111. CATEGORIZE — Place in a particular class or group.

112. CHARLES DARWIN — English natural scientist who formulated a theory of evolution by natural selection.

113. ANIMISM — Assigning human qualities to objects "the sun was mad and burned me".

114. CONTRAST — The state of being strikingly different from something else.

115. MACROSYSTEM — The whole socio-cultural context.

116. ILLUSTRATE — Explain or make (something) clear by using examples, charts, pictures, etc.

117. MICROSYSTEM — Family of classroom.

118. DISTINGUISH — Recognize or treat (someone or something) as different.

119. CEREBRAL PALSY — A condition characterized by paralysis, weakness, lack of coordination.

120. EXOSYSTEM — Influence of external aspects on development.

121. DISTINGUISH — Recognize or treat (someone or something) as different.

122. DEMONSTRATE — Clearly show the existence or truth of (something) by giving proof or evidence.

123. CALCULATE — Determine (the amount or number of something) mathematically.

124. DRAMATIZE — Adapt a novel or present a particular incident as a play or movie.

125. APPLICATION — Bloom's 3rd level, take previous learning and use it in a new way.

A. Bloom
B. Distinguish
C. Integration
D. Mesosystem
E. Affect
F. Biography
G. Animism
H. Criticize
I. Contrast
J. Exosystem
K. Calculate
L. Application
M. Analogy
N. Macrosystem
O. Distinguish
P. Illustrate
Q. Examine
R. Categorize
S. Compare
T. Classification
U. Microsystem
V. Cerebral Palsy
W. Charles Darwin
X. Demonstrate
Y. Dramatize

Provide the word that best matches each clue.

126. CRITICIZE — Indicate the faults of (someone or something) in a disapproving way.

127. BLOOM — Detailed classification of critical thinking and learning skills and objectives into tiered levels.

128. EXAMINE — inspect (someone or something) in detail to determine their nature or condition.

129. COMPARE — Estimate, measure, or note the similarity or dissimilarity between.

130. ANIMISM — Assigning human qualities to objects "the sun was mad and burned me".

131. BROFENBRENNER — Leader in field of child psychology and development, outlined 4 types of nested systems.

132. BIOGRAPHY — Reports events about someone's life.

133. INTEGRATION — Combine one thing with another so that they become a whole.

134. TANTRUM — An uncontrolled outburst of anger and frustration, typically in a young child.

135. IMPULSIVE — Acting or done without forethought.

136. EXPERIMENT — A scientific procedure undertaken to make a discovery, test a hypothesis, or demonstrate a fact.

137. ANALYSIS — Breakdown information into parts and use those parts.

138. DEMONSTRATE — Clearly show the existence or truth of (something) by giving proof or evidence.

139. CELLULAR RESPIRATION — The process by which cells use oxygen to produce energy from food.

140. MACROSYSTEM — The whole socio-cultural context.

141. MESOSYSTEM — Interaction of two microsystems.

142. ANALOGY — A comparison of two things based on their being alike in some way.

143. MICROSYSTEM — Family of classroom.

144. CHLOROPHYLL — A green photosynthetic pigment found in the chloroplasts of plants, algae, and some bacteria.

145. CEREBRAL PALSY — A condition characterized by paralysis, weakness, lack of coordination.

146. DISTINGUISH — Recognize or treat (someone or something) as different.

147. DISTINGUISH — Recognize or treat (someone or something) as different.

148. PERCEPTION — The ability to see, hear, or become aware of something through the senses.

149. CONTRAST — The state of being strikingly different from something else.

150. HYPERACTIVITY — The condition of being abnormally or extremely active.

A. Distinguish
B. Animism
C. Chlorophyll
D. Microsystem
E. Cerebral Palsy
F. Analysis
G. Integration
H. Biography
I. Hyperactivity
J. Cellular Respiration
K. Tantrum
L. Macrosystem
M. Experiment
N. Contrast
O. Criticize
P. Compare
Q. Examine
R. Mesosystem
S. Perception
T. Analogy
U. Demonstrate
V. Impulsive
W. Distinguish
X. Bloom
Y. Brofenbrenner

Provide the word that best matches each clue.

151. ILLUSTRATE — Explain or make (something) clear by using examples, charts, pictures, etc.

152. CONTRAST — The state of being strikingly different from something else.

153. APPLICATION — Bloom's 3rd level, take previous learning and use it in a new way.

154. ASPERGER — A type of autism characterized by normal cognitive and language development and impaired social skills.

155. DEMONSTRATE — Clearly show the existence or truth of (something) by giving proof or evidence.

156. TANTRUM — An uncontrolled outburst of anger and frustration, typically in a young child.

157. ANALOGY — A comparison of two things based on their being alike in some way.

158. HYPERACTIVITY — The condition of being abnormally or extremely active.

159. MACROSYSTEM — The whole socio-cultural context.

160. DISTINGUISH — Recognize or treat (someone or something) as different.

161. CELLULAR RESPIRATION — The process by which cells use oxygen to produce energy from food.

162. CALCULATE — Determine (the amount or number of something) mathematically.

163. DISCREPANCY — A lack of compatibility or similarity between two or more facts.

164. INTEGRATION — Combine one thing with another so that they become a whole.

165. MICROSYSTEM — Family of classroom.

166. COMPARE — Estimate, measure, or note the similarity or dissimilarity between.

167. EXOSYSTEM — Influence of external aspects on development.

168. CEREBRAL PALSY — A condition characterized by paralysis, weakness, lack of coordination.

169. MESOSYSTEM — Interaction of two microsystems.

170. AFFECT — Emotion or desire, especially as influencing behavior or action.

171. IMPULSIVE — Acting or done without forethought.

172. BLOOM — Detailed classification of critical thinking and learning skills and objectives into tiered levels.

173. DRAMATIZE — Adapt a novel or present a particular incident as a play or movie.

174. ANIMISM — Assigning human qualities to objects "the sun was mad and burned me".

175. CHLOROPHYLL — A green photosynthetic pigment found in the chloroplasts of plants, algae, and some bacteria.

A. Demonstrate
B. Microsystem
C. Impulsive
D. Analogy
E. Tantrum
F. Asperger
G. Cerebral Palsy
H. Dramatize
I. Cellular Respiration
J. Bloom
K. Contrast
L. Application
M. Affect
N. Macrosystem
O. Distinguish
P. Exosystem
Q. Chlorophyll
R. Compare
S. Calculate
T. Illustrate
U. Integration
V. Animism
W. Discrepancy
X. Hyperactivity
Y. Mesosystem

Provide the word that best matches each clue.

176. COMPARE — Estimate, measure, or note the similarity or dissimilarity between.

177. CLASSIFICATION — Assignment of objects or people to categories on the basis of shared characteristics.

178. EXOSYSTEM — Influence of external aspects on development.

179. CATEGORIZE — Place in a particular class or group.

180. CONTRAST — The state of being strikingly different from something else.

181. IMPULSIVE — Acting or done without forethought.

182. MESOSYSTEM — Interaction of two microsystems.

183. DISCREPANCY — A lack of compatibility or similarity between two or more facts.

184. ANIMISM — Assigning human qualities to objects "the sun was mad and burned me".

185. ANALYSIS — Breakdown information into parts and use those parts.

186. MICROSYSTEM — Family of classroom.

187. CRITICAL THINKING — The objective analysis and evaluation of an issue in order to form a judgment.

188. HYPERACTIVITY — The condition of being abnormally or extremely active.

189. BLOOM — Detailed classification of critical thinking and learning skills and objectives into tiered levels.

190. CEREBRAL PALSY — A condition characterized by paralysis, weakness, lack of coordination.

191. CRITICIZE — Indicate the faults of (someone or something) in a disapproving way.

192. BIOGRAPHY — Reports events about someone's life.

193. INTEGRATION — Combine one thing with another so that they become a whole.

194. CHARLES DARWIN — English natural scientist who formulated a theory of evolution by natural selection.

195. EXPERIMENT — A scientific procedure undertaken to make a discovery, test a hypothesis, or demonstrate a fact.

196. APPLICATION — Bloom's 3rd level, take previous learning and use it in a new way.

197. ASPERGER — A type of autism characterized by normal cognitive and language development and impaired social skills.

198. MACROSYSTEM — The whole socio-cultural context.

199. CALCULATE — Determine (the amount or number of something) mathematically.

200. DRAMATIZE — Adapt a novel or present a particular incident as a play or movie.

A. Microsystem
B. Critical thinking
C. Integration
D. Contrast
E. Calculate
F. Bloom
G. Criticize
H. Compare
I. Dramatize
J. Cerebral Palsy
K. Categorize
L. Exosystem
M. Impulsive
N. Charles Darwin
O. Discrepancy
P. Biography
Q. Animism
R. Experiment
S. Macrosystem
T. Classification
U. Analysis
V. Asperger
W. Application
X. Mesosystem
Y. Hyperactivity

Word Search

1. Find the hidden words. The words have been placed horizontally, vertically, or diagonally. When you locate a word, draw an ellipse around it.

S H W K I E N N F Y X C O N T R A S T N S B H
B C L E T V I D P N S A K H M P Y M G Q D B G
L M F N R F L Z W H R X F F M H E C Y A O R J
O S H T G B P Z K G C C O M P A R E Y N F W Y
O Y F D D M R C R I T I C I Z E P R K A J N B
M H D R I I E S O J X U X U L D W A M L A P Z
D Z I N J C C A T E G O R I Z E Z Y U O W B R
R H Y G E R U M H B C J J W Z E A L S G Z V P
A E K U O O A P P L I C A T I O N C Y Y Q I J
M F X D I S T I N G U I S H R H F N Z N G I J
A S K Y F Y P D I I I O G M E S O S Y S T E M
T U A M M S X E R B V W Z S W M R O U R A X L
I R L W U T L P Y Z Q H Z V Z D Q V S Q V W F
Z N N T S E C T X P N R I Q V D O P S L O T C
E F O Z X M W J B S C A F B G E X A M I N E D
Y D B J V B J C P R E E Z B F A E G C C H Z U

1. inspect (someone or something) in detail to determine their nature or condition.
2. The state of being strikingly different from something else.
3. Bloom's 3rd level, take previous learning and use it in a new way.
4. Recognize or treat (someone or something) as different.
5. A comparison of two things based on their being alike in some way.
6. Indicate the faults of (someone or something) in a disapproving way.
7. Family of classroom.
8. Adapt a novel or present a particular incident as a play or movie.
9. Estimate, measure, or note the similarity or dissimilarity between.
10. Interaction of two microsystems.
11. Place in a particular class or group.
12. Detailed classification of critical thinking and learning skills and objectives into tiered levels.

A. Microsystem
B. Application
C. Bloom
D. Mesosystem
E. Criticize
F. Compare
G. Distinguish
H. Contrast
I. Categorize
J. Examine
K. Dramatize
L. Analogy

2. Find the hidden words. The words have been placed horizontally, vertically, or diagonally. When you locate a word, draw an ellipse around it.

V F K W W L Q E C P O Z Q M Q C S S S C Z H S
S J Z N B V Y X Y D V Y J G D L E N Q Y P O P
D Z L S J C N O K J F A M C C O N T R A S T N
R A X I J U E S R L D R D K Z G N F L A I S E
A C K A N A L Y S I S O U S T K N U Q Y L W E
M A P L H E H S D B I O G R A P H Y K X L E V
A S T P Y D G T X E T Z U Y L Q I O R B U T D
T P Q N T G G E J V G A E W H H C X O V S F U
I E Q D Q P X M Z B F E V Y Q Q O C R T T N I
Z R Z I C A T E G O R I Z E S T M L R D R O C
E G N Q N B N J W A N A L O G Y P K P N A B P
U E F A F A H K O U P N K F V W A B X S T Y L
I R W D I S T I N G U I S H N O R R T K E H T
C A L C U L A T E R B F M T F D E R O L J T Z
I Y D C W S M V N X O P G X R L N G W C V C N
H X M P T J J H P S I N P L O X S V X E E Q X

1. Place in a particular class or group.
2. Explain or make (something) clear by using examples, charts, pictures, etc.
3. Determine (the amount or number of something) mathematically.
4. Influence of external aspects on development.
5. A type of autism characterized by normal cognitive and language development and impaired social skills.
6. A comparison of two things based on their being alike in some way.
7. Breakdown information into parts and use those parts.
8. Estimate, measure, or note the similarity or dissimilarity between.
9. Adapt a novel or present a particular incident as a play or movie.
10. The state of being strikingly different from something else.
11. Reports events about someone's life.
12. Recognize or treat (someone or something) as different.

A. Contrast
B. Asperger
C. Analogy
D. Biography
E. Analysis
F. Compare
G. Illustrate
H. Categorize
I. Exosystem
J. Distinguish
K. Dramatize
L. Calculate

3. Find the hidden words. The words have been placed horizontally, vertically, or diagonally. When you locate a word, draw an ellipse around it.

M	H	L	G	A	E	M	Q	A	D	F	K	C	A	T	E	G	O	R	I	Z	E	V
E	J	E	D	S	L	E	Q	N	Z	W	X	K	C	Z	Z	J	E	H	Y	Y	I	R
A	A	X	H	I	D	J	C	A	B	R	O	F	E	N	B	R	E	N	N	E	R	C
B	E	A	H	E	Q	J	N	L	O	C	L	A	O	R	A	O	X	I	G	A	V	H
I	F	M	H	B	E	E	J	Y	V	K	I	V	N	X	V	S	C	X	J	P	V	Q
F	M	I	Y	U	Z	Z	M	S	J	Z	W	I	H	U	A	S	P	E	R	G	E	R
C	O	N	T	R	A	S	T	I	S	Z	A	D	I	L	L	U	S	T	R	A	T	E
M	F	E	E	T	R	D	F	S	A	T	F	V	V	L	X	K	Z	R	D	T	J	H
E	E	W	M	L	L	M	G	D	C	T	B	T	X	K	R	A	N	A	L	O	G	Y
X	N	E	X	P	E	R	I	M	E	N	T	I	T	T	G	U	R	N	N	Z	X	H
C	P	F	R	W	H	A	H	G	G	R	S	U	Q	C	B	U	R	A	A	I	U	P
L	P	N	C	A	L	C	U	L	A	T	E	X	J	F	Y	X	M	P	Y	A	N	O
K	X	P	J	J	Q	H	Q	A	Z	P	R	P	T	W	Z	X	Z	I	Z	U	B	I
J	Q	C	I	J	F	D	V	Q	P	N	K	U	K	Q	Z	E	I	U	O	O	H	S
Q	E	A	N	S	Z	S	N	T	I	O	D	R	A	M	A	T	I	Z	E	F	T	G
H	X	L	X	D	Z	B	C	J	C	O	D	I	S	T	I	N	G	U	I	S	H	G

1. Breakdown information into parts and use those parts.
2. A comparison of two things based on their being alike in some way.
3. inspect (someone or something) in detail to determine their nature or condition.
4. Explain or make (something) clear by using examples, charts, pictures, etc.
5. Adapt a novel or present a particular incident as a play or movie.
6. Determine (the amount or number of something) mathematically.
7. A scientific procedure undertaken to make a discovery, test a hypothesis, or demonstrate a fact.
8. Recognize or treat (someone or something) as different.
9. Leader in field of child psychology and development, outlined 4 types of nested systems.
10. Place in a particular class or group.
11. A type of autism characterized by normal cognitive and language development and impaired social skills.
12. The state of being strikingly different from something else.

A. Categorize
B. Experiment
C. Distinguish
D. Calculate
E. Analogy
F. Illustrate
G. Examine
H. Dramatize
I. Brofenbrenner
J. Contrast
K. Analysis
L. Asperger

4. Find the hidden words. The words have been placed horizontally, vertically, or diagonally. When you locate a word, draw an ellipse around it.

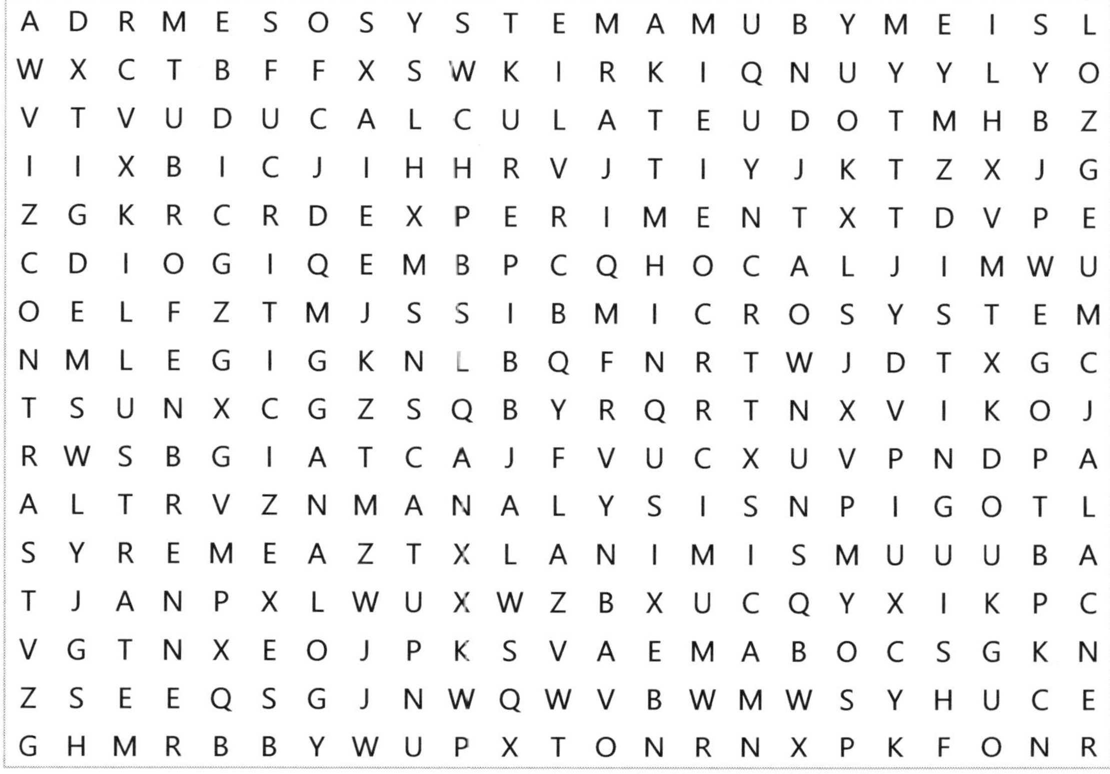

1. Leader in field of child psychology and development, outlined 4 types of nested systems.
2. Assigning human qualities to objects "the sun was mad and burned me".
3. A comparison of two things based on their being alike in some way.
4. The state of being strikingly different from something else.
5. Determine (the amount or number of something) mathematically.
6. Breakdown information into parts and use those parts.
7. A scientific procedure undertaken to make a discovery, test a hypothesis, or demonstrate a fact.
8. Recognize or treat (someone or something) as different.
9. Indicate the faults of (someone or something) in a disapproving way.
10. Explain or make (something) clear by using examples, charts, pictures, etc.
11. Family of classroom.
12. Interaction of two microsystems.

A. Criticize
B. Experiment
C. Microsystem
D. Brofenbrenner
E. Calculate
F. Animism
G. Distinguish
H. Mesosystem
I. Contrast
J. Illustrate
K. Analysis
L. Analogy

5. Find the hidden words. The words have been placed horizontally, vertically, or diagonally. When you locate a word, draw an ellipse around it.

M	Y	N	X	C	U	D	R	P	H	D	T	Z	C	E	F	M	Q	P	W	P	Y	Z
D	X	I	H	A	K	J	P	G	I	T	G	P	N	T	I	E	Y	E	G	S	C	Z
E	P	P	U	T	N	P	I	R	D	T	Q	S	Y	S	N	X	B	F	P	K	U	C
M	J	Z	J	E	C	A	L	C	U	L	A	T	E	N	K	A	P	K	X	O	M	I
O	D	M	Z	G	D	R	A	M	A	T	I	Z	E	J	H	M	N	A	U	V	A	Y
N	D	O	D	O	N	Q	U	A	F	H	S	O	W	X	A	I	Q	S	P	G	H	D
S	A	Y	U	R	O	H	H	N	O	L	A	T	D	U	S	N	V	P	P	U	E	F
T	K	G	Z	I	T	U	E	I	P	V	N	X	L	F	M	E	I	E	T	B	F	Q
R	V	B	E	Z	O	H	V	M	Z	E	A	B	B	N	Z	T	H	R	D	V	K	F
A	Z	H	J	E	F	T	E	I	S	J	L	W	I	Z	K	K	S	G	M	E	U	S
T	A	Q	D	L	A	O	S	S	B	I	O	G	R	A	P	H	Y	E	D	C	W	E
E	E	C	Q	Y	O	C	Y	M	H	P	G	I	A	V	X	Y	Q	R	F	R	R	U
A	P	P	L	I	C	A	T	I	O	N	Y	N	O	N	L	V	T	B	N	G	U	M
Q	B	W	F	S	G	I	M	V	Q	O	X	E	J	Z	V	F	M	K	J	B	L	H
J	Q	Q	Q	U	E	M	O	M	E	S	O	S	Y	S	T	E	M	R	M	C	R	Y
Z	S	G	B	R	O	F	E	N	B	R	E	N	N	E	R	J	W	E	W	E	Y	Q

1. A type of autism characterized by normal cognitive and language development and impaired social skills.
2. Leader in field of child psychology and development, outlined 4 types of nested systems.
3. inspect (someone or something) in detail to determine their nature or condition.
4. Place in a particular class or group.
5. Interaction of two microsystems.
6. Determine (the amount or number of something) mathematically.
7. Clearly show the existence or truth of (something) by giving proof or evidence.
8. Adapt a novel or present a particular incident as a play or movie.
9. A comparison of two things based on their being alike in some way.
10. Bloom's 3rd level, take previous learning and use it in a new way.
11. Assigning human qualities to objects "the sun was mad and burned me".
12. Reports events about someone's life.

A. Mesosystem
B. Brofenbrenner
C. Analogy
D. Dramatize
E. Biography
F. Examine
G. Animism
H. Demonstrate
I. Application
J. Asperger
K. Categorize
L. Calculate

6. Find the hidden words. The words have been placed horizontally, vertically, or diagonally. When you locate a word, draw an ellipse around it.

1. Assigning human qualities to objects "the sun was mad and burned me".
2. Family of classroom.
3. Clearly show the existence or truth of (something) by giving proof or evidence.
4. Recognize or treat (someone or something) as different.
5. inspect (someone or something) in detail to determine their nature or condition.
6. Leader in field of child psychology and development, outlined 4 types of nested systems.
7. Explain or make (something) clear by using examples, charts, pictures, etc.
8. Reports events about someone's life.
9. Recognize or treat (someone or something) as different.
10. Breakdown information into parts and use those parts.
11. A scientific procedure undertaken to make a discovery, test a hypothesis, or demonstrate a fact.
12. A type of autism characterized by normal cognitive and language development and impaired social skills.

A. Illustrate
B. Animism
C. Microsystem
D. Distinguish
E. Brofenbrenner
F. Asperger
G. Biography
H. Analysis
I. Experiment
J. Demonstrate
K. Examine
L. Distinguish

7. Find the hidden words. The words have been placed horizontally, vertically, or diagonally. When you locate a word, draw an ellipse around it.

C C W Q L X Q H A K F L D X L H L A E A F D E

Y D C B Y C T N S C M N J P Q X X M L O H L F

J M L B W S C I P W V B X D S O K Y O N W D Y

Q E O V Q O C R E A P Q V T S U Q Q X F B L T

Q X R I R M F J R N C A P P L I C A T I O N M

A P T O C K W W G A F F E Z R H F F E C K Y Y

T E B I M K K I E L Y F A N I M I S M R D D I

T R O C P C E Q R Y K U T R E A W C M I B J M

D I N M E S O S Y S T E M B X H L A I T L S H

D M S B X Q C B V I F C E P A C Z L U I O E A

J E I P Y I Z M C S Q B B I M G Q C X C U B Y

I N W C P B L O O M Y A G Z I E X U A I N H T

G T I D I S T I N G U I S H N C K L R Z F J C

L O L Z U X W O R I Y V F H E X U A J E O S J

V O C C U I B X O N D W O G L O D T Y G I C Q

F S P L N E X O S Y S T E M Z K H E A C M A G

1. A scientific procedure undertaken to make a discovery, test a hypothesis, or demonstrate a fact.
2. Interaction of two microsystems.
3. Breakdown information into parts and use those parts.
4. inspect (someone or something) in detail to determine their nature or condition.
5. Bloom's 3rd level, take previous learning and use it in a new way.
6. Assigning human qualities to objects "the sun was mad and burned me".
7. Determine (the amount or number of something) mathematically.
8. Recognize or treat (someone or something) as different.
9. Indicate the faults of (someone or something) in a disapproving way.
10. A type of autism characterized by normal cognitive and language development and impaired social skills.
11. Detailed classification of critical thinking and learning skills and objectives into tiered levels.
12. Influence of external aspects on development.

A. Animism
B. Criticize
C. Experiment
D. Distinguish
E. Analysis
F. Calculate
G. Examine
H. Mesosystem
I. Application
J. Asperger
K. Bloom
L. Exosystem

8. Find the hidden words. The words have been placed horizontally, vertically, or diagonally. When you locate a word, draw an ellipse around it.

1. Assigning human qualities to objects "the sun was mad and burned me".
2. inspect (someone or something) in detail to determine their nature or condition.
3. A scientific procedure undertaken to make a discovery, test a hypothesis, or demonstrate a fact.
4. Indicate the faults of (someone or something) in a disapproving way.
5. Determine (the amount or number of something) mathematically.
6. Breakdown information into parts and use those parts.
7. Recognize or treat (someone or something) as different.
8. Clearly show the existence or truth of (something) by giving proof or evidence.
9. Reports events about someone's life.
10. Place in a particular class or group.
11. Adapt a novel or present a particular incident as a play or movie.
12. Influence of external aspects on development.

A. Examine
B. Criticize
C. Biography
D. Distinguish
E. Calculate
F. Experiment
G. Analysis
H. Animism
I. Exosystem
J. Demonstrate
K. Dramatize
L. Categorize

9. Find the hidden words. The words have been placed horizontally, vertically, or diagonally. When you locate a word, draw an ellipse around it.

K	P	O	J	U	D	Z	G	T	C	Y	Q	L	E	E	A	K	V	P	Y	O	Q	S
Q	Q	N	H	Q	D	V	K	H	A	W	A	I	P	C	W	B	R	M	I	D	R	M
H	T	C	W	G	K	X	X	A	P	P	L	I	C	A	T	I	O	N	L	P	C	F
D	U	D	I	S	T	I	N	G	U	I	S	H	W	Y	D	T	H	V	L	J	O	D
I	Y	R	R	Q	P	E	W	L	H	Y	O	H	C	N	E	B	D	I	U	T	M	E
S	E	C	U	X	K	N	K	K	Q	G	L	Q	J	P	M	F	I	J	S	F	P	Z
T	X	A	U	R	E	Y	Z	U	D	Z	I	I	C	G	O	U	U	K	T	N	A	R
I	P	T	P	F	N	E	H	F	Y	X	K	U	Y	A	N	B	J	I	R	Z	R	T
N	E	E	H	C	J	Q	P	F	U	C	H	O	B	N	S	I	B	N	A	Z	E	Q
G	R	G	W	Y	B	O	S	D	R	V	M	M	F	I	T	O	B	O	T	A	E	P
U	I	O	A	J	J	Y	S	K	U	X	L	U	D	M	R	G	F	Q	E	G	D	K
I	M	R	X	T	Y	A	H	U	G	P	Q	H	W	I	A	R	E	K	E	F	C	D
S	E	I	Y	A	S	E	A	Y	L	D	E	D	Y	S	T	A	Z	L	F	F	I	V
H	N	Z	E	U	B	D	H	G	D	T	I	L	O	M	E	P	P	N	G	P	B	C
R	T	E	F	L	G	W	V	N	W	D	R	I	P	E	C	H	Q	W	P	A	K	A
Z	B	L	O	O	M	Q	C	R	I	T	I	C	I	Z	E	Y	U	P	K	S	N	X

1. Reports events about someone's life.
2. Estimate, measure, or note the similarity or dissimilarity between.
3. Detailed classification of critical thinking and learning skills and objectives into tiered levels.
4. Explain or make (something) clear by using examples, charts, pictures, etc.
5. Indicate the faults of (someone or something) in a disapproving way.
6. Recognize or treat (someone or something) as different.
7. Clearly show the existence or truth of (something) by giving proof or evidence.
8. Place in a particular class or group.
9. Recognize or treat (someone or something) as different.
10. A scientific procedure undertaken to make a discovery, test a hypothesis, or demonstrate a fact.
11. Bloom's 3rd level, take previous learning and use it in a new way.
12. Assigning human qualities to objects "the sun was mad and burned me".

A. Criticize
B. Distinguish
C. Demonstrate
D. Application
E. Illustrate
F. Animism
G. Experiment
H. Bloom
I. Distinguish
J. Biography
K. Compare
L. Categorize

10. Find the hidden words. The words have been placed horizontally, vertically, or diagonally. When you locate a word, draw an ellipse around it.

N	Q	W	I	A	Y	B	R	O	F	E	N	B	R	E	N	N	E	R	I	N	A	W
O	H	Z	O	N	G	E	O	V	D	D	I	X	T	X	G	E	A	D	A	B	L	W
V	E	H	Q	A	I	A	M	U	Z	R	V	O	Q	Z	A	S	L	M	S	L	M	F
T	G	O	E	L	Z	P	U	S	P	E	X	F	M	P	A	T	D	R	X	O	Y	R
U	V	M	I	O	U	P	G	U	X	N	T	O	K	O	F	C	O	P	D	O	Q	O
T	F	V	T	G	Q	L	B	B	Z	G	A	N	I	M	I	S	M	P	T	M	O	A
U	C	U	L	Y	X	I	U	G	K	T	Z	C	R	I	T	I	C	I	Z	E	V	N
B	A	K	J	U	Y	C	J	X	E	N	O	H	J	X	O	A	S	S	D	S	E	A
V	T	Q	Y	A	Z	A	Q	T	T	E	U	J	S	X	P	Y	D	K	R	J	V	L
C	E	R	B	C	C	T	E	H	K	X	W	W	B	O	R	O	E	E	A	D	K	Y
K	G	E	F	Q	D	I	S	T	I	N	G	U	I	S	H	S	K	D	M	V	K	S
U	O	Y	L	Q	I	O	W	P	N	T	D	E	M	O	N	S	T	R	A	T	E	I
O	R	W	V	R	F	N	W	C	A	L	C	U	L	A	T	E	W	I	T	S	V	S
B	I	I	K	U	A	A	Z	Q	X	B	J	S	Y	J	X	Q	Y	L	I	G	T	R
B	Z	A	K	Q	G	P	T	Y	I	T	K	S	I	T	B	J	E	L	Z	Q	J	G
S	E	M	K	W	X	L	U	P	X	L	B	Y	D	Z	H	A	D	T	E	K	G	R

1. Detailed classification of critical thinking and learning skills and objectives into tiered levels.
2. Indicate the faults of (someone or something) in a disapproving way.
3. A comparison of two things based on their being alike in some way.
4. Breakdown information into parts and use those parts.
5. Determine (the amount or number of something) mathematically.
6. Adapt a novel or present a particular incident as a play or movie.
7. Bloom's 3rd level, take previous learning and use it in a new way.
8. Recognize or treat (someone or something) as different.
9. Place in a particular class or group.
10. Assigning human qualities to objects "the sun was mad and burned me".
11. Clearly show the existence or truth of (something) by giving proof or evidence.
12. Leader in field of child psychology and development, outlined 4 types of nested systems.

A. Distinguish
B. Application
C. Categorize
D. Analogy
E. Analysis
F. Bloom
G. Criticize
H. Calculate
I. Brofenbrenner
J. Animism
K. Dramatize
L. Demonstrate

11. Find the hidden words. The words have been placed horizontally, vertically, or diagonally. When you locate a word, draw an ellipse around it.

O	H	Y	A	Q	P	V	G	T	A	Q	K	L	J	O	Z	U	J	D	Z	J	L	I
I	T	E	B	U	T	C	I	B	A	P	P	L	I	C	A	T	I	O	N	R	F	D
O	D	E	R	L	W	A	H	W	Y	I	E	L	L	O	S	Q	T	A	J	K	H	G
I	D	Z	O	Q	G	L	L	D	R	A	M	A	T	I	Z	E	V	B	X	S	I	K
G	X	G	F	J	N	C	Y	B	H	A	B	G	X	X	E	L	D	A	I	R	H	E
X	W	F	E	Z	F	U	A	N	A	L	Y	S	I	S	V	P	V	A	W	K	M	X
C	A	C	N	I	V	L	J	J	M	L	I	A	G	G	X	C	T	C	A	R	A	P
P	A	A	B	B	N	A	K	R	D	E	M	O	N	S	T	R	A	T	E	H	E	E
S	I	T	R	F	G	T	A	E	R	U	U	W	W	Q	U	R	V	G	Y	X	Q	R
Z	C	E	E	D	C	E	N	M	V	J	V	U	L	B	N	X	E	C	F	U	C	I
D	T	G	N	C	P	D	I	H	W	G	J	I	L	L	U	S	T	R	A	T	E	M
X	J	O	N	U	U	C	M	P	U	R	F	A	Q	W	J	X	I	X	I	T	I	E
Y	M	R	E	R	M	B	I	D	V	D	O	K	Y	C	O	M	P	A	R	E	V	N
F	G	I	R	M	M	M	S	Z	R	Y	X	D	M	X	E	E	G	T	W	T	S	T
V	O	Z	N	H	X	F	M	X	T	R	H	M	G	H	G	F	K	P	X	K	W	X
Q	U	E	L	D	I	S	T	I	N	G	U	I	S	H	U	Z	T	H	W	W	B	G

1. A scientific procedure undertaken to make a discovery, test a hypothesis, or demonstrate a fact.
2. Adapt a novel or present a particular incident as a play or movie.
3. Breakdown information into parts and use those parts.
4. Leader in field of child psychology and development, outlined 4 types of nested systems.
5. Determine (the amount or number of something) mathematically.
6. Estimate, measure, or note the similarity or dissimilarity between.
7. Place in a particular class or group.
8. Bloom's 3rd level, take previous learning and use it in a new way.
9. Clearly show the existence or truth of (something) by giving proof or evidence.
10. Assigning human qualities to objects "the sun was mad and burned me".
11. Explain or make (something) clear by using examples, charts, pictures, etc.
12. Recognize or treat (someone or something) as different.

A. Illustrate
B. Brofenbrenner
C. Experiment
D. Compare
E. Categorize
F. Analysis
G. Animism
H. Dramatize
I. Calculate
J. Distinguish
K. Application
L. Demonstrate

12. Find the hidden words. The words have been placed horizontally, vertically, or diagonally. When you locate a word, draw an ellipse around it.

U	S	D	H	R	Y	O	G	D	E	M	O	N	S	T	R	A	T	E	O	G	A	R
L	X	E	R	Z	T	Q	W	C	A	T	E	G	O	R	I	Z	E	M	W	V	E	T
C	M	X	M	P	W	U	F	F	L	P	C	X	S	R	I	E	H	Q	Q	D	Z	X
U	C	I	D	F	E	U	X	W	Z	N	P	L	Q	U	Y	J	F	L	F	L	P	O
A	N	A	L	Y	S	I	S	B	B	Z	N	H	P	E	N	Q	C	P	D	J	H	T
O	A	L	O	S	D	D	J	D	B	I	O	G	R	A	P	H	Y	G	R	K	I	G
L	R	U	M	F	I	O	G	B	R	O	F	E	N	B	R	E	N	N	E	R	B	G
Q	I	L	L	U	S	T	R	A	T	E	N	D	I	S	T	I	N	G	U	I	S	H
I	S	L	X	M	T	W	N	K	R	Q	Q	M	I	C	R	O	S	Y	S	T	E	M
K	T	X	W	K	I	R	Y	T	W	W	G	X	B	Y	I	C	X	V	A	S	I	K
Y	F	A	R	M	N	A	P	P	L	I	C	A	T	I	O	N	Q	K	E	A	R	Q
V	G	A	O	J	G	D	P	D	N	U	Q	C	U	J	Y	E	T	Q	O	R	Y	I
A	V	R	W	S	U	F	H	B	L	O	O	M	D	R	A	M	A	T	I	Z	E	J
R	W	P	H	G	I	R	H	N	O	S	L	O	V	P	I	D	F	H	N	M	Q	N
L	A	S	M	G	S	F	X	M	K	K	V	D	D	T	N	N	D	H	W	F	B	W
F	J	M	L	N	H	O	R	K	R	V	S	D	L	P	O	T	L	C	Q	B	H	B

1. Explain or make (something) clear by using examples, charts, pictures, etc.
2. Recognize or treat (someone or something) as different.
3. Bloom's 3rd level, take previous learning and use it in a new way.
4. Leader in field of child psychology and development, outlined 4 types of nested systems.
5. Clearly show the existence or truth of (something) by giving proof or evidence.
6. Adapt a novel or present a particular incident as a play or movie.
7. Breakdown information into parts and use those parts.
8. Family of classroom.
9. Reports events about someone's life.
10. Recognize or treat (someone or something) as different.
11. Place in a particular class or group.
12. Detailed classification of critical thinking and learning skills and objectives into tiered levels.

A. Demonstrate
B. Distinguish
C. Distinguish
D. Categorize
E. Brofenbrenner
F. Dramatize
G. Biography
H. Bloom
I. Microsystem
J. Illustrate
K. Application
L. Analysis

13. Find the hidden words. The words have been placed horizontally, vertically, or diagonally. When you locate a word, draw an ellipse around it.

T	R	M	O	Q	R	E	G	Q	L	L	P	U	I	A	N	A	L	Y	S	I	S	A
U	R	B	R	O	F	E	N	B	R	E	N	N	E	R	I	U	Z	S	Z	C	L	Z
I	X	Y	J	V	T	O	A	O	E	P	V	Z	Z	X	Z	F	L	F	G	R	R	V
D	V	G	T	Q	L	H	G	H	I	U	F	M	F	S	E	S	V	K	W	I	X	L
R	C	O	M	P	A	R	E	A	P	T	E	V	S	L	X	V	U	G	U	T	E	H
A	M	C	S	P	E	I	G	T	G	V	V	P	M	T	P	F	H	K	B	I	I	J
M	F	V	D	E	M	O	N	S	T	R	A	T	E	F	E	M	P	M	V	C	S	W
A	L	N	C	A	L	C	U	L	A	T	E	C	Z	A	R	F	S	E	P	I	A	G
T	F	O	Q	S	T	T	X	O	I	Z	F	N	J	F	I	L	V	S	B	Z	R	W
I	F	A	I	P	J	H	T	T	V	P	H	A	P	H	M	D	V	O	T	E	S	N
Z	B	M	P	A	I	L	L	U	S	T	R	A	T	E	E	N	T	S	Q	Y	D	X
E	O	F	D	B	S	U	F	W	Y	G	L	A	Z	B	N	Z	A	Y	Y	Q	G	F
J	S	C	O	E	X	O	S	Y	S	T	E	M	P	K	T	Q	Z	S	V	W	T	J
P	W	H	J	D	Z	W	M	Y	Z	U	E	X	A	M	I	N	E	T	M	B	B	M
N	A	N	U	A	R	X	O	W	D	P	L	I	D	G	B	C	N	E	C	L	D	U
Q	W	Z	U	T	H	J	X	Q	M	O	X	C	Y	I	C	S	R	M	R	H	L	G

1. Explain or make (something) clear by using examples, charts, pictures, etc.
2. A scientific procedure undertaken to make a discovery, test a hypothesis, or demonstrate a fact.
3. Indicate the faults of (someone or something) in a disapproving way.
4. Interaction of two microsystems.
5. inspect (someone or something) in detail to determine their nature or condition.
6. Breakdown information into parts and use those parts.
7. Determine (the amount or number of something) mathematically.
8. Leader in field of child psychology and development, outlined 4 types of nested systems.
9. Estimate, measure, or note the similarity or dissimilarity between.
10. Influence of external aspects on development.
11. Clearly show the existence or truth of (something) by giving proof or evidence.
12. Adapt a novel or present a particular incident as a play or movie.

A. Calculate
B. Demonstrate
C. Experiment
D. Illustrate
E. Analysis
F. Examine
G. Compare
H. Brofenbrenner
I. Exosystem
J. Criticize
K. Dramatize
L. Mesosystem

14. Find the hidden words. The words have been placed horizontally, vertically, or diagonally. When you locate a word, draw an ellipse around it.

1. Estimate, measure, or note the similarity or dissimilarity between.
2. Bloom's 3rd level, take previous learning and use it in a new way.
3. Recognize or treat (someone or something) as different.
4. Explain or make (something) clear by using examples, charts, pictures, etc.
5. Leader in field of child psychology and development, outlined 4 types of nested systems.
6. Influence of external aspects on development.
7. Reports events about someone's life.
8. A scientific procedure undertaken to make a discovery, test a hypothesis, or demonstrate a fact.
9. Place in a particular class or group.
10. Interaction of two microsystems.
11. Family of classroom.
12. Breakdown information into parts and use those parts.

A. Categorize
B. Exosystem
C. Experiment
D. Microsystem
E. Application
F. Distinguish
G. Mesosystem
H. Biography
I. Analysis
J. Illustrate
K. Brofenbrenner
L. Compare

15. Find the hidden words. The words have been placed horizontally, vertically, or diagonally. When you locate a word, draw an ellipse around it.

Q	G	Q	C	F	E	K	M	X	W	G	K	U	K	Y	O	E	Y	P	U	D	M	X
C	Y	C	A	T	E	G	O	R	I	Z	E	Z	K	A	D	E	G	N	Y	J	K	K
B	D	E	M	O	N	S	T	R	A	T	E	O	S	N	H	B	L	O	O	M	O	S
A	N	G	I	G	F	U	T	F	F	U	Z	Q	I	A	E	I	O	D	F	U	B	D
H	B	I	O	G	R	A	P	H	Y	I	Q	J	H	L	A	J	A	X	Z	M	R	I
Q	A	C	D	C	Y	M	R	T	S	U	Q	K	Z	O	B	S	Z	S	B	G	O	S
S	A	O	C	A	U	I	L	S	X	W	B	G	V	G	T	W	G	S	E	Y	F	T
O	F	G	R	L	V	C	C	O	M	P	A	R	E	Y	L	K	E	W	J	O	E	I
R	H	H	H	C	T	R	E	Z	X	M	E	S	O	S	Y	S	T	E	M	O	N	N
G	Q	K	A	U	U	O	R	M	Y	W	O	T	I	N	B	E	W	A	A	E	B	G
D	R	P	P	L	J	S	J	F	T	Y	N	A	R	G	V	Q	S	Y	U	F	R	U
X	D	Y	L	A	I	Y	I	Q	F	D	I	S	T	I	N	G	U	I	S	H	E	I
D	G	D	L	T	T	S	D	U	T	W	Q	B	B	R	P	X	N	L	W	W	N	S
M	N	X	I	E	F	T	C	U	D	B	E	F	G	G	T	D	B	N	V	C	N	H
G	O	M	C	T	B	E	X	T	O	I	F	L	A	M	M	D	S	G	X	X	E	I
Z	A	S	O	R	J	M	U	H	N	O	K	R	I	P	I	Z	K	D	H	I	R	I

1. Leader in field of child psychology and development, outlined 4 types of nested systems.
2. Interaction of two microsystems.
3. Recognize or treat (someone or something) as different.
4. Reports events about someone's life.
5. Family of classroom.
6. A comparison of two things based on their being alike in some way.
7. Estimate, measure, or note the similarity or dissimilarity between.
8. Determine (the amount or number of something) mathematically.
9. Clearly show the existence or truth of (something) by giving proof or evidence.
10. Place in a particular class or group.
11. Recognize or treat (someone or something) as different.
12. Detailed classification of critical thinking and learning skills and objectives into tiered levels.

A. Brofenbrenner
B. Biography
C. Demonstrate
D. Mesosystem
E. Analogy
F. Distinguish
G. Distinguish
H. Bloom
I. Compare
J. Microsystem
K. Categorize
L. Calculate

1. Find the hidden words. The words have been placed horizontally, vertically, or diagonally. When you locate a word, draw an ellipse around it.

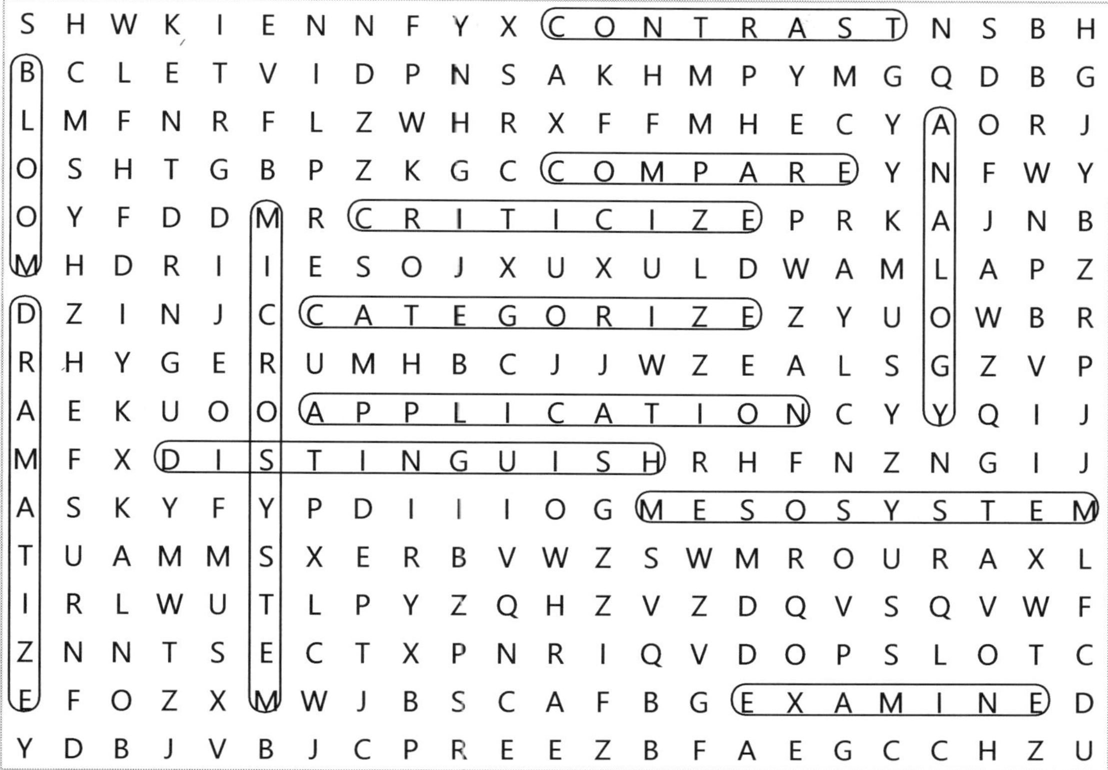

1. inspect (someone or something) in detail to determine their nature or condition.
2. The state of being strikingly different from something else.
3. Bloom's 3rd level, take previous learning and use it in a new way.
4. Recognize or treat (someone or something) as different.
5. A comparison of two things based on their being alike in some way.
6. Indicate the faults of (someone or something) in a disapproving way.
7. Family of classroom.
8. Adapt a novel or present a particular incident as a play or movie.
9. Estimate, measure, or note the similarity or dissimilarity between.
10. Interaction of two microsystems.
11. Place in a particular class or group.
12. Detailed classification of critical thinking and learning skills and objectives into tiered levels.

A. Microsystem	B. Application	C. Bloom	D. Mesosystem	E. Criticize
F. Compare	G. Distinguish	H. Contrast	I. Categorize	J. Examine
K. Dramatize	L. Analogy			

2. Find the hidden words. The words have been placed horizontally, vertically, or diagonally. When you locate a word, draw an ellipse around it.

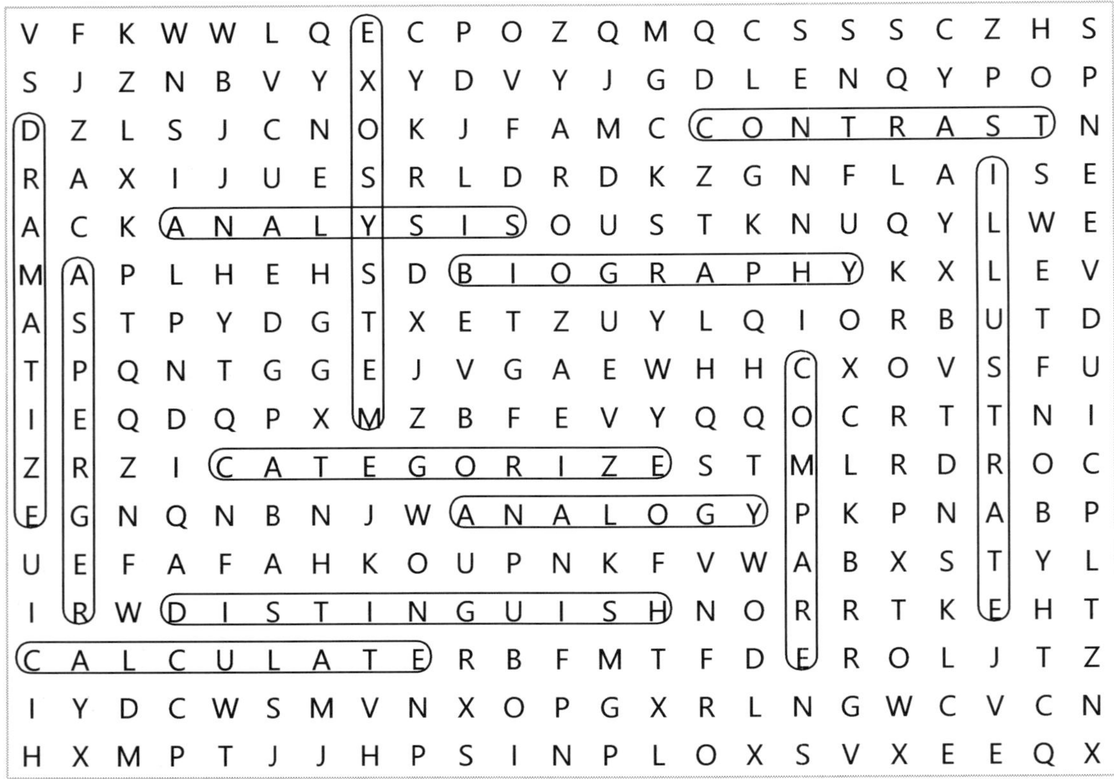

1. Place in a particular class or group.
2. Explain or make (something) clear by using examples, charts, pictures, etc.
3. Determine (the amount or number of something) mathematically.
4. Influence of external aspects on development.
5. A type of autism characterized by normal cognitive and language development and impaired social skills.
6. A comparison of two things based on their being alike in some way.
7. Breakdown information into parts and use those parts.
8. Estimate, measure, or note the similarity or dissimilarity between.
9. Adapt a novel or present a particular incident as a play or movie.
10. The state of being strikingly different from something else.
11. Reports events about someone's life.
12. Recognize or treat (someone or something) as different.

A. Contrast	B. Asperger	C. Analogy	D. Biography	E. Analysis	F. Compare
G. Illustrate	H. Categorize	I. Exosystem	J. Distinguish	K. Dramatize	L. Calculate

3. Find the hidden words. The words have been placed horizontally, vertically, or diagonally. When you locate a word, draw an ellipse around it.

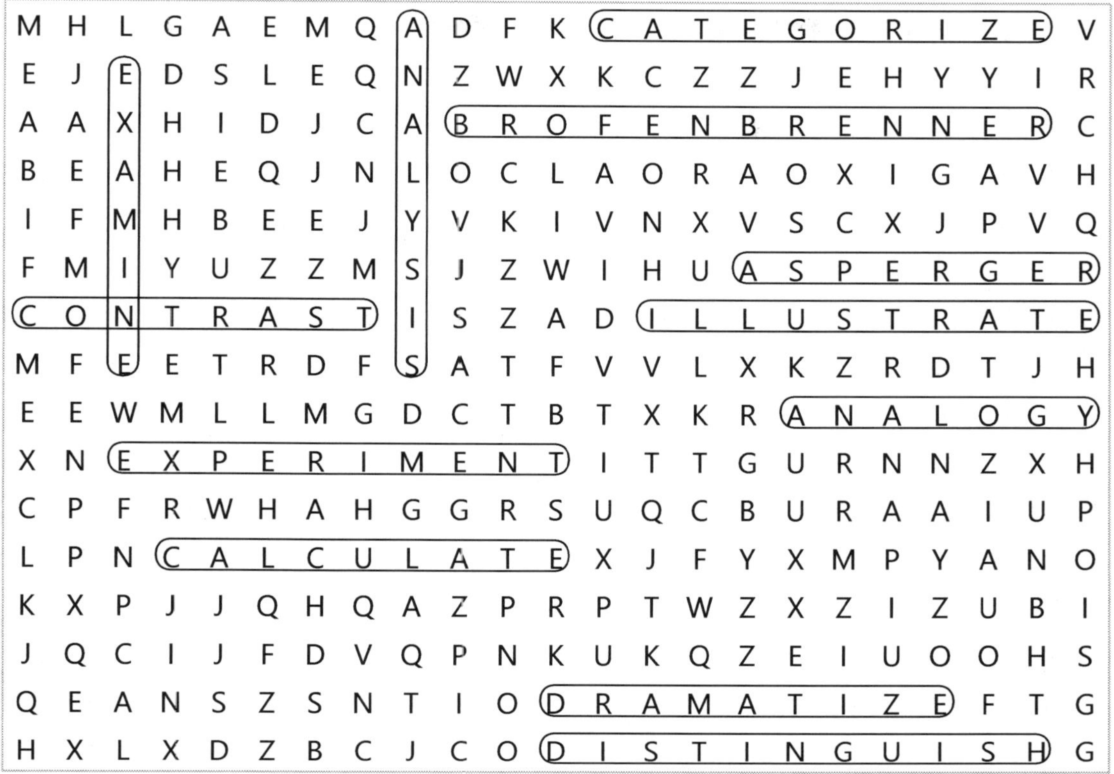

1. Breakdown information into parts and use those parts.
2. A comparison of two things based on their being alike in some way.
3. inspect (someone or something) in detail to determine their nature or condition.
4. Explain or make (something) clear by using examples, charts, pictures, etc.
5. Adapt a novel or present a particular incident as a play or movie.
6. Determine (the amount or number of something) mathematically.
7. A scientific procedure undertaken to make a discovery, test a hypothesis, or demonstrate a fact.
8. Recognize or treat (someone or something) as different.
9. Leader in field of child psychology and development, outlined 4 types of nested systems.
10. Place in a particular class or group.
11. A type of autism characterized by normal cognitive and language development and impaired social skills.
12. The state of being strikingly different from something else.

A. Categorize
B. Experiment
C. Distinguish
D. Calculate
E. Analogy
F. Illustrate
G. Examine
H. Dramatize
I. Brofenbrenner
J. Contrast
K. Analysis
L. Asperger

4. Find the hidden words. The words have been placed horizontally, vertically, or diagonally. When you locate a word, draw an ellipse around it.

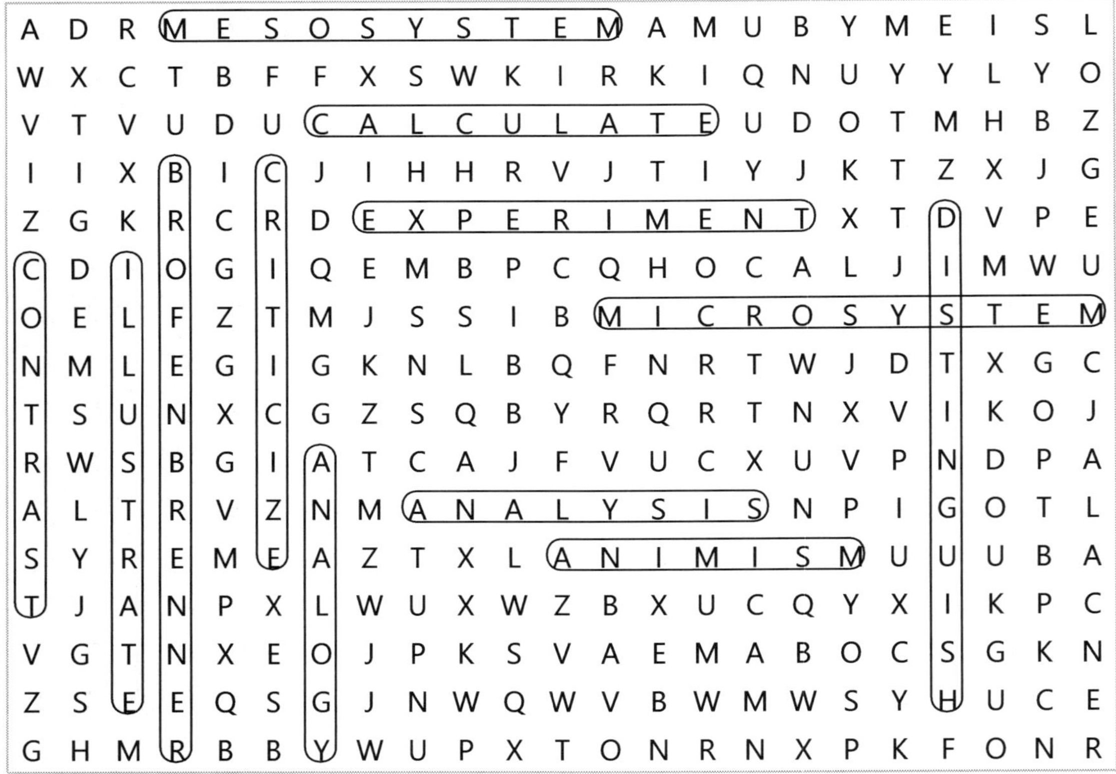

1. Leader in field of child psychology and development, outlined 4 types of nested systems.
2. Assigning human qualities to objects "the sun was mad and burned me".
3. A comparison of two things based on their being alike in some way.
4. The state of being strikingly different from something else.
5. Determine (the amount or number of something) mathematically.
6. Breakdown information into parts and use those parts.
7. A scientific procedure undertaken to make a discovery, test a hypothesis, or demonstrate a fact.
8. Recognize or treat (someone or something) as different.
9. Indicate the faults of (someone or something) in a disapproving way.
10. Explain or make (something) clear by using examples, charts, pictures, etc.
11. Family of classroom.
12. Interaction of two microsystems.

A. Criticize
B. Experiment
C. Microsystem
D. Brofenbrenner
E. Calculate
F. Animism
G. Distinguish
H. Mesosystem
I. Contrast
J. Illustrate
K. Analysis
L. Analogy

5. Find the hidden words. The words have been placed horizontally, vertically, or diagonally. When you locate a word, draw an ellipse around it.

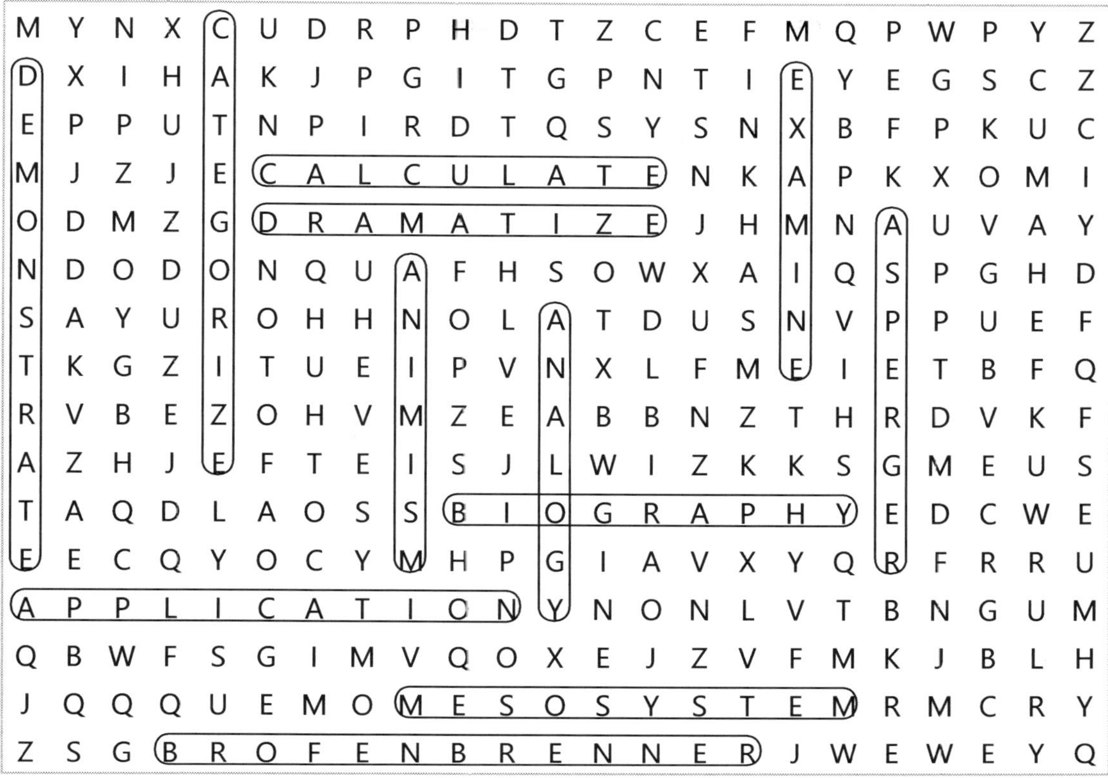

1. A type of autism characterized by normal cognitive and language development and impaired social skills.
2. Leader in field of child psychology and development, outlined 4 types of nested systems.
3. inspect (someone or something) in detail to determine their nature or condition.
4. Place in a particular class or group.
5. Interaction of two microsystems.
6. Determine (the amount or number of something) mathematically.
7. Clearly show the existence or truth of (something) by giving proof or evidence.
8. Adapt a novel or present a particular incident as a play or movie.
9. A comparison of two things based on their being alike in some way.
10. Bloom's 3rd level, take previous learning and use it in a new way.
11. Assigning human qualities to objects "the sun was mad and burned me".
12. Reports events about someone's life.

A. Mesosystem
B. Brofenbrenner
C. Analogy
D. Dramatize
E. Biography
F. Examine
G. Animism
H. Demonstrate
I. Application
J. Asperger
K. Categorize
L. Calculate

6. Find the hidden words. The words have been placed horizontally, vertically, or diagonally. When you locate a word, draw an ellipse around it.

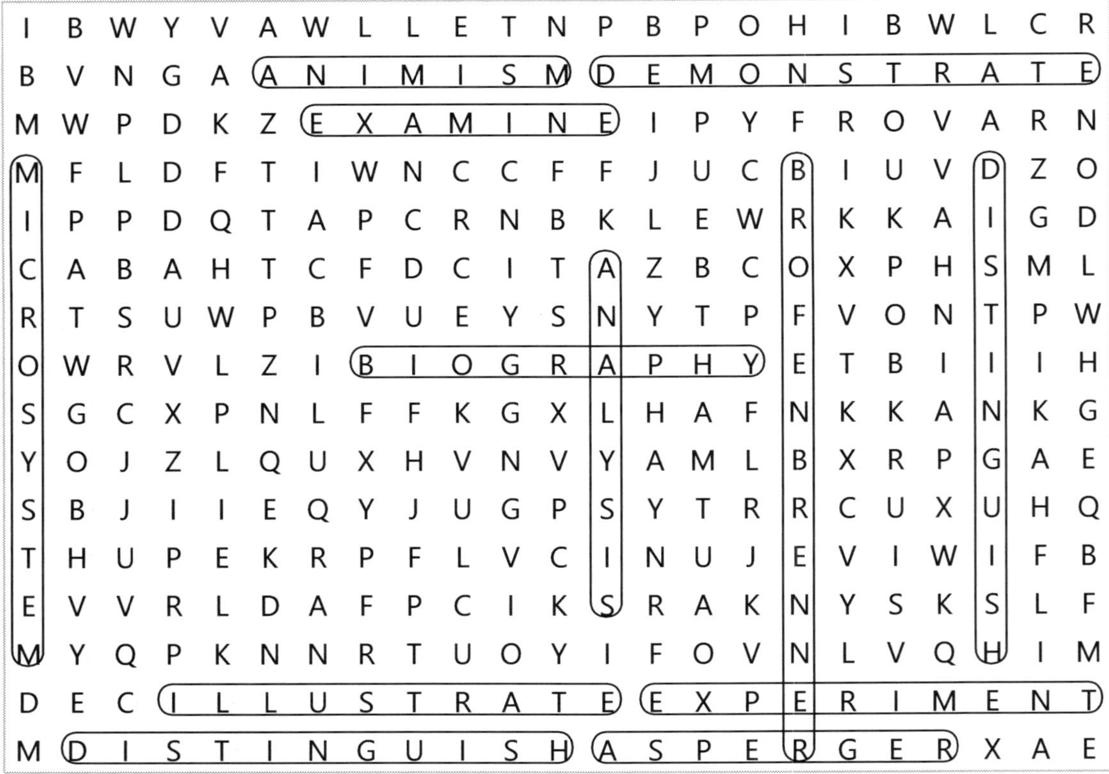

1. Assigning human qualities to objects "the sun was mad and burned me".
2. Family of classroom.
3. Clearly show the existence or truth of (something) by giving proof or evidence.
4. Recognize or treat (someone or something) as different.
5. inspect (someone or something) in detail to determine their nature or condition.
6. Leader in field of child psychology and development, outlined 4 types of nested systems.
7. Explain or make (something) clear by using examples, charts, pictures, etc.
8. Reports events about someone's life.
9. Recognize or treat (someone or something) as different.
10. Breakdown information into parts and use those parts.
11. A scientific procedure undertaken to make a discovery, test a hypothesis, or demonstrate a fact.
12. A type of autism characterized by normal cognitive and language development and impaired social skills.

A. Illustrate	B. Animism	C. Microsystem	D. Distinguish	E. Brofenbrenner
F. Asperger	G. Biography	H. Analysis	I. Experiment	J. Demonstrate
K. Examine	L. Distinguish			

7. Find the hidden words. The words have been placed horizontally, vertically, or diagonally. When you locate a word, draw an ellipse around it.

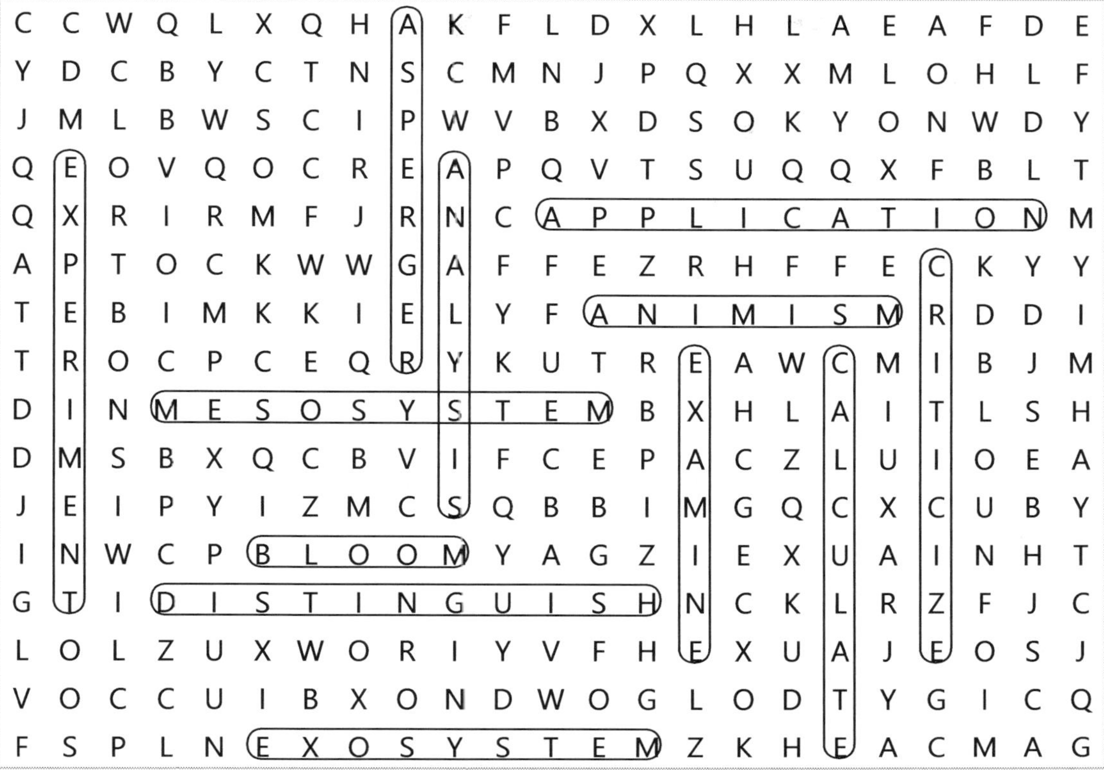

1. A scientific procedure undertaken to make a discovery, test a hypothesis, or demonstrate a fact.
2. Interaction of two microsystems.
3. Breakdown information into parts and use those parts.
4. inspect (someone or something) in detail to determine their nature or condition.
5. Bloom's 3rd level, take previous learning and use it in a new way.
6. Assigning human qualities to objects "the sun was mad and burned me".
7. Determine (the amount or number of something) mathematically.
8. Recognize or treat (someone or something) as different.
9. Indicate the faults of (someone or something) in a disapproving way.
10. A type of autism characterized by normal cognitive and language development and impaired social skills.
11. Detailed classification of critical thinking and learning skills and objectives into tiered levels.
12. Influence of external aspects on development.

A. Animism B. Criticize C. Experiment D. Distinguish E. Analysis
F. Calculate G. Examine H. Mesosystem I. Application J. Asperger
K. Bloom L. Exosystem

8. Find the hidden words. The words have been placed horizontally, vertically, or diagonally. When you locate a word, draw an ellipse around it.

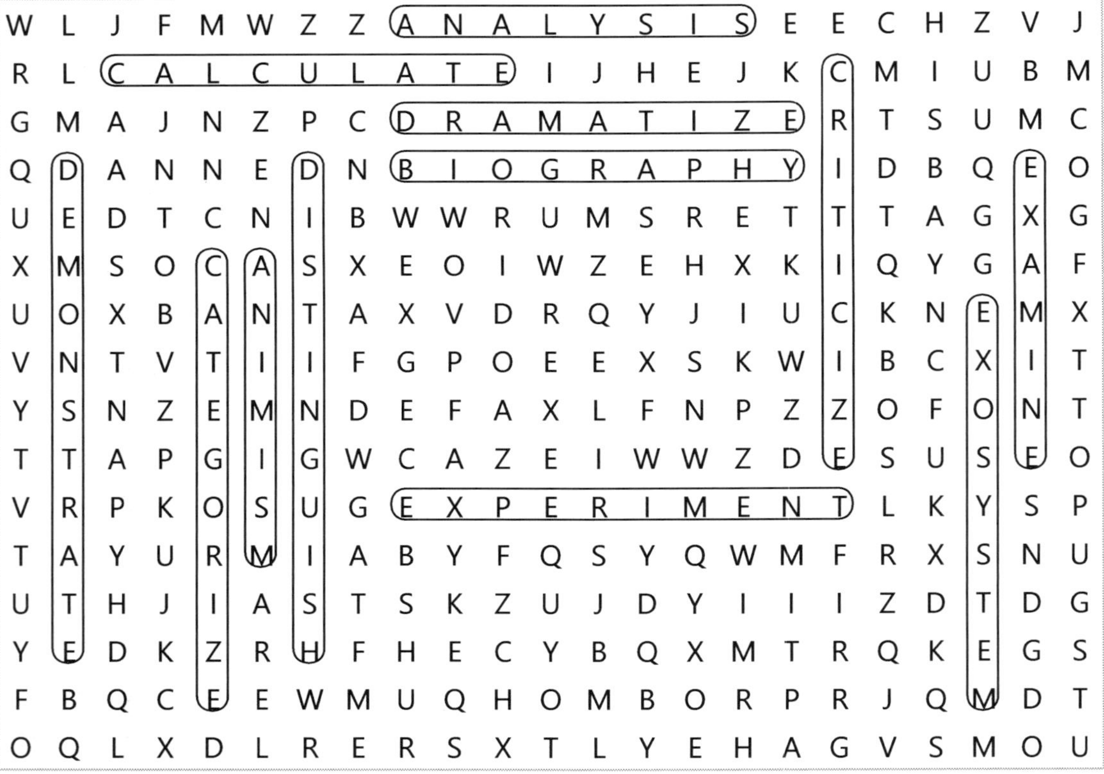

1. Assigning human qualities to objects "the sun was mad and burned me".
2. inspect (someone or something) in detail to determine their nature or condition.
3. A scientific procedure undertaken to make a discovery, test a hypothesis, or demonstrate a fact.
4. Indicate the faults of (someone or something) in a disapproving way.
5. Determine (the amount or number of something) mathematically.
6. Breakdown information into parts and use those parts.
7. Recognize or treat (someone or something) as different.
8. Clearly show the existence or truth of (something) by giving proof or evidence.
9. Reports events about someone's life.
10. Place in a particular class or group.
11. Adapt a novel or present a particular incident as a play or movie.
12. Influence of external aspects on development.

A. Examine	B. Criticize	C. Biography	D. Distinguish	E. Calculate
F. Experiment	G. Analysis	H. Animism	I. Exosystem	J. Demonstrate
K. Dramatize	L. Categorize			

9. Find the hidden words. The words have been placed horizontally, vertically, or diagonally. When you locate a word, draw an ellipse around it.

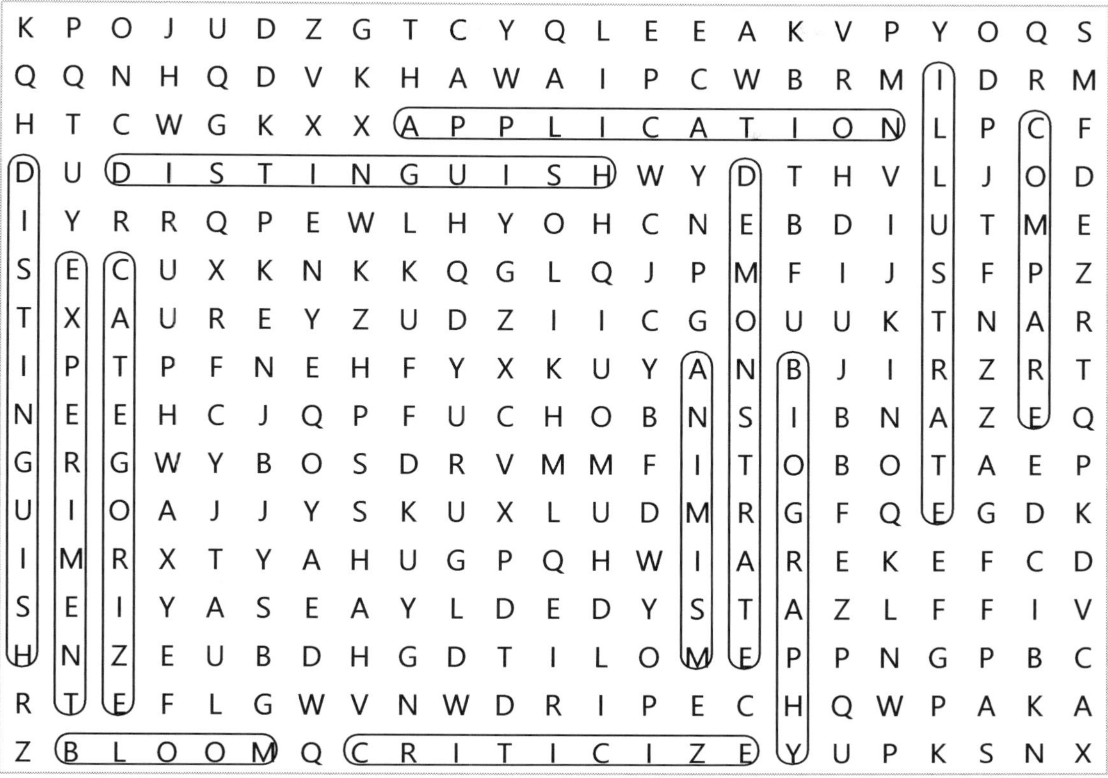

1. Reports events about someone's life.
2. Estimate, measure, or note the similarity or dissimilarity between.
3. Detailed classification of critical thinking and learning skills and objectives into tiered levels.
4. Explain or make (something) clear by using examples, charts, pictures, etc.
5. Indicate the faults of (someone or something) in a disapproving way.
6. Recognize or treat (someone or something) as different.
7. Clearly show the existence or truth of (something) by giving proof or evidence.
8. Place in a particular class or group.
9. Recognize or treat (someone or something) as different.
10. A scientific procedure undertaken to make a discovery, test a hypothesis, or demonstrate a fact.
11. Bloom's 3rd level, take previous learning and use it in a new way.
12. Assigning human qualities to objects "the sun was mad and burned me".

A. Criticize	B. Distinguish	C. Demonstrate	D. Application	E. Illustrate
F. Animism	G. Experiment	H. Bloom	I. Distinguish	J. Biography
K. Compare	L. Categorize			

10. Find the hidden words. The words have been placed horizontally, vertically, or diagonally. When you locate a word, draw an ellipse around it.

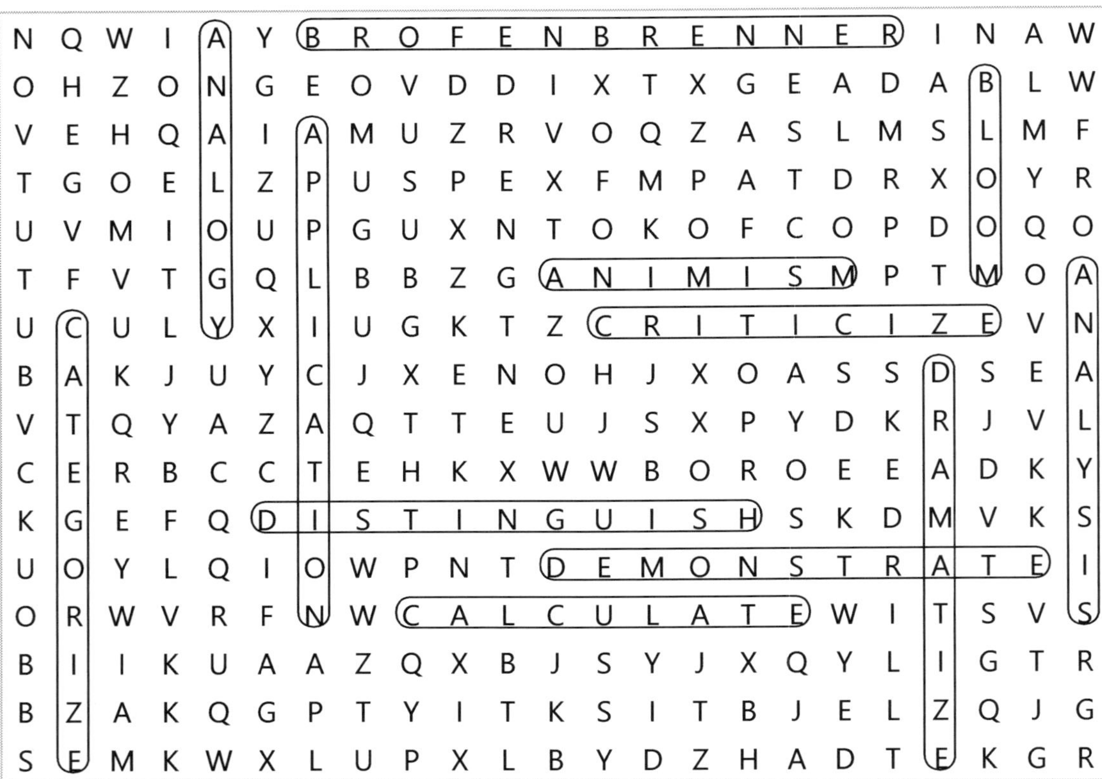

1. Detailed classification of critical thinking and learning skills and objectives into tiered levels.
2. Indicate the faults of (someone or something) in a disapproving way.
3. A comparison of two things based on their being alike in some way.
4. Breakdown information into parts and use those parts.
5. Determine (the amount or number of something) mathematically.
6. Adapt a novel or present a particular incident as a play or movie.
7. Bloom's 3rd level, take previous learning and use it in a new way.
8. Recognize or treat (someone or something) as different.
9. Place in a particular class or group.
10. Assigning human qualities to objects "the sun was mad and burned me".
11. Clearly show the existence or truth of (something) by giving proof or evidence.
12. Leader in field of child psychology and development, outlined 4 types of nested systems.

A. Distinguish	B. Application	C. Categorize	D. Analogy	E. Analysis
F. Bloom	G. Criticize	H. Calculate	I. Brofenbrenner	J. Animism
K. Dramatize	L. Demonstrate			

11. Find the hidden words. The words have been placed horizontally, vertically, or diagonally. When you locate a word, draw an ellipse around it.

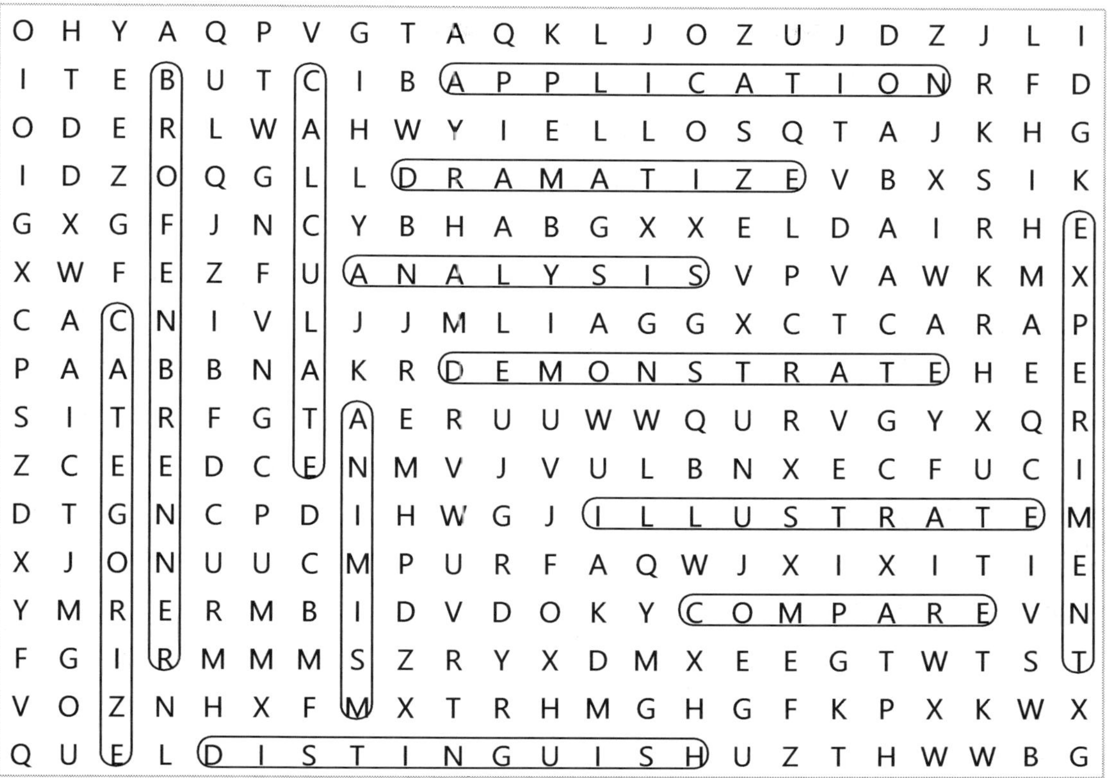

1. A scientific procedure undertaken to make a discovery, test a hypothesis, or demonstrate a fact.
2. Adapt a novel or present a particular incident as a play or movie.
3. Breakdown information into parts and use those parts.
4. Leader in field of child psychology and development, outlined 4 types of nested systems.
5. Determine (the amount or number of something) mathematically.
6. Estimate, measure, or note the similarity or dissimilarity between.
7. Place in a particular class or group.
8. Bloom's 3rd level, take previous learning and use it in a new way.
9. Clearly show the existence or truth of (something) by giving proof or evidence.
10. Assigning human qualities to objects "the sun was mad and burned me".
11. Explain or make (something) clear by using examples, charts, pictures, etc.
12. Recognize or treat (someone or something) as different.

A. Illustrate
B. Brofenbrenner
C. Experiment
D. Compare
E. Categorize
F. Analysis
G. Animism
H. Dramatize
I. Calculate
J. Distinguish
K. Application
L. Demonstrate

12. Find the hidden words. The words have been placed horizontally, vertically, or diagonally. When you locate a word, draw an ellipse around it.

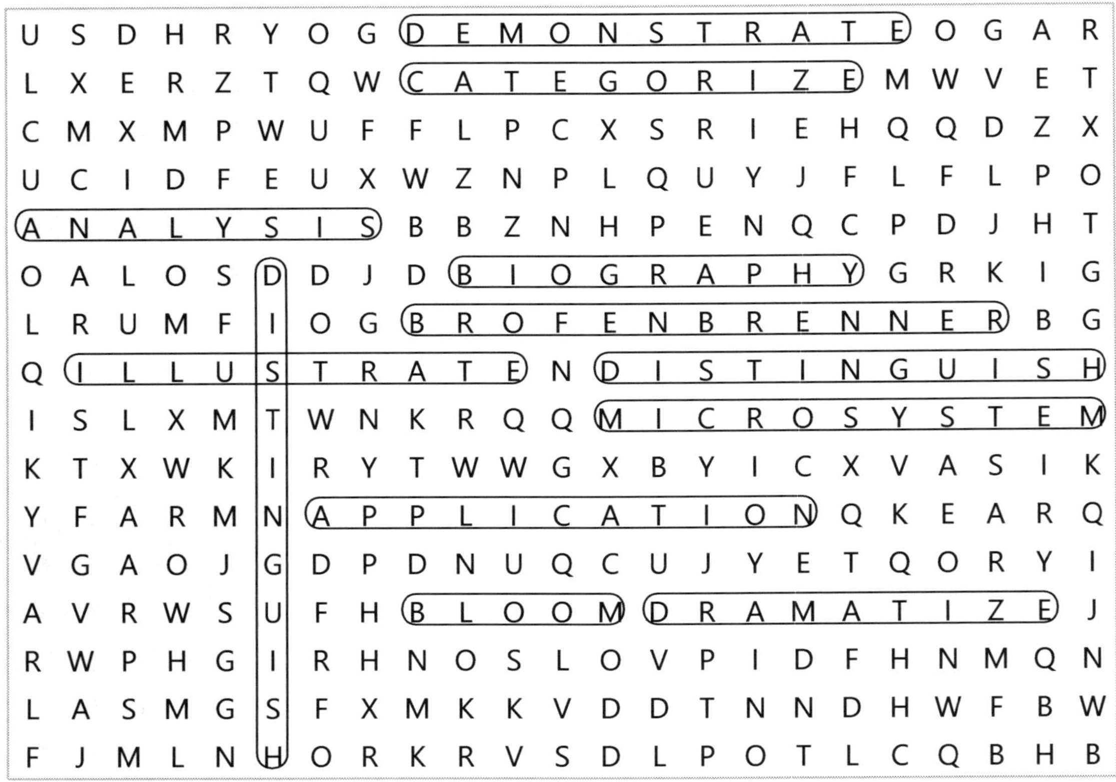

1. Explain or make (something) clear by using examples, charts, pictures, etc.
2. Recognize or treat (someone or something) as different.
3. Bloom's 3rd level, take previous learning and use it in a new way.
4. Leader in field of child psychology and development, outlined 4 types of nested systems.
5. Clearly show the existence or truth of (something) by giving proof or evidence.
6. Adapt a novel or present a particular incident as a play or movie.
7. Breakdown information into parts and use those parts.
8. Family of classroom.
9. Reports events about someone's life.
10. Recognize or treat (someone or something) as different.
11. Place in a particular class or group.
12. Detailed classification of critical thinking and learning skills and objectives into tiered levels.

A. Demonstrate
B. Distinguish
C. Distinguish
D. Categorize
E. Brofenbrenner
F. Dramatize
G. Biography
H. Bloom
I. Microsystem
J. Illustrate
K. Application
L. Analysis

13. Find the hidden words. The words have been placed horizontally, vertically, or diagonally. When you locate a word, draw an ellipse around it.

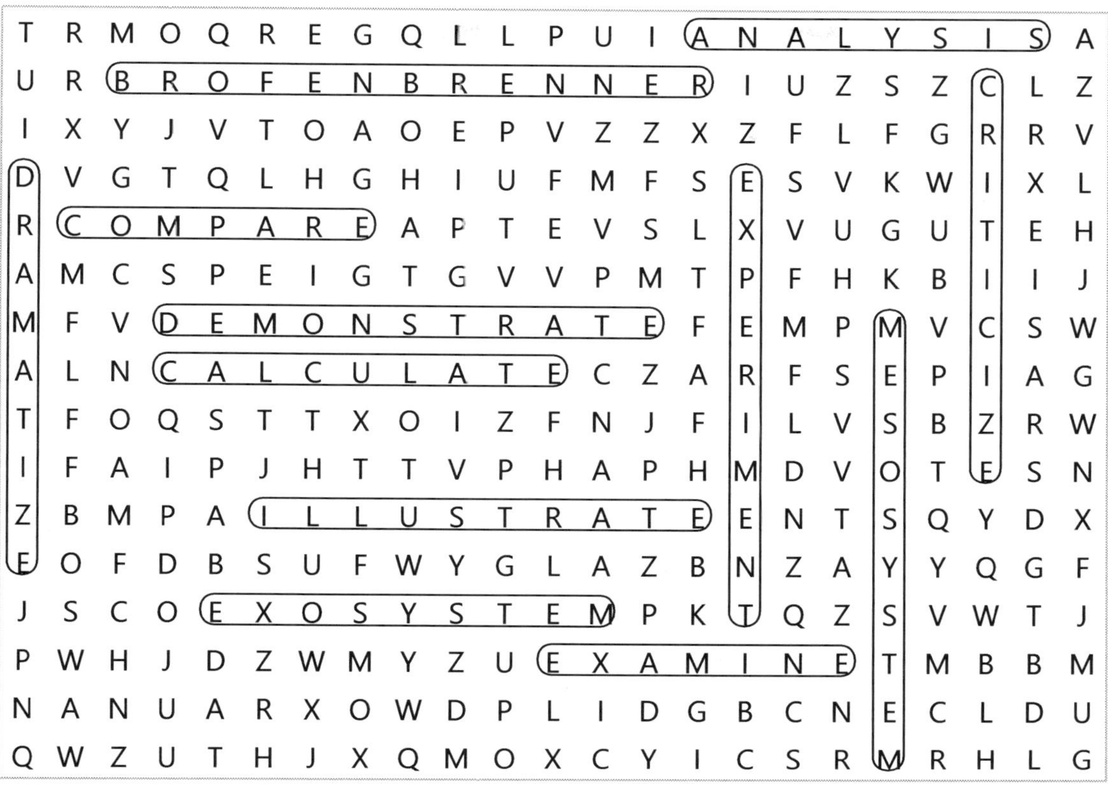

1. Explain or make (something) clear by using examples, charts, pictures, etc.
2. A scientific procedure undertaken to make a discovery, test a hypothesis, or demonstrate a fact.
3. Indicate the faults of (someone or something) in a disapproving way.
4. Interaction of two microsystems.
5. inspect (someone or something) in detail to determine their nature or condition.
6. Breakdown information into parts and use those parts.
7. Determine (the amount or number of something) mathematically.
8. Leader in field of child psychology and development, outlined 4 types of nested systems.
9. Estimate, measure, or note the similarity or dissimilarity between.
10. Influence of external aspects on development.
11. Clearly show the existence or truth of (something) by giving proof or evidence.
12. Adapt a novel or present a particular incident as a play or movie.

A. Calculate
B. Demonstrate
C. Experiment
D. Illustrate
E. Analysis
F. Examine
G. Compare
H. Brcfenbrenner
I. Exosystem
J. Criticize
K. Dramatize
L. Mesosystem

14. Find the hidden words. The words have been placed horizontally, vertically, or diagonally. When you locate a word, draw an ellipse around it.

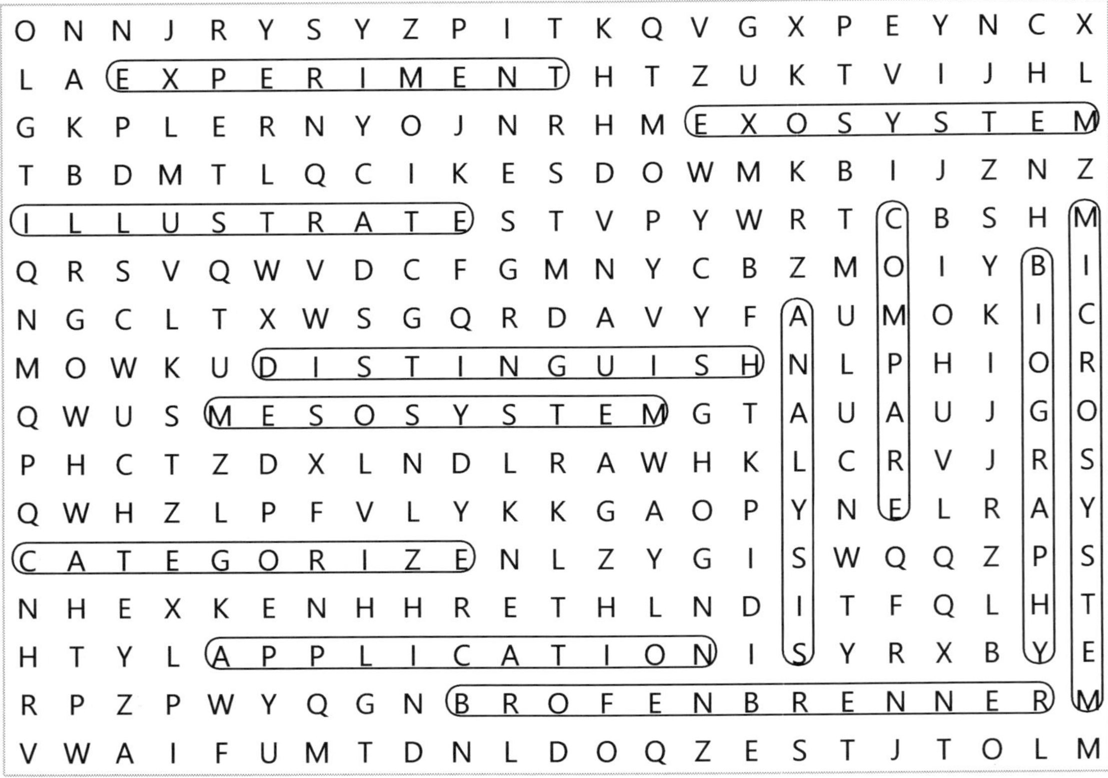

1. Estimate, measure, or note the similarity or dissimilarity between.
2. Bloom's 3rd level, take previous learning and use it in a new way.
3. Recognize or treat (someone or something) as different.
4. Explain or make (something) clear by using examples, charts, pictures, etc.
5. Leader in field of child psychology and development, outlined 4 types of nested systems.
6. Influence of external aspects on development.
7. Reports events about someone's life.
8. A scientific procedure undertaken to make a discovery, test a hypothesis, or demonstrate a fact.
9. Place in a particular class or group.
10. Interaction of two microsystems.
11. Family of classroom.
12. Breakdown information into parts and use those parts.

A. Categorize
B. Exosystem
C. Experiment
D. Microsystem
E. Application
F. Distinguish
G. Mesosystem
H. Biography
I. Analysis
J. Illustrate
K. Brofenbrenner
L. Compare

15. Find the hidden words. The words have been placed horizontally, vertically, or diagonally. When you locate a word, draw an ellipse around it.

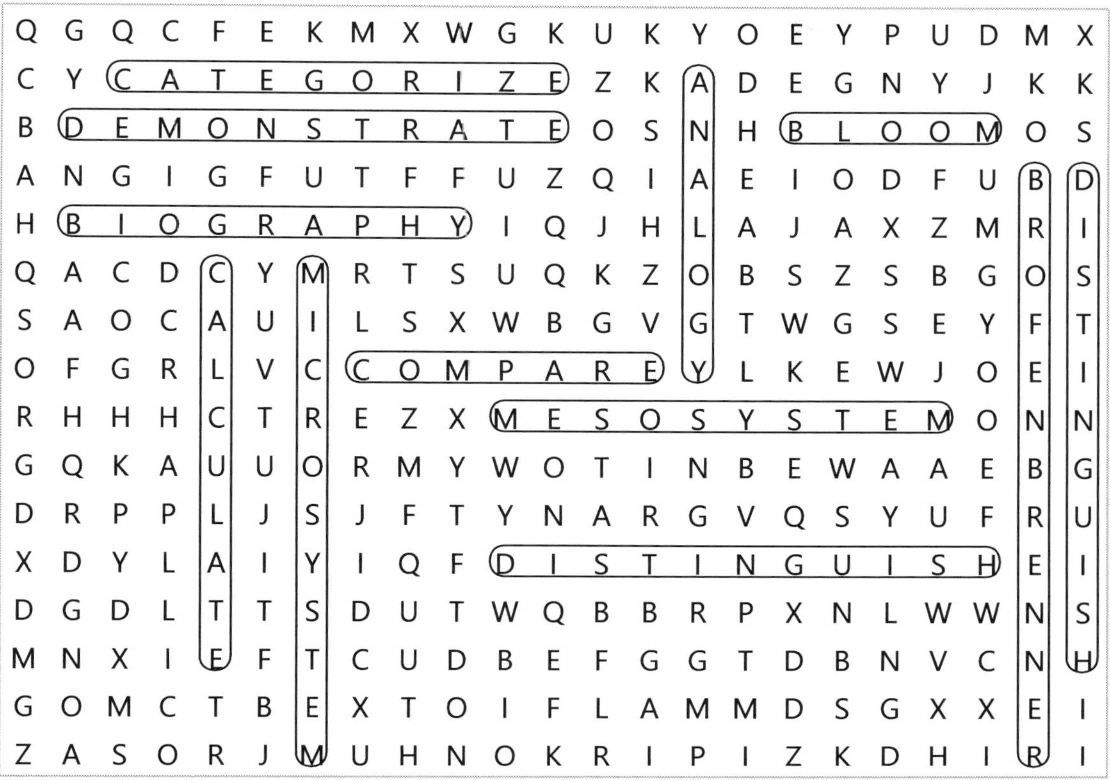

1. Leader in field of child psychology and development, outlined 4 types of nested systems.
2. Interaction of two microsystems.
3. Recognize or treat (someone or something) as different.
4. Reports events about someone's life.
5. Family of classroom.
6. A comparison of two things based on their being alike in some way.
7. Estimate, measure, or note the similarity or dissimilarity between.
8. Determine (the amount or number of something) mathematically.
9. Clearly show the existence or truth of (something) by giving proof or evidence.
10. Place in a particular class or group.
11. Recognize or treat (someone or something) as different.
12. Detailed classification of critical thinking and learning skills and objectives into tiered levels.

A. Brofenbrenner
B. Biography
C. Demonstrate
D. Mesosystem
E. Analogy
F. Distinguish
G. Distinguish
H. Bloom
I. Compare
J. Microsystem
K. Categorize
L. Calculate

Made in the USA
Middletown, DE
19 January 2020